how to boil

a potato

… and everything else
you need to know in
the kitchen

Carolyn Humphries

foulsham

LONDON • NEW YORK • TORONTO • SYDNEY

foulsham

The Publishing House, Bennetts Close,
Cippenham, Slough, Berkshire, SL1 5AP

ISBN 0-572-02618-8

Printed in Great Britain by The Bath Press, Bath.

contents

introduction

Do you wander around the supermarket not really knowing what you're buying or why? Do you sometimes open the fridge, freezer or larder and think *'What are we going to eat?'* or *'How am I going to cook it?'*

This invaluable book will tell you all you need to know. To start with, there's a simple glossary that explains all the terms used in recipes. Then you'll find a list of the most useful equipment and of items to keep in your storecupboard, so you always have something on hand to put together a nourishing and interesting meal in no time. There are tips on essential food hygiene, reheating and cooking from frozen, quantities per person, meal planning – and even how to cheat, using convenience foods.

Each of the main chapters tells you about a particular type of food – from eggs and meat to vegetables and fruit – and then gives clear and straightforward advice on the best ways to buy, prepare and cook it. You'll learn how to choose the freshest produce, and the best ways to cook each ingredient. There's also a selection of delicious recipes at the end of each chapter, which illustrates the best ways to prepare and cook the foods, including using up leftovers and making the best of your storecupboard. What's more, the whole book is designed to be easy to dip into so that you can find exactly what you need to know, when you need to know it.

How to Bake a Potato will enlighten you when you are confused, inform you when you want to learn, and inspire you when you just can't think what to cook. Whether you're on your own or have a family to feed, if you want to be a good cook but just don't know where to start, this is the book for you.

glossary of food terms

A

Al dente: An Italian term, literally meaning 'to the tooth'. Widely used to describe the texture of pasta or vegetables cooked until just tender but still with some 'bite'.

Antipasto: The Italian equivalent of hors d'oeuvres. A 'starter' course, often consisting of a selection of delicatessen meats, seafood, salads and vegetables marinated in olive oil.

Au gratin: A dish that is (usually) precooked, topped with sauce, breadcrumbs and grated cheese, and browned under the grill (broiler).

B

Bain marie: A pan containing gently simmering water in which a container of food is cooked without boiling.

Bake: To cook uncovered in the oven.

Bake blind: To cook before filling, usually of a pastry case (pie shell). *See* **Pastry**.

Bard: To cover lean meat or poultry with strips of fat pork or bacon, to stop it drying out during cooking.

Baste: To spoon cooking fat, juices or marinade over food as it cooks, to keep it moist. A bulb baster can also be used. See Equipment, page 15.

Beat: To mix ingredients together in a circular motion with a wooden spoon or electric beaters to incorporate air to make the mixture light and fluffy. The same technique is also used with a wire whisk to eliminate lumps in batters and sauces.

Bind: To add eggs, milk, cream or a sauce to dry ingredients to make them stick together.

Blanch: To plunge foods in boiling water briefly. Can be used to loosen the skin of nuts, fruit or vegetables; to remove any bitter or strong flavour from foods, especially from vegetables or salty meats; to kill enzymes and preserve the colour of vegetables prior to freezing.

Blend: To stir wet and dry ingredients together thoroughly until smooth.

Boil: To cook in liquid at a temperature of at least 100°C/212°F.

Bouquet garni: Traditionally a bunch of herbs tied together and added to a braise, stew or casserole during cooking and removed before serving. Dried bouquet garni sachets are a convenient alternative.

Braise: To brown food in hot fat, then cook slowly, on a bed of vegetables (mirepoix), in a minimum of liquid in a tightly covered container.

Brine: A strong solution of salt and water used for pickling and preserving.

Brochette: *See* **Kebab.**

Broiling: American term for grilling. *See* **Grill**.

Brown: To sear the outside of meat quickly in a little hot fat or a non-stick pan to seal in the juices.

C

Carve: To cut joints of meat or poultry into slices with a sharp knife.

Casserole (Dutch oven): An ovenproof or flameproof cooking pot with a lid, used to slow-cook fish, meat and/or vegetables in liquid.

Chill: To cool food in the fridge until very cold before serving. **Note:** Hot or warm food should be allowed to cool to room temperature BEFORE placing in the fridge.

Chop: To cut ingredients into small pieces with a sharp knife.

Clarify: To clean fat, particularly butter, of any residue. The fat is melted, then the clear liquid poured off for use and any solid residue is discarded.

Coat: To cover completely with seasoned flour, egg and breadcrumbs, batter or a sauce.

Coulis: Literally means a sauce. Nowadays, usually a purée, often of fruit.

Crimp: To pinch the pastry (paste) edge of a pie all round between the finger and thumb to decorate.

Cream: To beat together, using a wooden spoon or an electric beater, until light and fluffy. Usually butter or margarine and sugar.

Croûtes: Pieces of bread fried (sautéed) in butter or oil until crisp, drained on kitchen paper (paper towels) and used as a garnish or base for other foods.

Croûtons: Small cubes of bread, fried (sautéed) in butter or oil until crisp, drained on kitchen paper (paper towels) and used to garnish soups and salads.

Curdle: To separate into solids and liquids. Milk, cream and egg dishes curdle when overheated or when too much acid, like lemon juice or vinegar, is added. Creamed butter or margarine and sugar will also curdle when too much egg is added all at once.

Cure: To preserve meat or fish by drying, salting or smoking.

D

Decorate: To add ingredients to sweet dishes before serving to make them look more attractive. *See also* **Garnish**.

Deep-fry: To cook food by immersing it in hot oil. For most foods, 190°C/375°F is the correct temperature. To test if the oil is hot enough, drop in a cube of day-old bread; it should brown in 30 seconds.

Dice: To cut food into small cubes.

Dilute: To add water or other liquid to make the flavour less strong.

Dissolve: To mix a soluble substance such as salt, sugar or gelatine with liquid until no grains are left. This is particularly important with gelatine. If you can still see tiny jelly-like granules in the liquid, the finished dish will have unpleasant, gelatinous lumps in it.

Dot: To put small pieces of an ingredient, usually butter or margarine, all over the surface of a dish before cooking.

Dough: Flour, fat (usually), milk or water and/or egg mixed to form a pliable mixture that can be kneaded, shaped or rolled. *See also* **Knead**.

Drain: To remove the liquid from food either through a colander or sieve (strainer) or by lifting the food out of liquid with a draining spoon and leave it to finish draining on kitchen paper (paper towels), if necessary.

Dredge: To sprinkle food liberally with flour or sugar.

Drizzle: To trickle liquids such as oil, syrup, melted butter or sauce over the surface of food.

Dry-fry: To cook foods in their own fat in a non-stick frying pan (skillet) without the addition of extra oil or other fat.

Dry ingredients: Grainy or powdery ingredients such as flour, sugar, spices, seasoning and so on.

Dust: To sprinkle lightly with flour, sugar, spices or other seasoning.

Dutch oven: *See* **Casserole**.

E

Emulsion: A mixture, such as mayonnaise, where the oil is held in suspension to form a smooth, glossy mass.

F

Ferment: The action of live yeast with moisture and sugar in a recipe.

Fillet: The leanest, most tender cuts of all meats: the undercut of the sirloin of beef; a cut taken from the fleshy part of the buttocks of pork; the 'eye' of meat in the thick end of the neck of lamb; also, the boned flesh of fish and the boned breasts of poultry.

Flute: To mark the pastry (paste) edge of a pie all round with a series of small cuts made with the back of a knife at regular intervals, usually about 1 cm/½ in apart for savoury pies, 5 mm/¼ in apart for sweet ones.

Flake: To separate cooked fish into individual flakes with a fork.

Flambé: To toss food in a shallow pan in flaming brandy or other spirit until the flames die down.

Fold in: To gently incorporate one ingredient or mixture into another, using a metal spoon in a cutting and turning 'figure of eight' movement.

Frost: To coat the rim of a glass or individual fruits in beaten egg white, then caster (superfine) sugar.

Frosting: *See* **Icing**.

Fry (sauté): To cook food over direct heat in a little oil or butter.

G

Garnish: To decorate a savoury dish before serving.

Glaze: A shiny finish given to some foods by brushing with beaten egg, cream, yoghurt or milk before baking. Foods may also be glazed after cooking by brushing with sugar syrup, aspic or sweet jelly (jello) or melted preserves such as redcurrant jelly (clear conserve). Also refers to the sticky, shiny finish given to meat, poultry, vegetables or fruit by cooking them in a reduced, clear sauce. *See* **Reduce**.

Goujons: Small thin strips of meat or fish.

Grate: To shred in small pieces on a grater. The fine mesh is used for nutmeg; the medium mesh for citrus rind, ginger, cheese, chocolate and breadcrumbs; the coarse side for cheese, chocolate, vegetables and fat such as animal suet.

Grill (broil): Cook food under direct heat.

H

Hand-hot: When liquid feels bearably hot to the touch, not scalding.

Hors d'oeuvres: First course of a meal; may be hot or cold.

Hull: To remove the green central calyx from strawberries, tomatoes, etc.

I

Icing (frosting): A sugary coating for cakes or biscuits (cookies).
Infuse: To steep herbs, spices or other flavourings in hot water or other liquid to extract the flavour. Flavourings are discarded before the liquid is used.

J

Joint: A large piece of meat that is cooked and cut into slices for serving. Also, to cut poultry or game into pieces at the joints.
Julienne: Food, usually vegetables, cut into very fine strips. A garnish of shredded vegetables.

K

Kebab: Meat, poultry, fish, vegetables or fruit on a skewer for grilling (broiling) or barbecuing.
Knead: To push and stretch a dough with the heel of the hand. For pastry (paste) this should be done briefly and gently, just to remove the cracks. For yeast dough it should be done much more firmly, for up to ten minutes, until the dough is smooth and elastic.
Knock back (punch down): To punch a risen yeast dough with the knuckles to knock out the air and return it to its original size. This makes it more elastic, ready to knead (see above) and shape before allowing it to rise again.
Knock up: Gently slash the top and bottom edges of a pie crust together, with the back of a knife, to seal them.

L

Lardons: Tiny pieces of fat pork or bacon, cooked until crisp and served in a salad. Also strips of fat, threaded through the surface of meat with a special needle, to keep it moist during roasting.

M

Macedoine: A mixture of sliced or diced fruits or vegetables.
Marinade: A mixture of liquids and flavourings, used to soak raw foods to add flavour and to tenderise them before cooking. Often spooned over the food during cooking; any remainder may also be made into a sauce to serve with the cooked dish. *See also* **Baste**.
Marinate: To soak foods in a **marinade** (see above).
Macerate: To steep foods in spirits, liqueurs, wine, fruit juice and/or sugar syrup. The food is then served in the liquid.

Mash: To use a fork or potato masher to crush and beat cooked or soft foods to a pulp.

Medallion: Small, round cut of tender meat, fish or pâté.

Mirepoix: A bed of sweated vegetables on which food is braised.

Mix: To stir ingredients together until combined.

N

Noisette: A best end of neck of lamb cutlet, boned and tied in a round.

P

Parboil: To partly cook in boiling water. The food is then finished by cooking another way: e.g. parboiled potatoes may then be roasted.

Pare: To cut off the outer skin thinly, particularly of citrus fruit.

Peel: To remove the skin of fruit and vegetables.

Pipe: To force soft mixtures such as icing (frosting), whipped cream, mashed potato, choux pastry (paste), biscuit (cookie) dough, melted chocolate or redcurrant jelly (clear conserve) through a bag with a plain or shaped tube (pipe) fitted to give a decorative finish.

Pith: The white layer between the rind and flesh of citrus fruit.

Poach: To simmer gently in just enough hot, not boiling, liquid to cover the food, until softly cooked.

Prove: To put yeast dough in a warm place to rise until doubled in bulk.

Pulses: Dried peas, beans and lentils.

Punch down: *See* **Knock back**.

Purée: To pass fruit or vegetables through a fine sieve (strainer) or process in a blender or food processor to make a smooth pulp.

R

Reduce: To boil rapidly to evaporate some moisture, making a liquid thicker and concentrating the flavour.

Rind: The tough skin of bacon or pork. The oily, coloured skin of citrus fruit.

Rise: To expand and puff up. May be caused by the effect of heat on dishes with a lot of air incorporated, e.g. soufflés, puff and choux pastry (paste), Yorkshire pudding, breads, cakes and scones (biscuits), or by fermentation of yeast.

Roast: To cook in the oven in fat or oil.

Roll out: To flatten and spread out dough with the help of a rolling pin.

Rub in: To incorporate fat into flour by working it gently between the fingertips and letting it drop back into the bowl until the mixture looks like breadcrumbs.

S

Sauté: *See* **Fry**.

Scald: To bring milk or cream to just below boiling point (when tiny bubbles rise to the surface) before use in a recipe.

Scrape: To use a knife to remove the skin from young vegetables, the scales of fish, etc. with a scraping movement without damaging the flesh.

Sear: To brown meat or poultry quickly over a high heat to seal in the juices before finishing cooking at a lower temperature.

Seasoned flour: Flour to which a little salt and pepper have been added, used to dust meat, poultry, fish or vegetables before cooking.

Seasoning: Usually salt and pepper (preferably freshly ground) but can also include other flavourings, such as ginger, chilli powder, etc.

Score: To make shallow cuts with a sharp knife at regular intervals over the surface of cuts of meat, such as steaks, to tenderise them before grilling (broiling) or frying (sautéing). Also over the rind of pork to help it to 'crackle' when roasted.

Shallow-fry: To cook food in about 5 mm/¼ in hot oil in a frying pan (skillet).

Sift: To rub flour, icing (confectioners') sugar or other powdery ingredients through a sieve (strainer) or a flour sifter to remove the lumps.

Sieve (strain): To rub soft ingredients, such as raspberries, through a wire- or nylon-meshed sieve (strainer) to remove lumps or seeds.

Simmer: To cook gently in liquid just below boiling point; occasional small bubbles will rise to the surface but the liquid should not boil fully.

Skim: To spoon off the fat or scum from the surface of a soup, stew, casserole or gravy. Floating fat can also be removed by laying a sheet of kitchen paper (paper towel) lightly on the surface until the fat is absorbed. This may need to be repeated with several sheets.

Skin: To remove the skin of a food before use. For whole fish, it is often best to cook the fish first, so that the skin may be pulled off easily before serving. For poultry and game, the skin may be removed before cooking, using a knife to help if necessary. *See also* **Blanch, Peel**.

Soft dropping consistency: A consistency best illustrated by lifting a spoonful of the mixture out of the bowl: it should drop softly off the spoon when tilted, without being shaken.

Steam: To cook in steam. The food may be suspended in a special steamer or a covered colander over a pan of simmering water. Alternatively, it may be placed in a well-covered container inside a pan containing enough boiling water to come halfway up the sides of the container; the pan is then also covered and the food simmered until cooked. It may be necessary to top up the boiling water during cooking. It is important that food being steamed does not actually come into contact with the water during cooking.

Stew: To cook food slowly in liquid, covered, on top of the stove.

Stir-fry: To cook small, even-sized pieces of food quickly in a little oil or other fat in a wok or frying pan (skillet), tossing over a high heat.

Strain: To remove solids from liquid through a sieve (strainer) in order to retain the liquid for further use.

Sweat: To soften vegetables in fat in a covered pan over a gentle heat.

T

Toss: To turn a pancake by tossing it into the air so it turns over, then catching it again in the pan to cook the other side. Also to turn foods over to coat them in a marinade, dressing, melted butter or sauce by gently lifting them slightly and letting them drop back into the bowl or pan, using a spoon and fork or salad servers.

Truss: To tie up a joint or bird with string to keep it in a neat shape for cooking.

W

Whip: To stir rapidly or beat with a fork or electric beater in order to incorporate air quickly into ingredients like cream.

Whisk: To beat with a wire whisk; usually used to add air to egg white or egg and sugar mixtures. Also to remove the lumps from a sauce, gravy, etc., during cooking.

Z

Zest: The oily coloured rind of citrus fruit.

useful equipment

There's no need to splash out on loads of kitchen equipment. Start with a few absolute basics, then gradually add to your collection as you decide what you want to cook.

Essentials

- Can opener
- Carving knife and fork
- Casserole dishes (Dutch ovens), including one flameproof one for use on top of the stove
- Chopping boards – buy several, of different shapes or colours, then keep one just for raw meat; one for strong smelling foods like onions; one for fruit and vegetables and one for bread
- Colander – for straining cooked vegetables, etc.
- Draining spoon – long-handled with holes in the bowl
- Fish slice
- Frying pans (skillets) – 1 medium or large and 1 small omelette pan (non-stick if possible)
- Grater – a round or four-sided one with a top handle is better than a flat one
- Kitchen scissors
- Measuring jug
- Measuring spoons
- Ovenproof dishes – various shapes and sizes and one with a lip for pies
- Potato masher
- Potato peeler
- Roasting tins (baking pans), preferably 1 large and 1 small
- Saucepans – at least 1 small, 1 medium and 1 large, all with lids
- Scales

- Sharp knives – at least 1 small vegetable knife and 1 large cook's knife (for cutting up meat, etc.) and a bread knife with a serrated edge
- Sieve (strainer) – metal or plastic with a fine mesh
- Whisk, preferably balloon-shaped
- Wooden spoons – several, of different sizes

Extras

These may be useful when you start to expand your culinary repertoire.
- Baking (cookie) sheet
- Baking tins (pans) – square and rectangular, various sizes
- Beater, electric, hand-held
- Biscuit (cookie) cutters – fluted and plain, in different sizes
- Blender or food processor
- Cake tins (pans) – deep, loose-bottomed, different sizes and shapes
- Fluted flan dish (pie pan)
- Loaf tins (pans) – 450 g/1 lb and 900 g/2 lb sizes
- Palette knife
- Pastry (paste) brush
- Piping (pastry) bag with tubes, large plain and star-shaped
- Ramekin dishes (custard cups)
- Ring tin (pan) – about 1.2 litre/2 pt/6 cup
- Rolling pin – not vital as a clean bottle will always do instead
- Sandwich tins (pans) 18 cm/7 in, plus other sizes if you're keen!
- Skewers – metal meat skewers and metal or wooden kebab skewers
- Soufflé dish – about 18 cm/7 in diameter
- Soup ladle
- Spatula, flexible plastic – for scraping out mixing bowls
- Springform cake tin (pan) with removable sides and base
- Swiss roll tin (jelly roll pan)
- Tartlet tins (patty pans)
- Wire cooling rack

Nifty gadgets

The items on this list are not essential but will make cooking a lot easier.
- Apple corer
- Basting spoon with a lip on the side
- Boning knife
- Canelling knife – for paring strips of rind from citrus fruit, cucumber, etc.

- Citrus juicer – I like the wooden, Victorian, hand-held kind
- Double saucepan
- Egg pricker – to pierce the egg before boiling, which prevents cracking
- Fish kettle with a trivet and lid for cooking large, whole fish
- Garlic press – you may be able to get one with a cherry stoner combined
- Grapefruit knife
- Hand-held blender
- Herb chopper
- Jar opener
- Knife sharpener – hand-held or electric
- Mandolin, for thinly slicing vegetables – not necessary if you have a blade on your grater or food processor
- Meat cleaver
- Meat mallet
- Melon baller
- Mincer (grinder) – not necessary if you have a food processor
- Mouli grater
- Nutmeg grater
- Olive oil can with narrow pouring spout
- Pastry (paste) wheel
- Pepper mill
- Pestle and mortar
- Pie funnel – unless you prefer to use an upturned egg cup instead
- Pizza wheel – for cutting up cooked pizzas
- Poultry shears
- Pressure cooker – I couldn't live without mine
- Salad crisper and shaker
- Spaghetti tongs – the chrome ones with teeth are best
- Steamer – the chrome, collapsible sort that fits any saucepan
- Toasted sandwich maker – preferably one that cuts and seals the sandwiches in halves
- Universal cooking thermometer, for sugar, oil, etc.

a well-stocked storecupboard

As with your equipment, just start with the things you know you will use and gradually add ingredients as you feel you need them.

Storecupboard standards

- Baking powder
- Bicarbonate of soda (baking soda)
- Chilli powder and/or cayenne
- Cocoa (unsweetened chocolate) powder
- Coffee granules
- Cranberry sauce
- Dried herbs – basil, chives, mint, oregano, sage, thyme and mixed herbs
- Dried milk (non-fat dry milk)
- Drinking (sweetened) chocolate powder – or any instant chocolate drink powder with added milk powder
- Flour – plain (all-purpose), self-raising (self-rising) and wholemeal
- Garlic purée (paste) in a tube – use about 1 cm/½ in per garlic clove
- Honey – clear, not set
- Horseradish sauce or cream
- Lemon juice – not vital but a bottle will keep in the fridge for ages
- Marmalade
- Marmite or other yeast extract
- Mayonnaise
- Mustard – made English, Dijon and wholegrain
- Oil – sunflower and olive (essential), plus a speciality variety, such as sesame and walnut
- Pasta, dried – spaghetti, lasagne sheets, quick-cook macaroni, etc.
- Pepper – black peppercorns to be ground and ready-ground white
- Red lentils

- Redcurrant jelly (clear conserve)
- Rice, long-grain
- Salt
- Sauces – ketchup (catsup), brown, Worcestershire, Tabasco, soy, and chilli
- Spices – ground cinnamon, cumin, ginger and mace; grated nutmeg
- Stock cubes – vegetable, chicken and beef
- Sugar – caster (superfine), granulated, light and dark brown
- Tomato purée (paste) in a tube
- Vinegar – red or white wine or cider; balsamic, malt

Canny cans

- Baked beans
- Condensed mushroom, chicken and tomato soup (ideal for sauces)
- Corned beef
- Custard
- Fish – mackerel, pilchards or sardines
- Fruit – buy the ones you like, but pineapple is particularly useful in cooking
- Pulses – red kidney beans, butter (lima) beans, etc., and brown lentils
- Rice pudding
- Sweetcorn (corn)
- Tomatoes
- Tuna (check the label for 'dolphin friendly')
- Vegetables – peas, carrots, green beans

Perishables

- Bread – loaves, rolls, pitta bread, naan, etc. can all be stored in the freezer
- Butter and/or margarine
- Cheese – Cheddar and Parmesan; fresh Parmesan has a far better flavour then dried, and you can grate and freeze it for use straight from the freezer
- Cream or cream substitute – single (light) and whipping
- Crème fraîche – for sauces, dressings and toppings
- Eggs – the recipes in this book use medium size
- Frozen peas and beans
- Milk – cartons freeze well. Shake once defrosted
- Plain yoghurt

basic food hygiene

A hygienic cook is a healthy cook, so please bear the following in mind when you're preparing food.

- Always wash your hands first.
- Always wash and dry fresh fruit and vegetables before use.
- Don't lick your fingers.
- Don't keep tasting and stirring with the same spoon. Use a clean spoon every time you taste the food.
- Don't put raw and cooked meat on the same shelf in the fridge. Store raw meat on the bottom shelf, so it can't drip over other foods. Keep all perishable foods wrapped separately. Don't overfill the fridge or it will remain too warm.
- Use separate cloths for wiping down chopping boards for meat and vegetables, and your work surfaces; if you use the same one, you will simply spread germs. Always wash your cloths well in hot, soapy water and, ideally, use an anti-bacterial kitchen cleaner on all surfaces too.
- Always transfer leftovers to a clean container and cover with a lid, clingfilm (plastic wrap) or foil. Leave until completely cold, then store in the fridge. Never put any warm food in the fridge.
- When reheating food, always make sure it is piping hot throughout, never just lukewarm (see page 20, Reheating and cooking from frozen).
- Never re-freeze foods that have defrosted unless you cook them first. Never reheat cooked food more than once.

reheating and cooking from frozen

You may occasionally need to reheat dishes, especially if you live on your own. You can use a microwave (page 23) or reheat conventionally.

Reheating

- Cooked food should be reheated only once.
- To make sure foods don't dry out while reheating, cover with a lid or wrap them in foil, or add a sauce or gravy.
- Dishes with a high moisture content, such as casseroles or Bolognese sauce, can be reheated gently in a saucepan, stirring frequently.
- To reheat a dish in the oven, place in a preheated oven at 200°C/400°F/gas mark 6 for about 10 minutes or longer until heated through.
- To reheat a plated meal on the hob, place the plate over a pan of gently simmering water, cover and steam for about 10 minutes until heated through.
- Always make sure it is piping hot right through, never just warm.
- To test if a ready-made dish is hot through, insert a knife down through the centre, wait 5 seconds and remove. The blade should feel burning hot. If not, heat for a little longer.

Cooking from frozen

- Fruit, vegetables and fish cook very well from frozen.
- Instructions for ready-prepared meals and convenience foods like pizzas, sausages and burgers often say 'Best cooked from frozen'. Always follow the manufacturer's instructions.

- Home-frozen dishes are best thawed first, ideally in the fridge overnight, or otherwise covered, at room temperature. If thawing at room temperature, cook as soon as possible after thawing.
- Never cook poultry or joints of meat from frozen. Thaw as for home-frozen dishes (see above).
- It is possible to cook chops or steaks from frozen. After quickly browning, cook at a more gentle heat than you would use for thawed meat, and for longer. You must make sure they are cooked right through before serving. It is always preferable to defrost them first.
- Minced (ground) meat can be cooked from frozen. If it's in a lump, scrape the browned meat away from the block as it cooks and break up the lump as soon as possible. Make sure every grain is no longer pink before adding the remaining ingredients.
- To speed up the thawing of poultry or meat, immerse the wrapped product in cold water and change the water frequently. NEVER put it in hot water.
- Don't refreeze thawed food unless it is cooked through first.

microwave and conventional cooking combination

If you have a microwave, make it work for you. I prefer to use mine in conjunction with my conventional cooker as I think you get best results all round. For instance, you can cook fish to perfection (and without that awful smell) in the microwave while grilling (broiling) some oven chips. While the fish is 'standing' to finish cooking, cook some peas in the microwave: the whole meal will be ready literally in minutes.

Most people use their microwave mainly for reheating foods, whether convenience or fresh. But you can use it to cook almost anything. Here is a guide to converting conventional recipes for cooking in the microwave, together with some handy tips on microwave reheating.

Converting your favourite recipes

Most conventional recipes can be cooked in the microwave but you will need to experiment to get the best results. Remember these general rules:

* For soups and casseroles, use only two-thirds the amount of liquid specified in the recipe.
* Don't use tough cuts of meat. For casseroles, cut meat into 2.5 cm/1 in cubes, divide poultry into even-sized portions and cut any vegetables up into small, even pieces.

- Reduce the conventional cooking time by three-quarters if cooking on High (100 per cent power).
- Reduce the conventional cooking time by half if cooking on Medium (50 per cent power).
- Reduce the conventional cooking time by a quarter if cooking on Medium-low (30 per cent power).
- Cover a dish in the microwave if you would cover it in a conventional oven.
- Food will continue cooking during standing time, so don't overcook it – you can always add on extra time if necessary, but you can't rescue dried-up leather. If, after standing time, food is still slightly underdone, give it a little extra cooking time, checking frequently as sometimes just seconds can make all the difference.

Reheating

Home-cooked foods (fresh or frozen)

- Ready-made dishes such as lasagne, cottage pie, etc. are best reheated on Medium (50 per cent power), if cooking from frozen, or High (100 per cent power), if they have been stored in the fridge, until piping hot throughout. Test as for reheating conventionally (page 20).
- Microwave ovens often heat unevenly, giving what are called 'cold spots'. To rectify this, turn the dish once or twice during heating, even if your oven has a turntable.

Convenience foods

- Many ready-made foods can be reheated in the microwave. Pizzas, baked beans, canned pasta, soups, stews and frozen and cook-chill meals all reheat well. Follow the manufacturer's instructions on the packet or can.
- Always remove any foil containers, and empty canned foods into a bowl.
- Stir canned foods several times during heating to distribute the heat evenly.
- Remember always to pierce the bag of boil-in-the-bag foods – place the bag in a dish first to prevent spillage.

tricks of the trade

Nowadays there are many storecupboard items that are an absolute boon for busy cooks.

Sauces

All these savoury ingredients can be used as sauces to pour over freshly cooked pasta, or to serve with grilled (broiled) meats or other simple dishes.
- Canned, condensed soups
- Passata (sieved tomatoes)
- Canned vegetables, drained and puréed, then thinned with the liquid or a little milk
- Creamed sweetcorn (corn)
- Creamed mushrooms
- Soft cheeses with garlic and herbs or black peppercorns, melted and thinned with milk

These are good with ice cream, rice pudding, fresh fruit, plain cakes, yoghurt and fromage frais.
- Mars bars (or other speciality chocolate bars), melted and thinned with milk
- Chocolate hazelnut (filbert) spread, thinned with a little milk and heated until smooth and hot. Add a spoonful of chopped nuts, if liked
- Canned fruit, puréed and sieved (strained) if necessary to remove pips
- Lemon or orange curd, warmed and thinned with a little apple or orange juice

Coatings

Coatings add extra flavour and texture to plain foods. Dip items such as strips of chicken or small fillets of fish in beaten egg or milk and then one of these coatings.

- Chopped nuts and crushed Weetabix
- Crushed cornflakes or branflakes
- Crushed Shredded Wheat
- Plain breadcrumbs
- Rolled oats, flavoured with herbs or spices (if liked)
- Stuffing mix

Toppings

Use these to add variety to savoury dishes before grilling (broiling) or baking.

- Crushed Weetabix moistened with a little melted butter or margarine
- Grated cheese and/or crushed cornflakes or branflakes
- Leftover cooked potatoes, sliced and dotted with butter or margarine, or mashed with a little milk and butter or margarine
- Rolled oats, moistened with a little melted butter or margarine and flavoured with herbs or spices
- Sliced buttered bread, cut into triangles or cubes

And for sweet dishes:

- Crushed Weetabix, moistened with a little melted butter or margarine and sweetened with sugar or honey
- Cubes or triangles of buttered bread, sprinkled with light brown sugar
- Halved scones (biscuits), buttered and sprinkled with sugar
- Rolled oats, moistened with a little melted butter or margarine, sweetened with sugar or honey and flavoured with cinnamon, nutmeg or mixed (apple-pie) spice

Thickeners

These will add body to soups, sauces or casseroles when you need a thicker texture.

- Crumbled Weetabix
- Instant oat cereal
- Instant mashed potato powder

quantities

It is important to calculate the right quantity of food you need before you start cooking; you don't want to waste money and food, but you certainly don't want to starve everyone! The list below gives a guide to the amount you will need per person for an average portion. Note that if you are serving more than one vegetable you will need only half the quantity stated per person.

- Artichokes, globe · 1
- Artichokes, Jerusalem · 225 g/8 oz
- Asparagus, large · 225 g/8 oz
- Asparagus, small, tender · 100 g/4 oz
- Apples, for cooking · 1 large
- Aubergine (eggplant) · ½
- Batter · use 25 g/1 oz/¼ cup flour
- Beans, broad (fava) – unshelled · 225 g/8 oz
  　　　　　　　　　　　– shelled · 100 g/4 oz
- Beans, French (green) or runner · · · · · · · · · · · · · 100–175 g/4–6 oz
- Broccoli · 100 g/4 oz
- Brussels sprouts/spring (collard) greens · · · · · · · · · · · · · 175 g/6 oz
- Cabbage · ¼ small
- Carrots · 1 large
- Cauliflower · ¼ small
- Chicken – portion/breast · 1
  　　　　　– thighs, legs · 1–2
  　　　　　– whole bird · 225 g/8 oz
  　　　　　– poussin (Cornish hen) · · · · · · · · · · · · · · 1 small, ½ large
- Cornish hen · *see* Chicken
- Courgettes (zucchini) · 1 large
- Crab · 1 small or ¼–½ large
- Custard · use 150 ml/¼ pt/⅔ cup milk
- Duck – whole · ¼–½
  　　　– breast · 1 small or ½ large
- Eggplant · *see* Aubergine

- Fish – fillets/steaks   175 g/6 oz
  - whole   225–350 g/8–12 oz
- Leeks   1 small
- Lobster   1 small or ½ large
- Mangetout (snow peas)   50–100 g/2–4 oz
- Marrow (squash)   225 g/8 oz
- Meat – raw, minced (ground)   100 g/4 oz
  - diced   100–175 g/4–6 oz
  - steak   175 g/6 oz
  - chops/cutlets   1 large/2 small
  - joint, bone in   225–350 g/8–12 oz
  - joint, boneless   100–175 g/4–6 oz
- Mushrooms   50–100 g/2–4 oz
- Mussels   350–450 g/12 oz–1 lb
- Parsnip   1 small
- Pasta   50–100 g/2–4 oz
- Pastry (paste)   use 50 g/2 oz/½ cup flour
- Pears   1 large
- Peas – unshelled   225 g/8 oz
  - shelled   100 g/4 oz
- Potatoes   1 large or 4 small
- Poussin   *see* Chicken
- Prawns (shrimp) – unshelled   175 g/6 oz
  - shelled   50–100 g/2–4 oz
- Pulses (dried peas, beans, lentils)   50 g/2 oz/½ cup
- Rice, long-grain, uncooked   50 g/2 oz/¼ cup
- Sauce   use 75–150 ml/5–10 tbsp liquid
- Soft fruit (strawberries, raspberries, etc.)   100 g/4 oz
- Soup   250–300 ml/8–10 fl oz/1–1¼ cups
- Shrimp   *see* Prawns
- Spinach   225 g/8 oz
- Squash   *see* Marrow
- Stone fruits (apricots, etc.)   100–175 g/4–6 oz
- Tomatoes   1–2
- Turkey – steaks   175 g/6 oz
  - whole   225–350 g/8–12 oz
  - boneless joint   100–175 g/4–6 oz
- Zucchini   *see* Courgettes

planning a meal

A healthy, balanced diet

We all know that it is important to have a healthy balanced diet. This is best achieved by eating foods from the different food groups in the correct proportions every day.

The largest part of every meal and snack should be made up of starchy foods such as cereals, potatoes, yams, bread, pasta and rice; these will give you energy, fibre, vitamins and minerals. Add to the starchy part a smaller portion of foods rich in protein, vitamins and minerals such as meat, fish, eggs, nuts, pulses and cheese, milk or other dairy produce. Accompany these with lots of fruit and vegetables to give you more fibre and extra vitamins and minerals.

Eat only a very limited amount of sugar and fats such as butter, margarine, cream and oil and restrict your intake of foods made with them – these include cakes, pastries, biscuits (cookies), jams (conserves) and relishes, sweets, chocolates, alcohol and anything fried (sautéed). These foods will give you warmth and energy, it is true, but if eaten in excess they will make you fat as they pile on extra calories you don't need.

Presentation and style

When you're deciding what to cook, think about what the finished meal will look and taste like. Here, variety is the key.

Colours and textures are important, as is a healthy balance of ingredients. For instance, you wouldn't want to serve steamed white fish with mashed potatoes and butter (lima) beans. The meal would look unappetisingly pale and it would also taste very bland. But if you served the fish with potatoes cooked in their skins, a tomato sauce and French (green) beans, the overall colour and flavour would be much more appealing. Also, if you are serving, say, roast pork with apple sauce for a main course, don't serve apple pie as dessert!

Remember, too, that expensive foods are not necessarily better for you. For example, mackerel, which is very inexpensive, is just as good for you as swordfish. The cheaper cuts of meat are as nutritious as the best steak. The only difference is that the cheaper ones may have more fat, which should be removed before cooking, and the meat will need longer, slower cooking. In the same way, nibbling asparagus won't make you fitter than eating cabbage!

However, you should beware of some so-called 'economy' ranges of convenience foods. Cheap minced (ground) meat, for instance, will have a large proportion of fat and the meat content will be of dubious quality and may contain added soya protein. Cheap sausages will have lots of fat and rusk (a bulk filler) and a very low proportion of actual meat. Cheap fish fingers and other similar products made with minced fish or meat rather than pure fillet could contain any part of the creature, so the quality is likely to be poor.

notes on the recipes

- Most recipes serve four people. It is easy to quarter or halve the quantities for one or two or make the full quantity, and store any extra in the fridge or freezer.
- All ingredients are given in metric, imperial and American measures. Follow one set only in a recipe. American terms are given in brackets.
- All spoon measures are level: 1 tsp = 5 ml; 1 tbsp = 15 ml. If you are using ordinary spoons, rather than a set of kitchen measuring spoons, you may need to add a little extra to the quantities given.
- Eggs are medium unless otherwise stated.
- Always wash, peel, core and seed, if necessary, fresh produce before use.
- Seasoning and the use of strongly flavoured ingredients such as garlic or chillies is a matter of personal taste. Adjust to suit your own palate.
- Use fresh herbs unless dried are specifically called for. If you wish to substitute dried for fresh, use only half the quantity or less, as they are very pungent. Frozen, chopped varieties have a better colour and flavour than dried and make a good alternative to fresh.
- All can sizes are approximate as they vary from brand to brand. If a recipe calls for a 400 g can of tomatoes and yours is a 397 g can, that's fine.
- I have given a choice of butter or margarine in most of the recipes except where butter gives a better flavour. Use a soft spread if you prefer, but check that it is suitable for general cooking, not just for spreading.
- Cooking times are approximate and should be used as a guide only. For foods cooked in the oven, the cooking time given will be the time you can leave the dish unattended. If you are stir-frying, however, you will need to stand over the food throughout the cooking time. Always check food is piping hot and cooked through before serving.
- Where cream cheese is called for, you can use low- or medium-fat alternatives if you prefer.

eggs

Eggs are one of the most useful and versatile foods we have. They are a source of protein and fat, and also provide vitamin A, some B vitamins, vitamin D and calcium. Eggs are rich in iron, too, but not in a form that is easily used by the human body.

Old wives' tales

Contrary to popular belief, there is absolutely no more goodness in a brown egg than a white one; the colour of the shell depends on the breed of bird. There is no more goodness in a deep yellow yolk than a pale one, either, and eating lots of eggs does not make you 'egg-bound'.

Choosing eggs

Eggs from birds raised on battery farms, in barns or free-range are all equally nutritious but I buy free-range eggs on humane grounds even though they are more expensive. Organic eggs, that is eggs from birds fed on purely organically grown foods, are also available and if you are fanatical about watching your cholesterol level, you'll be interested in the lower-fat eggs. However, whichever type you buy, choose those with the longest sell-by date you can find and never exceed the use-by date. Avoid any that are cracked. Always buy from a reputable source. If you buy from a local farmer, ask when the eggs were laid – they should be preferably no more than a week old, and certainly not more than two weeks old, when you buy them. Do not wash them unless they are actually dirty when you buy them.

Egg types and sizes

Hens' eggs are the ones we use every day. They are now graded in four sizes: small, medium, large and jumbo (extra large). You can also try duck and goose eggs, which are extremely rich and are best for custards, mousses and other puddings. I use one duck egg to two small hens' eggs and one goose egg to two large hens' eggs. Tiny, speckled quails' eggs are a popular delicacy and are particularly good served hard-boiled as a starter.

As ostriches are now being farmed, their eggs may become more popular – but I offer this information more out of interest than as a suggestion for everyday cooking. Suffice it to say that one ostrich egg is equivalent to about 24 hens' eggs – so not it's really a practical option for breakfast!

Storing eggs

Eggs will keep for 10 days at room temperature and up to two months in the fridge. For best results, take out of the fridge about 45 minutes before use.

The freshness test

If your eggs are not date-stamped, you may not remember when you bought them. To test for freshness, put the egg (in its shell) in a glass of water. If it floats, it is stale. If sinks and lies on its side, it is fresh, if it sinks and stays upright, it is less fresh but still fine to eat. When you break a fresh egg, the yolk will appear firm and round and the white thick and jelly-like. A less fresh egg will have a slight smell and the white will be runny.

Basic egg preparation

To separate eggs

If you need to separate egg whites for whisking, it is essential that you do not allow even the tiniest amount of yolk to get into the white. You can buy an egg separator (it looks like a small metal bowl, with slots in it) but the easiest way is to break the egg on to a saucer. Place an eggcup over the yolk to hold it in place and then drain the white off into a separate bowl.

To whisk egg whites

Always make sure the bowl and the beater or whisk are clean and dry. Also make sure there is no yolk left in the whites. Whisk until you have the consistency stated in the recipe – 'softly peaking' means that the egg whites are no longer liquid, but just holding a solid shape; 'stiff' means that the bowl can be tipped upside down without them falling out!

To whisk eggs and sugar

Traditionalists will tell you to put the bowl of eggs and sugar over a pan of hot water and whisk with a balloon whisk to get the best volume. Nowadays you can forget the hot water and use an electric beater. The results are perfect and take far less effort.

Cooking eggs

Boiled eggs

- SOFT-BOILED:

Everyone has different a method. The one I am recommending here works well, but don't try to cook more than six at once.

1 Prick the air sac with an egg pricker.
2 Place in a saucepan just large enough to hold the eggs in a single layer.
3 Add enough cold water to just cover the eggs. Put on a lid. Bring to the boil.
4 As soon as the water bubbles, time the eggs for 3½ minutes.
5 At the end of this time, lift the eggs out of the water immediately with a draining spoon and place in eggcups.
6 Tap the tops gently with a spoon to prevent further cooking.

- HARD-BOILED (HARD-COOKED):

Prepare as for soft-boiled but cook for 7 minutes. If the eggs are to be served cold, drain off the boiling water and cover with cold water to prevent a black ring forming round the yolk. Leave until cold before shelling.

Fried (sautéed) eggs

1 Melt enough butter or add just enough oil in a heavy-based or non-stick frying pan (skillet) to cover the base.
2 Break the eggs, one at a time, into a cup, then gently slide into the pan.
3 Tilt the pan slightly and spoon the hot fat over (baste) the eggs as they cook.
4 Cook until the whites are just firm but the yolk is still soft. If you like crispy edges, cook over a fairly high heat (but be careful of spluttering). If you like them soft, use a lower heat.
5 Remove from the pan with a fish slice, to allow the fat to drain off, then transfer to warm plates.

Poached eggs

This method produces soft, delicate eggs.

1 Put about 2.5 cm/1 in water in a heavy-based frying pan (skillet) and add 15 ml/1 tbsp lemon juice.
2 Bring to the boil, then reduce the heat until the water is just simmering.
3 Break the eggs, one at a time, into a cup, then gently slide into the water.

4 Cover with a lid and poach for about 3 minutes for soft-cooked eggs, 4–5 minutes for firm ones.

- TO USE AN EGG POACHER:
1 Half-fill the pan with water.
2 Put a knob of butter or margarine in each egg holder and melt by bringing the water to the boil.
3 Break an egg into each holder and season with salt and pepper.
4 Cover and cook for 2–4 minutes until cooked to your liking.
5 Carefully loosen the eggs round the edges with a round-bladed knife before sliding them out.

Scrambled eggs

Allow 2 eggs per person.

- TO SCRAMBLE IN A PAN:
1 Break the eggs in a pan with 15 ml/1 tbsp milk or cream per egg and a small knob of butter or margarine. Season lightly.
2 Cook over a gentle heat, stirring all the time, until the mixture is just set but still creamy. Do not allow to boil or the mixture will curdle.

- TO COOK IN THE MICROWAVE:
1 Place the ingredients (as above) in a non-metallic bowl.
2 Microwave on High (100 per cent power) for about 45 seconds per egg, stirring every 30 seconds until almost set.
3 Leave to stand for 2 minutes to complete cooking.

Omelettes

There are two types of omelette: plain (French-style) and fluffy (soufflé).

- PLAIN OMELETTE:

Allow 2–3 eggs per person. Make one omelette at a time.

1 Beat the eggs in a bowl with a little salt and pepper and 15 ml/1 tbsp water.
2 Melt a small knob of butter in an omelette pan.
3 Add the egg mixture. Cook, lifting the edge of the mixture as it sets to let the runny egg trickle under, until the bottom of the omelette is golden brown and the mixture is just set.
4 Fold the omelette, then slide out on to a warm plate.

- CHEESE OMELETTE:

Prepare as before; scatter 25 g/1 oz/¼ cup grated Cheddar cheese over half of the omelette about halfway through the cooking time, or stir it into the eggs before cooking.

- MUSHROOM OMELETTE:

Prepare as before; stew 50 g/2 oz sliced mushrooms in a little water, then, when the omelette is just cooked, scatter the mushrooms over one half before folding and sliding it on to a plate.

- HAM OMELETTE:

Prepare as before; sprinkle 30 ml/2 tbsp chopped ham over the surface when the omelette is almost cooked. Heat through before folding and sliding on to a plate.

- CHICKEN OMELETTE:

Prepare as before; scatter with 30 ml/2 tbsp chopped, cooked chicken and a pinch of dried thyme when the omelette is almost cooked. Heat through, then fold and slide on to a plate.

- TOMATO OMELETTE:

Prepare as before; arrange a sliced tomato over half the omelette when it is almost cooked. Heat through, sprinkle with a few chopped, fresh basil leaves, fold and slide on to a plate.

- PRAWN OMELETTE:

Prepare as before; scatter 30 ml/2 tbsp cooked, peeled prawns (shrimp) over half the almost-cooked omelette. Sprinkle with a few drops of soy sauce. Heat through, then fold and slide on to a plate.

- FLUFFY OMELETTE:

Allow 2 eggs per person. Make one at a time.

1 Separate the eggs.
2 Beat the yolks with a pinch of salt and some freshly ground black pepper and 30 ml/2 tbsp water.
3 Whisk the egg whites until stiff, then fold in the yolk mixture.
4 Heat a knob of butter or margarine in an omelette pan. Add the egg mixture.
5 Cook over a moderate heat until the base of the omelette is golden brown.

6 Place the pan under a preheated grill (broiler) until the omelette has risen and is golden on top.
7 Fold in half and slide on to a plate.

● TO MAKE A FILLED FLUFFY OMELETTE:

Use any of the fillings on page 35; either fold the filling into the egg mixture before cooking or spread over the omelette, put under the grill (broiler) to heat through, then fold and serve.

● SWEET FLUFFY OMELETTE:

Prepare as for a fluffy omelette (above) but omit the salt and pepper and whisk 15 ml/1 tbsp caster (superfine) sugar into the whisked egg whites. When cooked, spread with a little warm jam (conserve) or fruit purée, then fold and serve. Dust with a little sifted icing (confectioners') sugar before serving.

Baked eggs

● TO BAKE IN THE OVEN:

1 Lightly butter ramekin dishes (custard cups).
2 Break an egg into each dish. Season lightly.
3 Top each with 15 ml/1 tbsp double (heavy) cream.
4 Stand the dishes in a shallow baking tin (pan) with enough boiling water to come halfway up the sides of the dishes.
5 Cook in a preheated oven at 180°C/350°F/gas mark 4 for 8–10 minutes.

● TO BAKE IN THE MICROWAVE:

1 Prepare as above but prick the yolk twice with a cocktail stick (toothpick).
2 Cook on High (100 per cent power) for 1–1½ minutes per egg (depending on the output of your microwave) and leave to stand for 2 minutes. For firmer eggs, cook for 30 seconds more per egg.

● BAKED EGGS WITH HAM:

Prepare as above; put 15 ml/1 tbsp chopped ham in the base of each dish before adding the egg.

● BAKED EGGS WITH ASPARAGUS:

Prepare as above; spread 15 ml/1 tbsp chopped, cooked asparagus in the base of each dish before adding the egg.

- BAKED EGGS WITH TOMATOES:

Prepare as above; put a skinned, chopped tomato in the base of each dish and sprinkle with 2 chopped, fresh basil leaves before adding the egg.

- SWISS BAKED EGGS:

Prepare as above; put 15 ml/1 tbsp grated Gruyère or Emmental (Swiss) cheese in the base of each dish before adding the egg.

Hot savoury and sweet soufflés

The basic soufflé mixture is the same; you simply add the flavouring of your choice to the sauce before adding the eggs.

- BASIC SOUFFLÉ MIXTURE:

This makes a soufflé for 4 people.

1 Grease a 1.2 litre/2 pt/5 cup soufflé or other shallow dish with 15 g/½ oz/ 1 tbsp butter or margarine.
2 Put 40 g/1½ oz/⅓ cup plain (all-purpose) flour in a saucepan.
3 Whisk in 300 ml/½ pt/1¼ cups milk until smooth. Add 25 g/1 oz/3 tbsp butter or margarine.
4 Cook over a moderate heat, stirring all the time, until very thick and smooth. Cool slightly, then stir in the flavouring of your choice (see below).
5 Separate 3 eggs and add the yolks to the mixture.
6 Whisk the egg whites until stiff.
7 Beat two spoonfuls of the egg white into the sauce to thin it slightly, then fold in the remainder with a metal spoon. Turn into the soufflé dish. Mark a small circle in the centre of the mixture with a knife.
8 Bake in a preheated oven at 190°C/375°F/gas mark 5 for about 30 minutes or until risen, golden brown and just set. Serve straight away.

- CALIFORNIAN CORN SOUFFLÉ:

Beat 200 g/7 oz/1 small can of sweetcorn (corn), drained, and 2 rashers (slices) of cooked, chopped bacon into the sauce with the egg yolks.

- CHEESE SOUFFLÉ:

Add 100 g/4 oz/1 cup grated Cheddar or Gruyère (Swiss) cheese to the sauce with the egg yolks and season with salt and freshly ground black pepper.

- CHICKEN SOUFFLÉ:

Add 100 g/4 oz/1 cup chopped, cooked chicken to the sauce with the egg yolks and a pinch of dried mixed herbs, some salt and freshly ground black pepper.

- CHOCOLATE SOUFFLÉ:

Beat 30 ml/2 tbsp caster (superfine) sugar and 50 g/2 oz/½ cup plain (semi-sweet) chocolate, melted, into the sauce with the egg yolks.

- COFFEE SOUFFLÉ:

Beat 45 ml/3tbsp caster (superfine) sugar and 15 ml/1 tbsp instant coffee powder or granules, dissolved in 10 ml/2 tsp water, into the sauce with the egg yolks.

- HAM SOUFFLÉ:

Stir 100 g/4 oz/1 cup cooked, chopped ham into the sauce with the egg yolks. Season with salt and freshly ground black pepper and 5 ml/1 tsp Dijon or English mustard.

- LEMON SOUFFLÉ:

Sweeten the sauce with 45 ml/3 tbsp caster (superfine) sugar and add the finely grated rind of 1 lemon.

- ORANGE SOUFFLÉ:

Add 45 ml/3 tbsp caster (superfine) sugar and the finely grated rind of 1 orange to the sauce with the egg yolks.

- SMOKED HADDOCK SOUFFLÉ:

Fold 100 g/4 oz cooked, flaked, smoked haddock (skin and bones removed) into the sauce and season with a squeeze of lemon juice and a little salt and freshly ground black pepper.

- SPINACH SOUFFLÉ:

Beat 225 g/8 oz cooked, chopped, well-drained spinach into the sauce with the egg yolks. Season with salt, freshly ground black pepper and a pinch of grated nutmeg.

- VANILLA SOUFFLÉ:

Sweeten the sauce with 45 ml/3 tbsp caster (superfine) sugar and add 5 ml/1 tsp vanilla essence (extract).

Cook's tips for eggs

- To rescue scrambled eggs that have gone watery through overcooking, pour off the liquid, then blot with kitchen paper (paper towels) to remove any liquid remaining. Beat in a good knob of butter or margarine.

- To stop an egg and sugar mixture from curdling when you add the eggs, beat in a little of the flour from the recipe.

- Don't open the oven door to check how a soufflé is cooking – it'll sink!

- If your hollandaise sauce curdles, remove from the heat and beat in 15 ml/1 tbsp hot water.

- If you are making mayonnaise and it curdles, you have added the oil too quickly. Put another egg yolk in a clean bowl, then gradually whisk in the curdled mixture a little at a time.

- Use very fresh eggs for hard-boiling (hard-cooking). It is difficult to remove the shells from staler ones.

- Some recipes contain raw eggs. They are not recommended for infants, toddlers, pregnant women or the infirm.

Recipes
Eggs Benedict

Serves 2–4

1 quantity of hollandaise sauce (page 262)
4 slices of bread
Butter or margarine
4 eggs
4 slices of ham

1 Make the hollandaise sauce.
2 Cut as large a round as possible from each slice of bread. Spread on both sides with butter or margarine and fry (sauté) until golden on both sides.
3 Meanwhile, poach the eggs.
4 Cut the ham to fit the fried bread and place on flameproof plates.
5 Top with the poached eggs, then spoon hollandaise sauce over. Flash under a hot grill (broiler) to lightly brown the top.

Eggs Florentine

Serves 1–2

225 g/8 oz spinach
15 ml/1 tbsp double (heavy) cream
Grated nutmeg
Salt and freshly ground black pepper
½ quantity of cheese sauce (page 260)
2 eggs

1 Wash and cook the spinach. Drain thoroughly. Snip with scissors to chop, then stir in the cream, a little nutmeg and salt and pepper to taste. Heat through. Spoon into one or two individual serving dishes.
2 Make the cheese sauce.
3 Poach the eggs.
4 Put an egg on each bed of spinach and spoon the cheese sauce over. Flash under a hot grill (broiler) to brown the top.

Piperade

Serves 2

15 ml/1 tbsp olive oil
15 g/½ oz/1 tbsp butter or margarine
2 onions, sliced
1 green (bell) pepper, sliced
1 red pepper, sliced
4 ripe tomatoes, roughly chopped
1 garlic clove, crushed
4 eggs, beaten
Salt and freshly ground black pepper

1 Heat the oil and butter or margarine in a large frying pan (skillet).
2 Add the onion, peppers, tomatoes and garlic and cook, stirring, for 5 minutes until soft.
3 Add the eggs, season with salt and pepper and cook over a gentle heat, stirring until scrambled. Serve straight from the pan.

Tortilla

Serves 2

30 ml/2 tbsp olive oil
1 onion, thinly sliced
1 large potato, thinly sliced
4 eggs
Salt and freshly ground black pepper

1 Heat the oil in a frying pan (skillet).
2 Add the onion and potato and cook gently, stirring, for 2 minutes. Cover with a lid and continue to cook very gently for about 8 minutes until softened but not browned, stirring occasionally. Spread out evenly.
3 Beat the eggs with a little salt and pepper and pour into the pan. Cook, lifting and stirring, until the egg is golden brown and set underneath. Slide out of the pan on to a plate, then tip back into the pan to cook the other side. Serve hot or cold.

Pancakes

Serves 4

These can be served filled with savoury or sweet fillings, or plain, sprinkled with sugar and lemon juice. They also freeze well: place individually between sheets of non-stick baking parchment, then seal in a plastic bag.

100 g/4 oz/1 cup plain (all-purpose) flour
A pinch of salt
1 egg
300 ml/½ pt/1¼ cups milk (or milk and water mixed)
15 g/½ oz/1 tbsp butter, melted (optional)
A little oil

1 Mix the flour and salt in a bowl. Make a well in the centre and add the egg and half the milk or milk and water. Beat well until thick and smooth. Stir in the melted butter, if using, and the remaining milk.
2 Leave to stand, for 30 minutes if possible, before use.
3 Put a little oil in a frying pan (skillet), pouring off any excess. Heat until very hot, then pour in just enough batter to coat the base of the pan when tipped and swirled gently. Cook until the mixture is set and the base is golden.
4 Toss or flip over with a palette knife. Cook the other side. Slide out and keep warm on a plate over a pan of hot water while cooking the remainder.

Beef Hash Pancakes

Serves 4

1 quantity of pancakes (page 41)
350 g/12 oz/1 large can of corned beef, chopped
30 ml/2 tbsp tomato ketchup (catsup)
15 ml/1 tbsp sweet pickle
1 quantity of cheese sauce (page 260)
Green salad, to serve

1 Make up the pancakes and keep warm on a plate over a pan of gently simmering water.
2 Make the cheese sauce.
3 Heat the corned beef with the ketchup and pickle in a saucepan, stirring.
4 Spread over the pancakes and roll up.
5 Place the pancakes on warm plates, spoon the cheese sauce over and serve hot with a green salad.

Crêpes Suzette

Serves 4

1 quantity of pancakes (page 41)
25 g/1 oz/2 tbsp butter
45 ml/3 tbsp light brown sugar
Grated rind and juice of 1 large orange
Grated rind and juice of ½ lemon
45 ml/3 tbsp brandy or orange liqueur

1 Make the pancakes.
2 Melt the butter in the frying pan (skillet) and add the sugar. Stir until the sugar dissolves.
3 Stir in the fruit rinds and juices. Simmer for 3–4 minutes, stirring, until the caramel dissolves and a smooth sauce is formed.
4 Fold the pancakes in quarters and add to the pan one at a time, bathing each one in the sauce and pushing to one side before adding the next.
5 Pour over the brandy or liqueur. Ignite and shake the pan gently until the flames subside. Serve straight away.

Yorkshire Pudding

Serves 4

100 g/4 oz/1 cup plain (all-purpose) flour
A pinch of salt
2 eggs
300 ml/½ pt/1¼ cups milk and water, mixed
A little oil, for greasing

1 Mix the flour and salt in a bowl and make a well in the centre.
2 Break in the eggs and make a well in the centre, add half the milk and water.
3 Gradually work in the flour, then beat with a wooden spoon until smooth.
4 Stir in the remaining milk and water. Leave to stand for 30 minutes.
5 Pour in enough oil to coat the base of each of 12 sections of a tartlet tin (patty pan) or an 18 cm × 28 cm/7 × 11 in shallow baking tin (pan). Heat in the oven at 220°C/425°F/gas mark 7 until sizzling.
6 Pour in the batter and bake at the top of the oven for 15–20 minutes for small puddings, 25–30 minutes for a large one, until puffy and golden.

Irish Eggs

Serves 4

450 g/1 lb potatoes, boiled and mashed
100 g/4 oz/1 cup Cheddar cheese, grated
Salt and freshly ground black pepper
30 ml/2 tbsp plain (all-purpose) flour
4 hard-boiled (hard-cooked) eggs
1 egg, beaten
85 g/3½ oz/1 packet of sage and onion stuffing mix
Oil, for deep-frying

1 Beat the mashed potatoes with the cheese and a little salt and pepper.
2 Shell the eggs and dip in the flour.
3 Shape a quarter of the potato mixture round each egg to cover completely.
4 Roll gently in the beaten egg, then the stuffing mix, to coat completely. Chill for 30 minutes.
5 Heat the oil until a cube of day-old bread browns in 30 seconds. Add the eggs and cook for about 4 minutes until crisp and golden. Drain on kitchen paper (paper towels) and leave to cool.

Scotch Eggs   Serves 4

4 hard-boiled (hard-cooked) eggs
30 ml/2 tbsp plain (all-purpose) flour
225 g/8 oz pork sausagemeat
5 ml/1 tsp dried onion granules
1 egg, beaten
75 g/3 oz/1½ cups breadcrumbs
Oil, for deep-frying

1 Shell the eggs. Roll in the flour.
2 Divide the sausagemeat into four pieces and flatten each to a round.
3 Dust with the onion granules, then shape each piece round an egg to cover completely. Roll in the beaten egg and then the breadcrumbs to coat completely. Chill for 30 minutes.
4 Heat the oil until a cube of day-old bread browns in 30 seconds. Add the eggs and cook for about 6 minutes until the outside is golden brown and crisp and the sausage is cooked through. Drain on kitchen paper (paper towels). Serve warm or cold.

Fool-proof Chocolate Mousse   Serves 6

4 eggs, separated
200 g/7 oz plain (semi-sweet) chocolate
75 ml/5 tbsp strong hot coffee
2.5 ml/½ tsp vanilla essence (extract)
A little whipped cream and grated chocolate, to decorate

1 Whisk the egg whites until stiff.
2 Break the chocolate up and place in a food processor or blender. Run the machine until the chocolate is completely crushed.
3 Add the hot coffee and continue to blend until the mixture is smooth.
4 Add the egg yolks and vanilla essence and blend for 1 further minute.
5 Pour slowly over the whites and fold in, lightly but thoroughly.
6 Spoon into individual dishes or a large serving dish and chill until set. Top with a little whipped cream and a sprinkling of grated chocolate.

Strawberry Pavlova

Serves 8

4 egg whites
225 g/8 oz/1 cup caster (superfine) sugar
15 ml/1 tbsp cornflour (cornstarch)
1.5 ml/¼ tsp vanilla essence (extract)
10 ml/2 tsp vinegar
150 ml/¼ pt/⅔ cup double (heavy) cream, whipped
225 g/8 oz small strawberries, halved or left whole

1 Whisk the egg whites until stiff.
2 Gradually whisk in the sugar, then the cornflour, vanilla and vinegar.
3 Spoon in a large circle on a sheet of non-stick baking parchment placed on a baking (cookie) sheet, making a slight hollow in the centre.
4 Bake in a preheated oven at 150°C/300°F/gas mark 2 for 1½ hours until a pale biscuit colour, crisp on the outside and slightly fluffy in the middle. Leave to cool.
5 Transfer to a serving plate and fill the centre with whipped cream and top with strawberries.

Swiss Baked Alaska

Serves 4–6

1 small Swiss (jelly) roll, filled with raspberry jam (conserve)
3 egg whites
175 g/6 oz/¾ cup caster (superfine) sugar
8 scoops of vanilla or raspberry ripple ice cream
3 glacé (candied) cherries, halved
6 angelica 'leaves'

1 Slice the Swiss roll in a single layer on an ovenproof plate.
2 Whisk the egg whites until stiff.
3 Whisk in half the sugar and continue whisking until stiff and glossy. Fold in the remaining sugar.
4 Pile the ice cream into the centre of the Swiss roll. Cover completely with the meringue and decorate with the cherries and angelica 'leaves'.
5 Bake immediately in a preheated oven at 230°C/450°F/gas mark 8 for 2 minutes until the meringue is turning pale golden. Serve immediately.

Chocolate Roulade

Serves 6

This makes a great Yule log for Christmas, decorated with a robin cake decoration or a sprig of holly.

175 g/6 oz/1½ cups plain (semi-sweet) chocolate
4 eggs, separated
150 g/5 oz/⅔ cup caster (superfine) sugar, plus a little extra for dusting
15 ml/1 tbsp hot water
150 ml/¼ pt/⅔ cup double (heavy) or whipping cream, whipped
A little sifted icing (confectioners') sugar, for dusting

1 Line an 18 × 28 cm/7 × 11 in Swiss roll tin (jelly roll pan) with non-stick baking parchment so that the paper stands about 2.5 cm/1 in above the tin all round.

2 Melt the chocolate in a bowl in a pan of hot water or in the microwave.

3 Whisk the egg yolks and caster sugar until thick and pale. Stir in the melted chocolate and hot water.

4 Whisk the egg whites until stiff and fold into the chocolate mixture with a metal spoon.

5 Turn into the prepared tin and spread out evenly. Bake near the top of a preheated oven at 180°C/350°F/gas mark 4 for about 15–18 minutes until firm to the touch.

6 Put a clean tea towel (dish cloth) on the work surface and cover with a sheet of baking parchment. Sprinkle with caster sugar.

7 Turn the roulade out on to the paper and carefully loosen the cooking paper but do not remove. Cover with another clean tea towel and leave until cold. Remove the top cloth and cooking paper.

8 Trim the edges if liked, then spread with the whipped cream. Carefully roll up from one short edge, using the paper underneath to help.

9 Wrap in the paper and chill until ready to serve. Unwrap, place on a serving plate, dust with sifted icing sugar and serve cut into slices.

Norwegian Cream   Serves 6

6 eggs, separated
100 g/4 oz/½ cup caster (superfine) sugar
15 ml/1 tbsp powdered gelatine
20 ml/4 tsp orange juice
45 ml/3 tbsp jam (conserve)
150 ml/¼ pt/⅔ cup double (heavy) cream, whipped
Grated chocolate or crumbled Flake bar

1 Whisk the egg whites until stiff. Add the caster sugar and whisk until peaking.
2 Whisk the yolks in a separate bowl and fold in the meringue.
3 Dissolve the gelatine in the orange juice in a bowl over a pan of hot water, or in the microwave. Fold into the egg mixture.
4 Turn into an 18 cm/7 in soufflé dish and chill until set.
5 When set, spread the top with jam, then whipped cream, and cover with grated chocolate or crumbled Flake bar.

. . . .

Vanilla Yoghurt Ice Cream   Serves 6–8

4 eggs, separated
175 g/6 oz/¾ cup caster (superfine) sugar
300 ml/½ pt/1¼ cups thick vanilla yoghurt
300 ml/½ pt/1¼ cups crème fraîche
2.5 ml/½ tsp vanilla essence (extract)

1 Whisk the egg yolks and sugar together until thick and pale.
2 Fold in the yoghurt, crème fraîche and vanilla essence.
3 Turn into a freezerproof container and freeze for 2 hours.
4 Turn the mixture into a large bowl. Whisk well with a fork to break up the ice crystals. Whisk the egg whites until stiff and fold into the yoghurt mixture.
5 Return to the freezer container and freeze until firm.

. . . .

Monday Magic Popovers

Serves 4

A delicious supper dish made of leftovers from the Sunday roast!

½ quantity of Yorkshire pudding batter (page 43)
175 g/6 oz leftover Sunday roast meat, diced
175 g/6 oz/1½ cups cooked vegetables, diced
2.5 ml/½ tsp dried oregano
Salt and freshly ground black pepper
45 ml/3 tbsp oil
Plain boiled potatoes, a green vegetable and gravy (pages 263 and 266),
    to serve

1 Make up the batter.
2 Mix the meat and vegetables with the herbs and a little salt and pepper.
3 Pour the oil into the 12 sections of a tartlet tin (pan). Heat in the oven at
  220°C/425°F/gas mark 7 until sizzling.
4 Add the meat and vegetables and return to the oven for 1 further minute.
5 Spoon in the batter and cook for about 20 minutes until puffy, crisp and
  golden. Serve hot with potatoes, a green vegetable and gravy.

Canny Savoury Soufflé

Serves 4

Ring the changes with different canned soups and appropriate vegetables,
depending on what you have in your storecupboard.

295 g/10½ oz/1 medium can of condensed asparagus soup
4 eggs, separated
75 g/3 oz/¾ cup Cheddar cheese, grated
295 g/10½ oz/1 medium can of cut asparagus spears, drained
A little butter or margarine, for greasing

1 Empty the soup into a bowl. Beat in the egg yolks and cheese.
2 Whisk the egg whites until stiff and fold into the mixture with a metal
  spoon.
3 Put the chopped asparagus in a lightly greased 18 cm/7 in soufflé dish.
  Spoon in the egg mixture.
4 Bake in a preheated oven at 200°C/400°F/gas mark 6 for about 25 minutes
  or until risen, golden and just set. Serve straight away.

cheese

Cheese is made from milk, separated into curds and whey by the use of an animal enzyme called rennet or a vegetarian equivalent. The whey is poured off and the curds processed and left to mature. Nowadays there are so many varieties with different textures, shapes, colours and flavours that it's impossible to list them. However, all cheese is a good source of protein and calcium (for strong bones and teeth). Full-fat cheeses are naturally high in fat, so don't eat too much too often, but there are many reduced- and low-fat varieties to enjoy as well.

Types of cheese

The main types of cheese are hard, semi-hard, soft, blue and fresh.

Hard cheeses

Hard varieties are made by pressing the curds to form hard, dense cheeses. They can be the firm, crumbly ones like Cheddar, Cheshire and Wensleydale; grainy ones like Parmesan and Pecorino; the firm, smooth, fat ones like Gouda and Edam and the rich, sweet, slightly rubbery ones like Gruyère and Emmental (Swiss). All hard cheeses melt well when heated.

Semi-hard cheeses

These tend to be firm but elastic, often with an open texture; others resemble soft cheeses but don't go runny when ripe. Good examples are Port Salut (French), Provolone (Italian), Monterey Jack (Californian) and Tilset (German). They can be used in cooking, but don't melt as well as the hard cheeses.

Soft cheeses

Many soft cheeses have a characteristic 'bloomy', white rind, others a pale gold or orange crust. When unripe, they have a firm, slightly grainy texture, turning smooth and creamy when perfect, and runny when over-ripe. As the cheese ripens, the flavour and smell intensify. Soft cheeses include the popular, mild, white-bloomed Brie and Camembert and the golden, much stronger, and richer Munster, Pont l'Évèque or Reblochon.

Blue cheeses

The blue veins that characterise these cheeses are actually mould. Nowadays most blue cheeses have penicillin mould injected into them but the original blue cheese, Roquefort, was made by accident. A shepherd boy left his lunch of sheep's milk cheese and bread in a cave at Roquefort while he went after a local girl. A week later he returned to the cave, to discover his cheese had gone 'blue'. It smelt and tasted so good that he passed on his find. To this day true Roquefort cheese is still matured in those same caves. Blue cheese can be hard or soft and popular varieties include Stilton, Dolcelatte, Gorgonzola and Danish Blue.

Fresh cheeses

These are the simplest cheeses. They are made from the curds, and sometimes the whey, of milk, either curdled with rennet or soured with a culture. Many fresh cheeses are made with skimmed milk and so are much lower in fat; others, like cream cheese, are full-fat. They are clearly labelled and there is a wide selection to choose from. They are delicious spread on bread and crackers, used as the base for a dip or mixed into a topping for jacket-baked potatoes and, of course, they are wonderful in many sumptuous desserts. The following are the best-known types of fresh cheese.

● CREAM CHEESE:

This is made from the curds of whole milk, often mixed with cream.

● CURD (SMOOTH COTTAGE), COTTAGE CHEESE AND QUARK:

These are made from the broken-down soft curds of skimmed milk. Cottage cheese is a lumpy curd cheese; curd cheese is smoother and quark is the smoothest.

● FETA:

Feta is white, crumbly and salty as it is pickled in brine. Originally made near Athens with sheep's milk, it is now also made in many countries with cows' milk.

● FROMAGE BLANC AND FROMAGE FRAIS:

Both of these are made from skimmed milk soured with a culture.

● MASCARPONE:

Originally made in Lombardy and Tuscany and sold in muslin bags, this is a rich, full-cream cheese.

- MOZZARELLA:

Originally made from water buffalo's milk but now also made from cows' milk, this is soft, spongy and bland. It is still usually sold in spheres packed its own whey to keep it moist, although it is sometimes sold in blocks. It is the cheese traditionally used in making pizza, and melts into gooey strings.

- RICOTTA:

A cottage-style cheese traditionally made from the whey of sheep's milk.

Choosing cheese

- If you are unsure of a cheese's flavour, it is quite acceptable to ask to taste before buying at your delicatessen counter.
- Hard cheese should have no dry-looking spots.
- Soft cheeses, like Camembert, should have a pure white bloom and should feel soft when gently pressed; they should not have a strong smell. Cut portions should be uniformly soft, not runny. Avoid soft cheeses that look chalky in the centre unless you intend to keep them for a few days to ripen. Similarly, the gold- or orange-rinded cheeses should have a uniform texture. Avoid those where the crust is discolouring or looks wet.
- Avoid any cheeses that have a strong smell of ammonia.

Buying and storing cheese

- Buy only one or two varieties at a time. Wrap each separately, and store in an airtight container in the fridge so they don't taint other foods.
- Cheese should be served at room temperature, so remove from the fridge a while before serving.
- Some cheeses can be frozen. Hard cheeses, such as Cheddar and Parmesan, are best grated first. Soft cheeses, like Camembert, will freeze whole, but not if overripe. Fresh cheeses don't freeze well.

Cook's tips for cheese

- Use a strong-flavoured cheese for cooking and you won't need so much.
- To avoid cheese in sauce going 'stringy', always add the cheese towards the end of the cooking time and stir just until it melts.
- Cheese grates more easily straight from the fridge.
- If cooking with Mozzarella, cook just until it melts and serve hot. It becomes leathery very quickly if overcooked and also when it cools.

Recipes
Savoury Smothered Pears   Serves 4

4 ripe pears, peeled, halved and cored
Lettuce leaves
1 quantity of blue cheese mayonnaise (page 266)
15 ml/1 tbsp milk
10 ml/2 tsp chopped fresh tarragon
Paprika, to garnish

1 Lay each pear half, rounded side up, on a bed of lettuce on a plate.
2 Make up the blue cheese mayonnaise, thinning with the milk, and stir in
   the tarragon. Spoon over the pears and sprinkle with paprika.

. . . .

Cottage Cheese Loaf   Serves 4

225 g/8 oz/1 cup cottage cheese
1 small onion, grated
50 g/2 oz/½ cup walnuts, chopped
2.5 ml/½ tsp dried mixed herbs
5 ml/1 tsp made English mustard
100 g/4 oz/2 cups fresh white breadcrumbs
2 eggs, beaten
Salt and freshly ground black pepper
A little oil, for greasing
Pickles and salad, to serve

1 Mix the cheese with all the other ingredients, seasoning to taste with salt
   and pepper.
2 Turn into a lightly oiled 450 g/1 lb loaf tin (pan), base-lined with greased
   greaseproof (waxed) paper.
3 Bake in a preheated oven at 180°C/350°F/gas mark 4 for about 40 minutes
   or until set.
4 Leave to cool in the tin for 5 minutes, then turn out, remove the paper and
   serve hot or cold, cut into slices with pickles and salad.

. . . .

English Cheese Pâtè

Serves 4

100 g/4 oz/1 cup Cheddar cheese, grated
100 g/4 oz Stilton cheese, crumbled
25 g/1 oz/2 tbsp butter or margarine, softened
45 ml/3 tbsp medium-dry sherry
A pinch of ground mace
Salt and freshly ground black pepper
Hot toast or crackers, to serve

1 Beat all the ingredients together until the mixture forms a paste.
2 Press into a small serving pot and chill until ready to serve with hot toast or crackers.

Swiss Cheese Fondue

Serves 4

1 garlic clove, halved
15 ml/1 tbsp cornflour (cornstarch)
15 ml/1 tbsp water
300 ml/½ pt/1¼ cups white wine
30 ml/2 tbsp kirsch
5 ml/1 tsp lemon juice
225 g/8 oz/2 cups Emmental or Gruyère (Swiss) cheese, grated
225 g/8 oz/2 cups Cheddar cheese, grated
25 g/1 oz/2 tbsp butter or margarine
Salt and freshly ground black pepper
A good pinch of grated nutmeg
Cubes of French bread, to serve

1 Rub the halved garlic clove round the bowl of a fondue pot or an attractive flameproof dish or saucepan, then discard.
2 Blend the cornflour with the water in the pot. Stir in the remaining ingredients.
3 Heat gently, stirring all the time, until the cheese melts and the mixture is smooth and glossy. Taste and adjust the seasoning, if necessary. Do not allow to boil.
4 Use forks to spear the pieces of bread and dip them into the fondue.

Golden Camembert with Cranberry Sauce

Serves 4

4 individual Camembert portions, chilled
1 large egg, beaten
40 g/1½ oz/¾ cup fresh white breadcrumbs
Oil, for deep-frying
Mixed salad leaves, to garnish
60 ml/4 tbsp cranberry sauce

1 Dip the cheese portions in beaten egg, then breadcrumbs. Repeat so they are thoroughly coated. Chill for at least 30 minutes.
2 Heat the oil until a cube of day-old bread browns in 30 seconds. Add the cheeses and cook for about 2 minutes until golden and crisp.
3 Drain on kitchen paper (paper towels). Place on plates, garnish with salad leaves and add a spoonful of cranberry sauce to the side of each. Serve straight away.

Everyday Rarebit

Serves 1–2

175 g/6 oz/1½ cups Cheddar cheese, grated
5 ml/1 tsp made English mustard
30 ml/2 tbsp apple juice
2 slices of toast
Sliced tomatoes, to serve

1 Put everything except the toast in a small pan and heat, stirring until melted and blended.
2 Spoon on to the toast and serve straight away with sliced tomatoes.

Buck Rarebit

Serves 1–2

Prepare as Everyday rarebit but top each with a poached egg.

Somerset Rarebit

Serves 1–2

Prepare as Everyday rarebit but substitute cider for the apple juice. Peel, core and slice an eating apple, place on the toast, and top with the cheese mixture.

··

Quick Cheese Straws

Makes 20

175 g/6 oz puff pastry (paste), thawed if frozen
100 g/4 oz/1 cup strong Cheddar cheese, finely grated
A good pinch of cayenne
Beaten egg, to glaze

1 Roll out the pastry thinly to form a rectangle.
2 Sprinkle half the cheese over half the pastry.
3 Fold the uncovered pastry over the top and roll again with the rolling pin.
4 Cover half with the remaining cheese and sprinkle with cayenne. Fold over, roll out and brush with beaten egg.
5 Cut into thin strips. Twist and place on a dampened baking (cookie) sheet.
6 Bake in a preheated oven at 190°C/375°F/gas mark 5 for about 15–20 minutes until crisp and golden brown. Serve warm.

··

Swiss Cheese Toasts

Serves 2 or 4

4 slices of wholemeal bread
Butter or margarine
30 ml/2 tbsp tomato purée (paste)
4 slices of ham
225 g/8 oz/1 small can of pineapple slices, drained
4 slices of Gruyère or Emmental (Swiss) cheese
1 tomato, cut into 4 slices
2.5 ml/½ tsp dried basil

1 Toast the slices of bread on one side only.
2 Butter the untoasted sides and spread with tomato purée.
3 Top with a slice each of ham, pineapple, cheese and finally tomato.
4 Sprinkle with basil and grill (broil) until the cheese melts. Serve hot.

··

Enriched Cheese Pudding

Serves 4

170 g/6 oz/1 small can of evaporated milk
2 eggs, beaten
100 g/4 oz/2 cups fresh white breadcrumbs
100 g/4 oz/1 cup Cheddar cheese, grated
2.5 ml/½ tsp dried oregano
Salt and freshly ground black pepper
A little butter or margarine, for greasing
300 ml/½ pt/1¼ cups passata (sieved tomatoes)

1 Make the milk up to 300 ml/½ pt/1¼ cups with water.
2 Add the eggs, breadcrumbs, 75 g/3 oz/¾ cup of the cheese, the herbs and a little salt and pepper and mix.
3 Lightly grease a 1.2 litre/2 pt/5 cup ovenproof dish.
4 Turn the mixture into the dish and leave to stand for 15 minutes. Sprinkle with the remaining cheese.
5 Bake in a preheated oven at 190°C/375°F/gas mark 5 for about 45 minutes until golden brown, risen and set.
6 Warm the passata and serve with the cheese pudding.

• •

Easy Strawberry Cheesecake

Serves 6

23 cm/9 in sponge flan case (pie shell)
200 g/7 oz/scant 1 cup cream cheese
50 g/2 oz/¼ cup caster (superfine) sugar
2.5 ml/½ tsp vanilla essence (extract)
150 ml/¼ pt/⅔ cup whipping cream
410 g/14½ oz/1 large can of strawberry pie filling

1 Put the flan case on a serving plate.
2 Beat the cheese with the sugar and vanilla essence. Whip the cream and fold in.
3 Turn into the flan case and chill until fairly firm. Spread the strawberry pie filling over before serving.

• •

Savoury Cheesecake

Serves 8

A little oil, for greasing
25 g/1 oz/1 small packet of plain crisps (potato chips)
25 g/1 oz/½ cup cornflakes
40 g/1½ oz/3 tbsp butter or margarine, melted
2 spring onions (scallions), finely chopped
600 ml/1 pt/2½ cups vegetable stock, made with 1 stock cube
15 ml/1 tbsp powdered gelatine
100 g/4 oz/½ cup curd (smooth cottage) cheese
15 ml/1 tbsp chopped fresh parsley
5 ml/1 tsp chopped fresh sage
1 egg, separated
150 ml/¼ pt/⅔ cup whipping cream

1 Lightly oil an 18 cm/7 in deep, loose-bottomed cake tin (pan).
2 Crush the crisps and cornflakes together. Stir in 25 g/1 oz/2 tbsp of the melted butter or margarine.
3 Press the mixture into the base of the tin and chill until firm.
4 Fry (sauté) the spring onions in the remaining butter or margarine for 2 minutes, stirring. Leave to cool.
5 Spoon 30 ml/2 tbsp of the stock into a small bowl. Sprinkle the gelatine over and leave to soften for 5 minutes. Stand the bowl in a pan of hot water or heat briefly in the microwave until the gelatine is completely dissolved. Stir into the remaining stock.
6 Mix the cheese with the spring onions, half the parsley and all of the sage. Beat in the egg yolk. Blend in the stock and chill until on the point of setting.
7 Whisk the egg white until stiff, then whip the cream until peaking.
8 Fold the cream, then the egg white into the cheese mixture with a metal spoon.
9 Turn into the cake tin and chill until set. Remove the tin. Garnish with the remaining parsley and serve cold.

Tiramisu

Serves 6

250 g/9 oz/good 1 cup Mascarpone cheese
2 eggs, separated
45 ml/3 tbsp caster (superfine) sugar
10 ml/2 tsp strong black coffee
120 ml/4 fl oz/½ cup medium strength black coffee
90 ml/6 tbsp Amaretto or coffee liqueur
20 sponge (lady) fingers
Drinking (sweetened) chocolate powder

1 Whisk the cheese and egg yolks together and gradually add the sugar.
2 Pour in the strong coffee and mix thoroughly. Whisk the egg whites until stiff and fold into the cheese mixture.
3 Mix the medium strength coffee with the liqueur and soak half the sponge fingers in it. Use to line the base of a shallow serving dish. Pour in half the cheese mixture.
4 Soak the remaining sponge fingers in the coffee and liqueur mixture and lay them on top. Top with the remaining cheese mixture.
5 Tap the dish on the work surface gently to settle the contents. Chill for at least 2 hours. Sprinkle with chocolate powder before serving.

Simple Lemon Cheesecake

Serves 4

1 packet of lemon-flavoured jelly (jello)
Boiling water
175 g/6 oz digestive biscuits (graham crackers), crushed
75 g/3 oz/⅓ cup butter or margarine, melted
25 g/1 oz/2 tbsp light brown sugar
200 g/7 oz/scant 1 cup cream cheese
50 g/2 oz/¼ cup caster (superfine) sugar
Finely grated rind and juice of 1 small lemon
150 ml/¼ pt/⅔ cup double (heavy) cream
Ground cinnamon, to decorate

1 Break up the jelly in a measuring jug and make up to 300 ml/½ pt/1¼ cups with boiling water. Stir until dissolved and leave to cool.

2 Meanwhile, mix the biscuits with the melted butter and brown sugar. Turn into a 20 cm/8 in flan tin (pie pan) and press down well.
3 Beat the cheese and caster sugar together with the lemon rind and juice. Whisk in the cold jelly.
4 When on the point of setting, whip the cream and fold in.
5 Turn into the flan case (pie shell) and chill until set. Decorate with a dusting of ground cinnamon.

....

Rich Vanilla Cheesecake   Serves 8–10

200 g/7 oz/1 small packet of digestive biscuits (graham crackers), crushed
75 g/3 oz/⅓ cup unsalted (sweet) butter, melted, plus a little extra
   for greasing
700 g/1½ lb/3 cups cream cheese
225 g/8 oz/1 cup caster (superfine) sugar
2 eggs
5 ml/1 tsp vanilla essence (extract)
150 ml/¼ pt/⅔ cup soured (dairy sour) cream
Grated nutmeg, to decorate

1 Mix the crushed biscuits into the butter. Press into the base and a little way up the sides of a 20 cm/8 in deep, round, loose-bottomed cake tin (pan).
2 Beat the cheese with the sugar, eggs and vanilla essence until smooth. Turn into the prepared tin and smooth the surface.
3 Bake in a preheated oven at 150°C/300°F/gas mark 2 for 1–1¼ hours or until just set. Turn off the oven and leave to cool in the oven.
4 Chill for at least 2 hours, overnight if possible. Decorate the top with the soured cream, swirling it over the surface and sprinkle with grated nutmeg.

....

fish and seafood

Fish and shellfish are great sources of protein and vitamins A and D, and fish oils, unlike meat fats, are now considered to be good for you. They are high in polyunsaturated Omega-3 fatty acids, which can help prevent heart disease. As an added bonus to cooks, all types of fish are quick to cook and easy to digest.

Types of fish

There is a vast range of fish available in fishmongers and on speciality counters in today's supermarkets. Apart from fresh fish and shellfish, we can buy prepared fish preserved in many different ways: smoked, salted, pickled and, of course, canned and frozen.

White fish

White fish is the term used to describe sea fish with white flesh; their oil is stored only in the liver. There are two types: round fish, such as cod, coley, haddock, whiting, hake, bream and bass; and flat fish, such as plaice, Dover sole, lemon sole, halibut, turbot, brill, flounder and skate. Interestingly, the main body of skate is not pleasant to eat – only the wings are used.

Oily fish

These have coarser, oily flesh ranging in colour from to beige to red. Some are caught at sea, while others are freshwater varieties found in rivers and lakes and now often farmed. Oily sea fish include conger eel, red and grey mullet, mackerel, herring, pilchard, sprat, snapper, tuna, swordfish and marlin and also small fry, such as whitebait (baby herring) and sardines (young pilchards). Freshwater varieties include salmon, rainbow and brown trout, carp, pike, perch and eel.

Shellfish

There are two types of shellfish.

- CRUSTACEANS:

These are shellfish with jointed shells, including crab (various types), lobster, crawfish, brown and pink shrimps, prawns (shrimp), Dublin Bay prawns (crayfish) and king prawns (jumbo shrimp).

- MOLLUSCS:

These are soft-bodied creatures encased in a hard shell; types include mussels, oysters, scallops, clams, whelks, winkles and cockles. The exceptions are squid and cuttlefish, where the shell is on the inside.

Smoked fish

Smoked fish may be cold- or hot-smoked. Fish that have been cold-smoked are still raw after smoking; they include cod, haddock, herrings (kippers), salmon and trout. Cold-smoked salmon and trout are sold thinly sliced and should be served without further cooking. The others should be cooked before eating. Hot smoked fish have been cooked in the smoking process, so do not need further cooking before eating. They include buckling (herring), mackerel, trout and some salmon. Smoked oysters and mussels are also sold in cans.

Some smoked fish, such as cod, haddock and kippers, may have colouring added to deepen the colour. I prefer the undyed varieties.

- ARBROATH SMOKIES:

Small, whole haddock, split, salted and hot-smoked over oak or birch wood. To eat, they are boned, spread with butter and pepper, closed up again and briefly grilled (broiled) until just hot through.

- COD'S ROE:

These are smoked, salted and pressed. They can be served sliced as a starter or made into taramasalata, a Greek dip. Also sold unsmoked, fresh and canned.

- RED HERRINGS:

Small, dried, salted herrings, smoked whole and dyed red. They have a very strong, salty flavour.

- SMOKED EEL FILLETS:

Serve these with brown bread and butter and lemon juice, or with scrambled egg, in the same way as smoked salmon.

Salt fish

- ANCHOVIES:

These can be bought salted and need brief soaking in cold water before use. Most of us, however, use salted anchovy fillets preserved in oil in cans or jars.

- BOMBAY DUCK:

This is not a variety of waterfowl, but dried, cured bommaloe fish fillets. It smells very strong but tastes delicious. It is not soaked before cooking. Grill (broil) it until crispy and serve as an appetiser or crumble over rice dishes.

- CAVIAR:

Considered a great delicacy, this is salted fish roe and may come from one of several varieties of fish, the most expensive being sturgeon. Beluga is one of the most famous but other roe like Sevuga and Osetra are also used. Keta is the red, salted roe of salmon. Lumpfish roe, or Danish or German caviar, is an inexpensive alternative. It is really pink but is dyed black or red and is good for serving as a starter with blinis, soured cream and chopped onion or to garnish smoked salmon or prawns (shrimp).

- DRIED SALT COD FILLET:

Soak in several changes of cold water for 24 hours before cooking.

- DRIED SALT HERRINGS:

Sold whole. Soak in several changes of cold water for 12 hours before use.

- DRIED SHARKS' FIN:

This unusual variety is used in oriental soups and stews. It looks like a dried old man's beard! Soak in several changes of cold water to give a firm jelly.

Pickled fish

- MACKEREL OR HERRING:

May be pickled, or soused, and sold as rolled fillets, cooked in vinegar with onion and spices. They can be served hot or cold. Bismark herrings are steeped whole in vinegar, then filleted, split and layered in a dish with onions, carrot and peppercorns and served with potatoes and soured (dairy sour) cream. Rollmops are herring fillets rolled up with sliced onions and peppercorns, preserved in jars in vinegar, sometimes with dill (dill weed).

- SALMON FILLETS (GRAVLAX):

These are pickled raw in vinegar with dill (dill weed), sugar, peppercorns and sometimes brandy.

Canned and frozen fish

Both canned and frozen fish are highly nutritious and very versatile. Canned fish of all kinds make an excellent basis for many very tasty meals and are worth keeping in your storecupboard at all times. Frozen fish, unlike frozen meat, has the advantage that it can be cooked very successfully without thawing first. Simply cook as fresh, allowing a few extra minutes, and take great care always to follow any packet instructions.

Choosing fish

- All fresh, whole fish should have a slippery, shiny skin; they should be bright in colour with firm, elastic flesh.
- Eyes should be bright and prominent with clear, black pupils. Fish with grey, sunken eyes with red rims will be stale and should be avoided.
- Gills should be bright red and clean.
- Fish and shellfish should always smell pleasant. Fishy, yes; offensive, no.
- Crustaceans should feel heavy and when shaken there should be no sound of water inside.
- Molluscs should be clean and unbroken; avoid batches which have lots of damaged shells or any that are open.
- Thawed, frozen fish should have the appearance of fresh fish. Dull, flabby flesh is a sign that the fish has been thawed badly and should be avoided.

Storing fish

Frozen fish

Fish that has been bought frozen should be taken home and placed in the freezer straight away.

Fresh fish

Much fresh (i.e. unfrozen) fish that you buy may actually have already been frozen and should therefore NEVER be stored in the freezer. Exceptions are:
- Fresh fish bought in a shop and marked as suitable for home freezing.
- Fish you have just caught.
- Fish bought straight off the trawler.

On the whole, domestic freezers can't freeze fish fast enough to prevent ice crystals forming between the flesh, which damages the texture. To be on the safe side and enjoy fresh or thawed, frozen fish at its best, it should be eaten on the day of purchase or, at most, kept in the fridge overnight.

Preparing fish

Cleaning fish is a rather unpleasant job, best left to your fishmonger. However, skinning and boning are quite simple to do yourself.

To skin fish

1 Place the fillet on a board, skin-side down.
2 Make a small cut between the flesh and skin at one end.
3 Hold the flap of skin firmly between your finger and thumb (dip your fingers in salt first to improve your grip), then ease the flesh away from the skin with a large, sharp knife, pulling the skin as you go. It should come away fairly easily.

To bone whole fish, e.g. mackerel

1 Cut off the head and tail.
2 Open the cleaned fish out flat and lay skin-side up on a board.
3 Run your thumb firmly up and down the backbone to loosen it.
4 Turn the fish over and pull away the backbone and any loose bones.

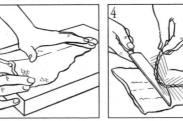

To fillet flat fish

1 Trim the fins and tail and cut off the head.
2 Make a slit along the length of the backbone (down the centre of the fish) from the head to the tail.
3 Slice a fillet away from one side of the backbone, cutting towards the outer edge, gently pulling the fillet free with the other hand. Repeat with the fillet on the other side of the backbone.
4 Turn the fish over and remove the other two fillets in the same way.

 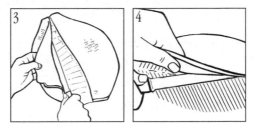

To fillet round fish

1 Cut off the head and tail.
2 Make a cut all the way down the backbone (opposite the slit where the fish was cleaned) from the head to the tail.

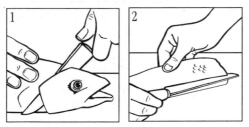

3 Gently slide the knife between the flesh and the bones, gently easing it away as you go, lifting the fillet with the other hand.
4 Turn the fish over and repeat on the other side.

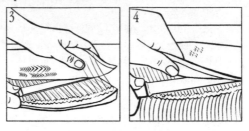

To scale fish

This is easy, but very messy, and so is best done over the sink, under running water to stop the scales from flying up.

1 Hold the fish by the tail.
2 Scrape away the scales with the back of a knife working firmly from the tail to the head.

To prepare a crab

Try not to mix the dark and white meat together as you remove them – they are usually served separately.

1 Twist off the legs. Pull the body away from the top shell.
2 Remove the bundle of intestines that you will find either stuck in the shell or clinging to the body. Scrape away any dark meat still clinging to it, then discard the bundle.
3 Scoop out the dark meat from the shell.
4 Discard the gills (dead men's fingers) from the body.
5 Twist off the legs and claws, crack and pick out all the white meat.
6 Pick out the little bits of white meat from the body (this is fiddly).

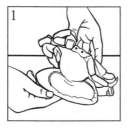
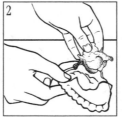
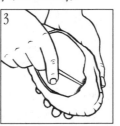

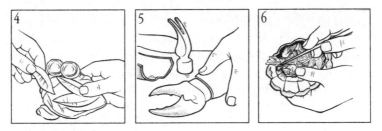

To prepare a lobster

1 Twist off the legs and claws. Crack them open and extract the meat.
2 Split the lobster in half down the back of the head and then along the centre of the back with a large, sharp knife.
3 Remove the black intestine that runs down the length of the body.
4 Remove the gills from behind the head. The red coral, any black roe and the greeny tomalley are all edible.

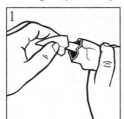
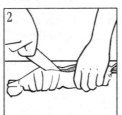
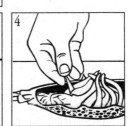

To clean mussels

1 If time allows, place the mussels in a large bowl and cover with water. Sprinkle with rolled oats or oatmeal. This will help clean the mussels on the inside.
2 Discard any that have damaged shells or are open and won't close when tapped sharply.
3 Scrub the mussels under running water and cut off any barnacles.
4 Pull off the beard hanging down from each mussel.

To prepare (shuck) oysters

1 Hold the oyster firmly in one hand, protected by a cloth or oven glove. Insert a sharp, pointed knife between the two shells, near the hinge.
2 Push the knife against the hinge, twisting until the hinge breaks.
3 Open the oyster carefully and loosen it from its shell with the knife.

  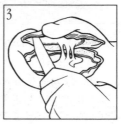

To peel prawns (shrimp)

1 Hold the prawn firmly in the middle and pull off the head and tail.
2 Turn it upside down, peel back the legs and slide off the body shell.
3 Remove the dark vein that runs along the length of the body.

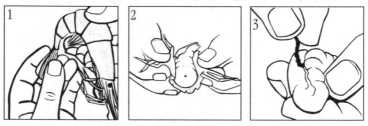

To open and clean scallops

1 Lever the two halves of the shell apart with a large, sharp knife.
2 Cut under the scallop where it is attached to the round shell to remove it. Pull off the round shell. Peel off the filmy membrane covering the scallop. Rinse under cold water.
3 Still holding the scallop in its half shell under the water, carefully cut away the black intestines, holding the rest of the scallop with your thumb.

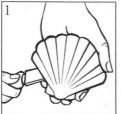  

To clean squid

1 Reach inside the body and pull away the head and tentacles. Cut off the tentacles and reserve. Discard the head.
2 Pull out the transparent quill from inside. Peel the skin off the body.
3 Pull away the side flaps and cut them up (they can be cooked too).
4 Rinse, cut the body into round slices or leave whole for stuffing.

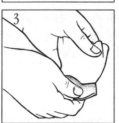
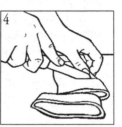

Cook's tips for fish

- Many varieties of fish are interchangeable. If cod is called for, you can use any round, white fish, and substitute any oily fish for mullet.

- Don't cook fish in very small pieces or it will disintegrate.

- If coating fish in egg and breadcrumbs or batter before frying (sautéing), make sure you cover it thoroughly or the fish will dry out.

- Beware of overcooking fish or it will become dry. Shellfish, in particular, go very tough if overcooked, so be careful.

- Overcooked fish may be rescued by flaking (or chopping if it is seafood) and mixing with a well-flavoured sauce.

- Oily fish can be grilled (broiled) without extra fat.

- Canned fish bones are very soft and need not be removed before serving.

- Most canned fish should be drained before using. Anchovy oil, however, is often drizzled over the dish or used as part of a dressing.

Cooking fish

To grill (broil) fish

- FISH FILLETS:

1 Place the fillets on foil on a grill (broiler) rack.
2 Drizzle with oil or dot with butter, sprinkle with lemon juice and season.
3 Cook quickly under a preheated grill for 3–5 minutes until golden and just tender – the fish should flake easily when tested with a knife. Do not turn the fish over. You can cook salmon and other oily fish without the oil or butter, if you prefer.

- FISH STEAKS OR CUTLETS:

Prepare as fillets but turn once during cooking for 4–6 minutes.

- WHOLE FISH:

1 Wipe inside and out with kitchen paper (paper towels).
2 Make several slashes through to the bone on each side with a sharp knife, then prepare and cook as fillets for 5–8 minutes, turning once.

To fry (sauté) fish

- FILLETS, STEAKS AND CUTLETS:

1 Heat a little butter or margarine and/or oil in a non-stick frying pan (skillet).
2 Dip the fish in seasoned flour or season lightly with salt and pepper.
3 Sprinkle with lemon juice. Fry (sauté) for 3–6 minutes, depending on thickness, turning once until golden brown and just cooked through. Drain on kitchen paper (paper towels) before serving.

- WHOLE FISH:

1 Wipe inside and out with kitchen paper (paper towels).
2 Make several slashes in the flesh through to the bone on each side.
3 Season and cook as for fillets (see above) for 5–8 minutes, depending on size.

To deep-fry fish

- FILLETS:

1 Heat oil for deep-frying in a deep-fat fryer or saucepan at 190°C/375°F on a thermometer or until a cube of day-old bread browns in 30 seconds.

2 Dust with seasoned flour, then dip in egg and breadcrumbs; alternatively, dip in a crisp batter made by mixing self-raising (self-rising) flour and a pinch of salt with just enough water to form a thick batter that will just drop off the spoon.

3 Lower into the hot oil and cook for about 4–5 minutes, until golden brown. Drain on kitchen paper (paper towels) before serving.

- SMALL FRY, E.G. WHITEBAIT:

1 Dip in milk, then seasoned flour and cook for about 2 minutes, until crisp and golden.

2 Drain on kitchen paper (paper towels).

To bake fish

1 Wrap in buttered foil or greaseproof (waxed) paper, or cover with a sauce.

2 Bake in a preheated oven at 190°C/375°F/gas mark 5 for 10–25 minutes, depending on thickness, until just tender. Do not overcook.

To poach fish

- FILLETS, STEAKS AND CUTLETS:

1 Place in a flameproof casserole (Dutch oven) or frying pan (skillet) with a lid.

2 Just cover with water, milk or stock. Add flavourings to taste – try a bay leaf or sprig of fresh herbs or bouquet garni sachet and/or a few slices of onion and a little salt and pepper.

3 Bring the liquid just to the boil, cover, reduce the heat and simmer gently until the fish is just tender – this should take 3–8 minutes, depending on the thickness.

4 Carefully lift out of the liquid, using a fish slice. Use the strained cooking liquid to make a sauce, if appropriate.

- LARGE WHOLE FISH:

Use a fish kettle if you have one. If not, any large, flameproof container that will hold the fish comfortably will do.

1 Wipe the fish inside and out with kitchen paper (paper towels). Remove the head, if preferred.

2 Place on a large sheet of foil and add flavourings of your choice (see above).

3 Wrap in the foil, leaving enough foil at each end to grip when you lift the fish in and out.

4 Place in the container. Add 300 ml/½ pt/1¼ cups white wine or cider, if liked, and enough water just to cover.

5 Bring the liquid just to the boil, cover, reduce the heat and poach for 4 minutes per 450 g/1 lb. Leave to stand for 10 minutes in the liquid if serving hot; if serving cold, leave to cool completely in the liquid.

6 Lift out of the liquid, remove the foil and flavourings. Peel off the skin, if liked, and garnish with parsley, watercress or cucumber slices.

To microwave fish

● FILLETS, CUTLETS OR STEAKS:

1 Place in a microwave-safe container with a lid. Arrange fish with the tails pointing towards the centre, and cutlets or steaks in a circle round the dish.

2 Add 60 ml/4 tbsp milk, water or a mixture of wine or cider and water.

3 Add flavourings of your choice (see To poach fish, page 71).

4 Cook on High (100 per cent power) for 3–6 minutes per 450 g/1 lb, depending on thickness and the output of your microwave, until the fish is just opaque. Do not overcook. Leave to stand for 2 minutes to finish cooking before serving.

● WHOLE FISH:

1 Wipe inside and out with kitchen paper (paper towels).

2 Make several slashes on each side and lay, head to tail, in a suitable container.

3 Add liquid and flavourings (see To poach fish, page 71).

4 Microwave on High (100 per cent power) for 4–6 minutes per 450 g/1 lb, gently turning once after 3 minutes until just cooked through (the flesh inside the body opening of the fish should look just opaque). Leave to stand for 2 minutes before serving.

Recipes

Moules Marinières

Serves 4

1.75 kg/4 lb mussels in their shells
40 g/1½ oz/3 tbsp butter or margarine
1 large onion, finely chopped
1 celery stick, finely chopped
2 wineglasses of white wine
1 wineglass of water
Freshly ground black pepper
30 ml/2 tbsp chopped fresh parsley

1 Clean the mussels.
2 Melt the butter or margarine in a large saucepan and add the onion and celery. Cover and cook gently for 3 minutes without browning.
3 Add the mussels, wine and water and a good grinding of pepper. Cover and cook for about 5 minutes, shaking occasionally until the mussels open.
4 Discard any that remain closed. Ladle into warm bowls and sprinkle with parsley.

• •

Piri Piri Prawns

Serves 4

24 raw tiger prawns (jumbo shrimp), peeled with the tails left on
1 green chilli, seeded and chopped
2.5 ml/½ tsp salt
Juice of 1 lime
Olive oil, for shallow-frying
Lime wedges, to garnish

1 Place the prawns in a shallow dish. Mix the chilli with the salt and lime juice and sprinkle over. Toss and leave to marinate for 1 hour.
2 Heat the oil in a large frying pan (skillet). Add the prawns and toss until pink. Do not overcook. Garnish with lime wedges.

• •

Dressed Crab

Serves 4

1 large crab, about 1.5 kg/3 lb
15 ml/1 tbsp fresh white breadcrumbs
A dash of lemon juice
2.5 ml/½ tsp Dijon mustard
A pinch of cayenne
Salt and freshly ground black pepper
Chopped fresh parsley
Lemon wedges and brown bread and butter, to serve

1 Prepare the crab.
2 Mix the dark meat with the breadcrumbs, lemon juice, the mustard, cayenne, salt and a good grinding of pepper.
3 Season the white meat with a little salt and pepper.
4 Wash the shell and arrange the white meat down each side with the dark meat in the centre. Sprinkle chopped parsley in lines along each side of the dark meat where it meets the white.
5 Place on a plate. Serve with lemon wedges and brown bread and butter.

Soused Mackerel

Serves 4

4 small mackerel
Salt and freshly ground black pepper
1 small onion, thinly sliced
5 ml/1 tsp dried dill (dill weed)
300 ml/½ pt/1¼ cups malt vinegar
300 ml/½ pt/1¼ cups water
10 ml/2 tsp light brown sugar
1 bay leaf

1 Bone the mackerel. Place skin-sides down and season with salt and pepper.
2 Add the onion, sprinkle with the dill and roll up.
3 Pack closely together in a shallow ovenproof dish. Pour the vinegar and water over and sprinkle with the sugar. Add the bay leaf.
4 Cover with foil and bake in a preheated oven at 180°C/350°F/gas mark 4 for 45 minutes until cooked through. Cool and chill before serving.

Golden Fish and Potato Fry

Serves 4

15 g/½ oz/1 tbsp butter or margarine
15 ml/1 tbsp sunflower oil
450 g/1 lb potatoes, grated
Salt and freshly ground black pepper
350 g/12 oz smoked haddock fillet, skinned and cubed, discarding any bones
200 g/7 oz/1 small can of sweetcorn (corn), drained
300 ml/½ pt/1¼ cups passata (sieved tomatoes)
A good pinch of caster (superfine) sugar
Leaf spinach, to serve

1 Melt the butter or margarine in a frying pan (skillet) and add the oil.
2 Add half the potatoes and press down well. Sprinkle with salt and pepper.
3 Scatter the fish and sweetcorn over the top, then add the remaining potatoes. Press down well again. Season lightly.
4 Cover with foil or a lid and cook for 30 minutes until cooked through.
5 Meanwhile, heat the passata with the sugar.
6 Turn the fish cake out on to a warm plate. Serve cut into wedges with the passata and leaf spinach.

....

Cod Provençal

Serves 4

15 ml/1 tbsp olive oil
1 large onion, finely chopped
1 large garlic clove, crushed
1 green (bell) pepper, diced
400 g/14 oz/1 large can of chopped tomatoes
15 ml/1 tbsp tomato purée (paste)
30 ml/2 tbsp white or red wine
450 g/1 lb cod fillet, skinned and cubed, discarding all bones
Salt and freshly ground black pepper
30 ml/2 tbsp sliced stuffed olives
Plain rice, to serve

1 Heat the oil in a saucepan. Add the onion, garlic and green pepper and cook gently for 3 minutes, stirring.

2 Add the tomatoes, tomato purée and wine. Bring to the boil, reduce the heat and simmer for 5 minutes.
3 Add the fish and a little salt and pepper and continue cooking for about 5 minutes or until the fish is tender.
4 Add the olives and spoon on to a bed of boiled rice to serve.

Salmon with Pesto
Serves 4

4 salmon tail fillets
1 quantity of simple pesto (page 222)
1 wineglass of dry white wine
Green tagliatelle tossed in a little olive oil and a tomato salad, to serve

1 Put the fish in a shallow dish.
2 Blend the pesto with the wine and pour over. Leave to marinate for 1 hour.
3 Place on foil on a grill (broiler) rack. Grill (broil) for about 8 minutes, basting with marinade until cooked through.
4 Pile on to tagliatelle tossed in olive oil. Heat the remaining marinade, spoon over and serve with a tomato salad.

Scallops with Bacon
Serves 4

12 shelled scallops
6 rashers (slices) of streaky bacon, rinded and halved
410 g/14 oz/1 large can of artichoke hearts, drained and halved
30 ml/2 tbsp olive oil
15 ml/1 tbsp lemon juice
Freshly ground black pepper

1 Halve the scallops and wrap each piece in half a bacon rasher.
2 Thread with the artichokes on four kebab skewers.
3 Mix the oil and lemon juice together with a little black pepper and brush all over the kebabs. Lay the kebabs on foil on the grill (broiler) rack.
4 Grill (broil), turning and brushing with the oil and lemon juice, until the bacon is just cooked. Serve hot.

Sizzling Oysters with Chilli Salsa   Serves 6

1 red chilli, seeded
3 ripe tomatoes, skinned
190 g/6¾ oz/1 small can of pimientos, drained
15 ml/1 tbsp tomato purée (paste)
15 ml/1 tbsp red wine vinegar
5 ml/1 tsp clear honey
Salt and freshly ground black pepper
18 fresh oysters in their shells

1 Put the chilli in a blender or food processor with all the remaining ingredients except the salt and pepper and the oysters.
2 Run the machine until fairly smooth. Season to taste. Turn into a small saucepan and warm over a gentle heat.
3 Open the oysters, remove the top shells. Add a good grinding of pepper to the oysters.
4 Carefully put the oysters in their shells on the grill (broiler) rack and cook for about 3 minutes until the oysters sizzle. Lift on to warmed plates. Spoon a little salsa over each and serve.

....

Chinese-style Swordfish Steaks   Serves 4

4 swordfish steaks
15 ml/1 tbsp Chinese five spice powder
30 ml/2 tbsp sesame oil
30 ml/2 tbsp sunflower oil
30 ml/2 tbsp lemon juice
100 g/4 oz beansprouts
1 red (bell) pepper, finely shredded
2 spring onions (scallions), finely sliced
30 ml/2 tbsp light soy sauce
Jacket-baked potatoes, to serve

1 Wipe the fish with kitchen paper (paper towels) and remove the skin.
2 Mix the five spice powder with half the oils and half the lemon juice. Brush all over the fish and leave to marinate for 2 hours.
3 Mix the beansprouts with the pepper and spring onion. Whisk together the soy sauce with the remaining oils and lemon juice.

4 Grill (broil) the fish for 3–4 minutes on each side, turning once and brushing with any remaining marinade, until cooked through.
5 Add the soy dressing to the beansprout mixture. Toss gently. Spoon on to plates.
6 Transfer the swordfish to the plates and serve with jacket-baked potatoes.

Mackerel with Horseradish   Serves 4

4 mackerel, cleaned
4 sprigs of fresh thyme
30 ml/2 tbsp sunflower oil
30 ml/2 tbsp horseradish sauce
5 ml/1 tsp lemon juice
A pinch of salt
Freshly ground black pepper
50 g/2 oz/¼ cup butter or margarine
30 ml/2 tbsp chopped fresh parsley
Plain boiled potatoes and French (green) beans, to serve

1 Wash the fish inside and out and pat dry with kitchen paper (paper towels). Make several slashes on each side with a sharp knife.
2 Push a sprig of thyme inside the body cavity of each. Lay in a shallow dish.
3 Mix the oil with half the horseradish sauce, the lemon juice, salt and lots of pepper.
4 Pour over the fish, turn to coat completely and leave to marinate in a cool place for at least 2 hours.
5 Remove from the marinade and lay on the grill (broiler) rack.
6 Grill (broil) for 10–15 minutes, turning once, until cooked through, brushing with any remaining marinade during cooking.
7 Meanwhile, put the butter or margarine in a small saucepan with the remaining horseradish sauce, the parsley and a good grinding of pepper. Heat until melted, stirring to blend.
8 Transfer the cooked fish to plates and spoon the horseradish sauce over. Serve with plain boiled potatoes and French beans.

Storecupboard Special Salmon and Tomato Puffs

Serves 4

425 g/15 oz/1 large can of pink or red salmon, drained
350 g/12 oz/1 packet of frozen puff pastry (paste), thawed
2 large tomatoes, chopped
5 ml/1 tsp dried oregano
Freshly ground black pepper
Milk, to glaze
170 g/6 oz/1 small can of creamed mushrooms
Lemon wedges and sprigs of fresh parsley, to garnish
New potatoes and peas, to serve

1 Empty the fish into a shallow dish. Carefully split into four portions, discarding the black skin and bones, if preferred.
2 Cut the pastry into quarters and roll out each to a thin square. Trim and make 'leaves' out of the trimmings.
3 Place a quarter of the chopped tomato in the centre of each pastry square and sprinkle with the oregano. Top with the fish.
4 Brush the edges with water and fold over the fish to cover completely.
5 Invert on to a dampened baking (cookie) sheet. Brush the parcels with milk, decorate with the pastry leaves and brush again.
6 Cook in a preheated oven at 200°C/400°F/gas mark 6 for about 15 minutes until puffy and golden brown.
7 Meanwhile, heat the mushrooms with 15 ml/1 tbsp milk in a saucepan. Transfer the puffs to warm plates and put a spoonful of the mushroom mixture to one side of each.
8 Garnish the plates with lemon wedges and sprigs of parsley, and serve with new potatoes and peas.

chicken and poultry

Chicken and turkey are inexpensive, versatile and highly nutritious. They are naturally lower in fat than red meats, especially if you remove the skin. They make tempting, easy family meals and are equally good for fabulous dinner party dishes. Duck and other birds, such as guinea fowl and pheasant, are more expensive but worth considering for a special meal.

Choosing your birds

It is up to you whether you choose frozen or fresh birds, free-range or intensively farmed. The flavour and texture are undoubtedly better from fresh, free-range birds and for those with a conscience, they are worth the extra cost. However, it is true that even a cheap, frozen chicken will be perfectly succulent and delicious once masked in a well-flavoured sauce.

Shopping for poultry

- Look out for special offers for your freezer. For instance, fresh birds are almost always reduced the day before their sell-by date; or you may be able to buy a large one and get a small one free. Provided that, once bought, they are taken home and frozen immediately, they will be perfect for use up to six months later.
- Duck breasts may look expensive but they are quite rich and one large one, cut into thin slices after frying (sautéing) or grilling (broiling), will be enough for two servings.

Preparing poultry

Unless you intend to cook the bird whole (e.g. roasting or pot-roasting), you must first cut it into portions.

To joint a bird

This is how to joint a bird into four or eight portions.

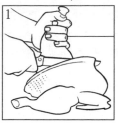

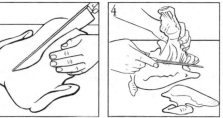

1 Gently pull the leg away from the body and cut through the skin and flesh down to the joint.
2 Break the leg joint, then cut through the remaining flesh and remove the leg portion. Repeat with the other side. For eight portions, separate the leg and thigh by cutting through the joint.
3 Cut down one side of the breastbone, easing the breast meat away from the carcass.
4 Find the wing joint and cut through, then cut away the remaining skin and remove the breast portion. Repeat with the other side. For eight portions, separate the breast from the wing.

Cooking poultry

To grill (broil) poultry

* BREASTS, PORTIONS, THIGHS, WINGS OR LEGS:
1 Place on foil on a grill (broiler) rack.
2 Brush with melted butter or margarine or oil and season lightly.
3 Cook under a preheated grill for 10–15 minutes, turning occasionally, until golden brown and cooked through.

To fry (sauté) poultry

● BREASTS, PORTIONS, THIGHS, WINGS OR LEGS:

The pieces can be dusted with seasoned flour or dipped in beaten egg and breadcrumbs first, if liked.

1 Heat a little oil, or oil and butter, in a frying pan (skillet) and brown the pieces quickly on all sides.
2 Reduce the heat and cook for a further 6–15 minutes, depending on thickness, until cooked through and golden.

To stir-fry poultry

1 Cut boneless chicken or turkey into thin strips (or buy ready-prepared).
2 Heat a little oil in a wok or frying pan (skillet).
3 Cook the meat, tossing over a high heat, for 3 minutes.
4 Add vegetables, cut into thin strips or small pieces, and continue to cook until tender, adding soy sauce and other flavourings of your choice.

To roast poultry

● BREASTS, PORTIONS, THIGHS, WINGS, LEGS:

1 Place in a roasting tin (pan). Brush with oil and season with salt. Sprinkle with herbs or other flavourings, if liked.
2 Roast in a preheated oven for 20–45 minutes, depending on size and thickness of pieces, until golden brown and cooked through.

● WHOLE BIRDS:

1 Prepare for roasting as for portions, etc.
2 Cook as follows:
   Chicken (up to 1.6 kg/3½ lb) – 190°C/375°F/gas mark 5 for 20 minutes per 450 g/1 lb plus 20 minutes over.
   Chicken (over 1.6 kg/3½ lb) – 160°C/325°F/gas mark 3 for 25 minutes per 450 g/1 lb plus 25 minutes over.
   Duck – 200°C/400°F/gas mark 6 for 20 minutes per 450 g/1 lb. Reduce the heat to 180°C/350°F/gas mark 4 and continue roasting for 30 minutes.
   Turkey (up to 4.5 kg/10 lb) – 190°C/375°F/gas mark 5 for 20 minutes per 450 g/1 lb. Remove foil and roast for a further 30 minutes.
   Turkey (over 4.5 kg/10 lb) – 190°C/375°F/gas mark 5 for 10 minutes per 450 g/1 lb, then remove the foil and roast for a further 30 minutes.
Always cover turkey with foil before roasting, removing it for the last 30 minutes to brown the skin.

To casserole or pot-roast poultry

- BREASTS, PORTIONS, THIGHS, WINGS, LEGS OR WHOLE BIRDS:

1 The meat and vegetables may be browned in a little oil or butter first. Place in a casserole dish (Dutch oven) with your choice of liquid. Season.
2 Cover and cook in a preheated oven at 180°C/350°F/gas mark 4 for 40 minutes for breasts, 1–1½ hours for other portions or whole birds, until tender and cooked through. Thicken the juices, if liked.

To poach poultry

- PORTIONS, BREASTS, THIGHS, WINGS OR LEGS:

1 Place in a saucepan or flameproof casserole (Dutch oven).
2 Pour in just enough stock, with or without wine or cider added, to cover. Add other flavourings of your choice.
3 Bring to the boil, reduce the heat, cover and simmer very gently for about 30 minutes or until tender. Use the cooking liquid to make a sauce, if appropriate.

- WHOLE BIRDS:

Prepare as for portions, but cook for 1–1½ hours.

Traditional accompaniments for poultry

- ROAST CHICKEN:

Bread sauce (page 260), parsley and thyme stuffing, (page 275), bacon-wrapped sausages.

- ROAST DUCK:

Sage and onion stuffing (page 275), apple sauce (page 259).

- ROAST GAME:

Bread sauce (page 260) or buttered breadcrumbs (page 240), game chips, redcurrant jelly (clear conserve).

- ROAST TURKEY:

Bread sauce (page 260), cranberry sauce, stuffing made with chestnut, sage and onion or parsley and thyme (page 275).

Cook's tips for poultry

- Poultry should NEVER be cooked from frozen as it is difficult to cook through properly.

- To thaw quickly, immerse the bird, still in its wrapper, in cold water. Change the water frequently. NEVER put it in hot water or germs can breed.

- To test whether poultry is cooked through, pierce the thickest part with a skewer: the juices should run clear.

- Chicken and turkey can dry out if over-cooked. When roasting a whole bird, start it off upside down, and turn it right way up halfway through cooking. This will keep the breast moist and help to cook the thighs thoroughly. Cover large birds with foil and remove for the last 30 minutes to brown the skin.

Recipes

Cheesy Chicken, Ham and Tomato Grill

Serves 4

4 skinless chicken breasts
30 ml/2 tbsp sunflower or olive oil
4 slices of lean ham
4 tomatoes, sliced
8 fresh basil leaves, chopped
50 g/2 oz/½ cup Cheddar cheese, grated
New potatoes and broccoli, to serve

1　Put the fillets one at a time into a plastic bag and beat with a rolling pin or meat mallet to flatten.
2　Brush with half the oil. Place under a hot grill (broiler) and grill (broil) for 3 minutes. Turn over, brush with the remaining oil and grill for a further 3 minutes.
3　Top each with a slice of ham, then a tomato slice and some chopped basil. Cover with the cheese.
4　Grill until the cheese is melted and bubbling.
5　Serve straight away with new potatoes and broccoli.

Coq au Vin

Serves 4

4 chicken portions
5 ml/1 tbsp olive oil
15 g/½ oz/1 tbsp butter or margarine
2 rashers (slices) of rindless streaky bacon, diced
12 button (pearl) onions
20 g/¾ oz/3 tbsp plain (all-purpose) flour
300 ml/½ pt/1¼ cups red wine
150 ml/¼ pt/⅔ cup chicken stock, made with ½ stock cube
100 g/4 oz button mushrooms
Salt and freshly ground black pepper
15 ml/1 tbsp brandy
1 bouquet garni sachet
15 ml/1 tbsp chopped fresh parsley, to garnish
French bread and a crisp green salad, to serve

1 Wipe the chicken with kitchen paper (paper towels).
2 Heat the oil with the butter in a large, flameproof casserole (Dutch oven).
3 Brown the chicken portions on all sides and remove.
4 Add the bacon and onions and brown quickly.
5 Stir in the flour and cook for 1 minute, stirring.
6 Remove from the heat and gradually blend in the wine and stock. Return to the heat and bring to the boil, stirring. Return the chicken to the casserole and add the mushrooms. Season and add the brandy and bouquet garni sachet.
7 Cover and place in a preheated oven at 180°C/350°F/gas mark 4 and cook for 1½ hours. When the chicken is cooked, stir gently, remove the bouquet garni sachet, taste and adjust the seasoning, if necessary.
8 Sprinkle with chopped parsley and serve hot with French bread and a crisp green salad.

Everyday Chicken Casserole   Serves 4

4 chicken portions
30 ml/2 tbsp sunflower oil
1 large onion, finely chopped
100 g/4 oz button mushrooms, quartered
15 ml/1 tbsp cornflour (cornstarch)
400 g/14 oz/1 large can of chopped tomatoes
30 ml/2 tbsp sherry, white wine or apple juice
1 bouquet garni sachet
Salt and freshly ground black pepper
Jacket-baked potatoes and peas, to serve

1 Brown the chicken portions in the oil in a flameproof casserole (Dutch oven). Remove from the pan with a draining spoon.
2 Add the onion and fry (sauté) for 2 minutes, stirring. Add the mushrooms and cook for 1 minute.
3 Sprinkle in the cornflour and stir well. Add the can of tomatoes and the sherry, wine or apple juice and stir in.
4 Return the chicken to the casserole. Add the bouquet garni and some salt and pepper. Bring to the boil.
5 Cover and cook in a preheated oven at 180°C/350°F/gas mark 4 for 1½ hours or until the chicken is really tender. Stir gently. Taste and adjust the seasoning if necessary. Discard the bouquet garni and serve with jacket-baked potatoes and peas.

• •

Chicken Maryland   Serves 6

6 chicken portions
A little milk
90 ml/6 tbsp plain (all-purpose) flour
Salt and freshly ground black pepper
75 g/3 oz/¾ cup toasted breadcrumbs
75 g/3 oz/⅓ cup butter or margarine
30 ml/2 tbsp sunflower oil
4 bananas
Sprigs of watercress, to garnish
Corn fritters (page 146), brown rice and a mixed green salad, to serve

1 Dip the chicken in milk, then coat in the flour, seasoned with a little salt and pepper.
2 Chill for 30 minutes. Dip in milk again, then coat in the breadcrumbs.
3 Melt 50 g/2 oz/¼ cup of the butter with 15 ml/1 tbsp of the oil in a large roasting tin (pan) in the oven at 190°C/375°F/gas mark 5.
4 When sizzling, add the chicken and turn over in the fat to coat completely.
5 Bake for 1 hour until golden brown and cooked through. Drain on kitchen paper (paper towels).
6 Meanwhile, halve the bananas. Melt the remaining butter and oil in a shallow baking tin (pan). Add the bananas, turn over in the fat.
7 Place on the shelf under the chicken and cook for about 30 minutes or until tender but still holding their shape.
8 Transfer the chicken and bananas to a large warm platter and garnish with watercress sprigs.
9 Serve with corn fritters, brown rice and a green salad.

Mild Spiced Chicken and Mushroom Casserole

Serves 4

25 g/1 oz/2 tbsp butter or margarine
4 chicken portions
1 onion, finely chopped
100 g/4 oz button mushrooms, sliced
15 ml/1 tbsp mild curry paste
295 g/10½ oz/1 medium can of condensed mushroom soup
Plain rice and a green vegetable, to serve

1 Melt the butter or margarine in a flameproof casserole (Dutch oven).
2 Add the chicken portions and fry (sauté) until browned. Remove with a draining spoon.
3 Add the onion and mushrooms and fry for 3 minutes to soften.
4 Add the curry paste and cook for 30 seconds, stirring.
5 Stir in the soup until well blended. Add the chicken portions and spoon the soup mixture over them.
6 Cover with a lid and cook in a preheated oven at 180°C/350°F/gas mark 4 for 1¼ hours until tender and bathed in a rich sauce.
7 Serve with plain rice and a green vegetable.

Savoury Turkey Escalopes

Serves 4

This recipe works equally well with chicken breasts or slices of pork fillet.

4 small turkey steaks, about 175 g/6 oz each
85 g/3½ oz/1 small packet of sage and onion stuffing mix
1 egg
15 ml/1 tbsp milk
Sunflower oil, for shallow-frying
Lemon wedges and sprigs of fresh parsley or sage, to garnish
Creamed potatoes (page 138) and French (green) beans, to serve

1 Put each turkey steak individually in a plastic bag and beat with a rolling pin or meat mallet until flattened and fairly thin.
2 Put the stuffing mix in a shallow dish and beat the egg and milk in a separate dish.
3 Dip the escalopes in the egg and then the stuffing to coat completely.
4 Fry (sauté) the escalopes for 3–4 minutes until golden brown underneath.
5 Turn over and fry the other sides until cooked through and golden.
6 Drain on kitchen paper (paper towels).
7 Garnish with lemon wedges and sprigs of fresh parsley or sage and serve with creamed potatoes and French beans.

••

Turkey with Wine and Cream

Serves 4

4 turkey steaks
25 g/1 oz/2 tbsp butter or margarine
150 ml/¼ pt/⅔ cup dry white wine
150 ml/¼ pt/⅔ cup chicken stock, made with ½ stock cube
100 g/4 oz button mushrooms, sliced
2.5 ml/½ tsp dried thyme
Salt and freshly ground black pepper
15 ml/1 tbsp cornflour (cornstarch)
15 ml/1 tbsp brandy
60 ml/4 tbsp crème fraîche
Chopped fresh parsley, to garnish
Plain rice and mangetout (snow peas), to serve

1 Brown the turkey steaks in the butter or margarine in a large frying pan (skillet).
2 Add the wine, stock and mushrooms and season with the thyme, salt and pepper. Bring to the boil, cover, reduce the heat and poach for about 8 minutes or until tender and cooked through.
3 Remove the turkey steaks and keep warm.
4 Blend the cornflour with the brandy and stir into the mixture in the frying pan. Bring to the boil, stirring, and simmer for 1 minute.
5 Stir in the crème fraîche and heat through. Taste and season.
6 Spoon over the turkey, sprinkle with parsley and serve with rice and mangetout.

· ·

Oriental Duck with Ginger · · · · · · · · Serves 4

20 g/¾ oz/1½ tbsp butter or margarine
2 large duck breasts
Salt and freshly ground black pepper
150 ml/¼ pt/⅔ cup chicken stock, made with ½ stock cube
30 ml/2 tbsp ginger wine
30 ml/1 tbsp light soy sauce
10 ml/ 2 tsp cornflour (cornstarch)
250 g/9 oz/1 packet of Chinese egg noodles
30 ml/2 tbsp snipped fresh chives, to garnish
Oriental salad (page 159), to serve

1 Heat the butter or margarine in a non-stick frying pan (skillet). Add the duck, season with salt and pepper and fry (sauté) for 8 minutes.
2 Turn the duck over, season again and fry for a further 7 minutes or until slightly pink in the centre. Cook a little longer for well done.
3 Remove from the pan and keep warm.
4 Add the stock and ginger wine to the pan and bring to the boil.
5 Blend the soy sauce with the cornflour and stir into the pan. Bring to the boil and cook for 2 minutes, stirring until thickened. Taste and season.
6 Meanwhile, cook the noodles according to the packet directions. Drain and toss in the remaining soy sauce. Pile on to warm plates.
7 Cut the duck into thin slices. Arrange on top of the noodles and spoon the sauce over. Sprinkle with the chives and serve with an Oriental salad.

· ·

Minted Duck with Peas

Serves 4

To make the giblets into stock, place in a pan and cover with 750 ml/1¼ pts/ 3 cups water. Bring to the boil, reduce the heat, cover and simmer gently for at least 30 minutes.

1.75 kg/4 lb oven-ready duck
25 g/1 oz/2 tbsp butter or margarine
2 onions, halved and thinly sliced
600 ml/1 pt/2½ cups duck or chicken stock, made with 1 stock cube
Salt and freshly ground black pepper
225 g/8 oz frozen peas
15 ml/1 tbsp chopped fresh mint
15 ml/1 tbsp chopped fresh oregano
15 ml/1 tbsp chopped fresh parsley
1.5 ml/¼ tsp grated nutmeg
1 round lettuce, shredded
45 ml/3 tbsp plain (all-purpose) flour
Sprigs of fresh mint, to garnish
Plain potatoes, to serve

1 Remove the giblets (use for the stock, if liked). Wipe the duck inside and out with kitchen paper (paper towels). Prick all over with a fork.
2 Melt the butter or margarine in a flameproof casserole (Dutch oven) and brown the duck on all sides.
3 Remove the duck and brown the onions. Pour off any fat.
4 Return the duck to the casserole. Add the stock and a little salt and pepper. Bring to the boil, cover and transfer to a preheated oven at 200°C/ 400°F/gas mark 6 for 30 minutes.
5 Skim the surface again to remove any fat. Add all the remaining ingredients except the flour. Reduce the oven to 180°C/350°F/gas mark 4 and cook for a further 1½ hours.
6 Remove the duck and keep warm. Skim off any fat. Blend the cornflour with the water. Stir into the casserole, place on top of the stove and simmer for 3 minutes, stirring. Taste and adjust the seasoning if necessary.
7 Cut the duck into portions. Transfer to warm plates. Spoon the pea sauce over each portion, garnish with sprigs of fresh mint and serve with plain potatoes.

Easy Duck with Orange

Serves 4

1.75 kg/4 lb oven-ready duck
2 small onions
Salt
300 ml/½ pt/1¼ cups water
1 chicken stock cube
5 ml/1 tsp light brown sugar
15 g/½ oz/1 tbsp butter or margarine
Thinly pared rind and juice of 1 orange
60 ml/4 tbsp port
Freshly ground black pepper
10 ml/2 tsp cornflour (cornstarch)
10 ml/2 tsp water
Orange slices and sprigs of fresh parsley, to garnish
New potatoes and mangetout (snow peas), to serve

1 Remove the giblets from the duck and reserve. Prick all over the skin with a fork. Push one of the onions into the cavity of the duck.
2 Place on a rack in a roasting tin (pan) and sprinkle with salt. Roast in a preheated oven at 200°C/400°F/gas mark 6 for 1 hour 20 minutes. Reduce the heat to 180°C/350°F/gas mark 4 and continue to roast for 30 minutes or until crisp, golden and tender.
3 Meanwhile, put the giblets in a saucepan with the water and stock cube. Bring to the boil, reduce the heat, cover and simmer for 40 minutes. Strain off the liquid and reserve.
4 Chop the remaining onion and fry (sauté) in the butter or margarine in a saucepan for about 5 minutes until richly browned, adding the sugar after 3 minutes. Add the orange rind and juice and the strained stock.
5 Bring to the boil, cover and simmer gently for 10 minutes. Remove the orange rind. Stir in the port and season to taste. Blend the cornflour with the water and stir in. Bring to the boil and simmer for 1 minute.
6 Transfer the duck to a carving dish and cut into portions. Transfer to warm plates.
7 Strain the sauce over, garnish with orange slices and sprigs of parsley and serve with new potatoes and mangetout.

Quick Chicken Curry   Serves 4

This speedy supper dish uses up the leftovers from your roast chicken dinner.

1 onion, chopped
1 garlic clove, crushed
30 ml/2 tbsp sunflower oil
175 g/6 oz button mushrooms, halved
15 ml/1 tbsp curry paste
450 ml/¾ pt/2 cups chicken stock, made with 1 stock cube
100 g/4 oz creamed coconut, cut into pieces
45 ml/3 tbsp raisins
225 g/8 oz/2 cups cooked chicken, cut into bite-sized pieces
175 g/6 oz/2 cups cooked leftover vegetables, chopped if necessary
Salt and freshly ground black pepper
30 ml/2 tbsp chopped fresh coriander (cilantro)
Naan bread, to serve

1 Cook the onion and garlic in the oil for 3 minutes until lightly golden.
2 Add the mushrooms and cook for 1 minute. Add the curry paste and stock. Bring to the boil and stir in the coconut and raisins. Cook until the coconut dissolves.
3 Add the chicken and vegetables and simmer very gently for 10 minutes. Season to taste and stir in the coriander. Serve with naan bread.

Cheat's Kentucky Fried Turkey with Barbecued Beans

Serves 3

6 crumb-coated, shaped, minced (ground) turkey drummers
A little sunflower oil
2.5 ml/½ tsp dried onion granules
2.5 ml/½ tsp ground cumin
2.5 ml/½ tsp dried mixed herbs
2.5 ml/½ tsp salt
A good pinch of white pepper
400 g/14 oz/1 large can of baked beans
15 ml/1 tbsp bottled barbecue or sweet brown sauce
Lettuce leaves, tomato slices, cucumber slices and lemon wedges, to garnish
Oven chips, to serve

1 Brush the turkey drummers with a little oil. Mix the onion granules, cumin, herbs, salt and pepper together and sprinkle all over the turkey.
2 Grill (broil), turning once, until golden brown and cooked through.
3 Meanwhile, put the beans in a saucepan and stir in the sauce. Heat through thoroughly, stirring occasionally.
4 Transfer the turkey drummers to warm plates and add the beans. Garnish with the salad and lemon wedges and serve with the oven chips.

meat

Meat reared in Britain has some of the highest quality controls in the world and, especially after the controversies of recent years, is something to be justly proud of. Beef, pork and lamb provide high-quality protein, B-vitamins, zinc and iron.

We are all advised to reduce our intake of animal fats and although animals nowadays are bred to produce lean meat, we are recommended to remove any excess fat. However, some fat is needed to help keep meat tender and succulent during cooking, so for joints or steaks, I suggest you leave some on whilst cooking and remove it before eating. When browning minced (ground) meat, dry-frying is better than cooking in added fat; spoon off any melted fat from it before continuing with the recipe. Obviously, stewing meat should be trimmed of fat before cooking – it's not possible to remove it once the meat is bathed in a sauce!

Cuts of meat vary not only with the type of animal but also from country to country, and even from region to region, so my definitions are only a rough guide. As a general rule, the most tender cuts are the most expensive and come from the fleshy part of the back end of the animal.

Beef

Choosing beef

Beef can range from a pinkish red through to a deep burgundy colour. This depends on the age, sex and breed of the animal but doesn't necessarily say much about the quality of the meat. Hanging meat results in a deeper red colour, and traditionalists say beef should be hung for 10–14 days to improve its flavour and tenderise the flesh. However, now that animals are killed much younger, the hanging time tends to be less, without compromising the quality. A good roasting joint should be lightly marbled with flecks of fat if it is to be succulently tender. The only cut that should have no fat on it at all is the fillet. Avoid cuts with large streaks of gristle as the meat will be tough.

Cuts of beef

- BRAISING STEAK:

Cut from the shoulder and traditionally called blade bone steak, or chuck steak, this is often sold with diced kidney for pies and puddings. It is also good for casseroles and stews.

- BRISKET:

Usually sold boned and rolled, this is cut from the top of the foreleg and used for slow pot-roasting or braising. Salted brisket should soaked and boiled, then served hot with mustard sauce (page 263). Alternatively, the cooked cut can be pressed with heavy weights and served cold, thinly sliced.

- FILLET:

The eye of the sirloin, the most tender of cuts. Roast quickly whole, or cut into steaks and grill (broil) or fry (sauté).

- RIBS:

Sold on the bone or boned and rolled, the wing (or prime rib) is considered the best. It is good roasted and pot-roasted.

- RUMP:

Cut from the buttock, rump is considered to have the best beef flavour. It is usually sold as steaks for grilling (broiling) or frying (sautéing).

- SILVERSIDE (ROUND):

Cut from the hind leg, this has a distinctive silvery sheen to the meat when roasted or pot-roasted. It is also sold salted; soak and boil the joint, then serve hot with mustard sauce (page 263) or press to serve cold.

- SIRLOIN:

The traditional cut for a Sunday roast, sirloin is sold either on the bone with the fillet attached (this can be removed to cook separately) or boned and rolled. Sirloin is marbled with fat and is very tender. It is also sold as steaks for grilling (broiling) or frying (sautéing).

- SKIRT BEEF (FLANK STEAK):

This heavy muscle is cut from inside the flank. It has an excellent flavour, and, although it has no fat attached, it must be trimmed of membranes and gristle before use. It is best used in casseroles.

- STEWING BEEF:

Cut from the shins or the neck, trim off any fat and gristle before use.

- T-BONE STEAK:

Large steaks on a T-shaped bone cut from the loin, behind the wing rib.

- TOP RUMP (TIP ROAST):

Also known as thick flank, top rump is sold in slices as frying steak and as joints for roasting or pot-roasting.

- TOPSIDE (ROUND):

A lean joint cut above the silverside on the hind leg, it is sold for roasting with a layer of fat tied round the joint to keep it moist during cooking. It is also good marinated, then braised or pot-roasted.

Traditional accompaniments for beef

- BOILED BEEF:

Mustard sauce (page 263).

- ROAST BEEF:

English mustard, horseradish sauce or cream, Yorkshire pudding (page 43) and roast parsnips.

- STEAKS:

French and/or English mustard, mushrooms and fried (sautéed) onions.

- STEWS:

Plain, herb or horseradish dumplings (page 181).

Lamb

Lamb can really only be called lamb if the animal is less than one year old so if you buy a large leg, it will really be hogget. Older still, it becomes mutton. Young lamb has pink flesh with milky white fat. Hogget is a little darker in colour with creamier fat. Mutton has dark red meat and very little fat. As a general rule, the older the meat, the stronger the flavour. Roast, grilled (broiled) or fried (sautéed) lamb should be served juicy and pink; if overcooked, it becomes stringy and dry. Slow-cooked lamb (such as Greek-style, page 106), however, will be thoroughly cooked but meltingly tender.

Choosing lamb

Pick the leanest pieces you can find – the less fat you have to trim off before cooking, the better value for money. All lamb has some fat, but it should not be discoloured or crumbly; it should be silky and resilient. The skin should look firm but not dry.

Cuts of lamb

- BEST END OF NECK:

This may be sold whole as a rack of lamb, tied into a crown roast, or two racks tied together to form a guard of honour. It is also sold cut into cutlets. Whole racks should be roasted; grill (broil) or fry (sauté) the cutlets.

- BREAST:

This sweet, slightly fatty meat is either cut into ribs for serving (see Barbecued lamb spare ribs, pages 107–8), or trimmed of as much fat as possible and stewed or pot-roasted. Alternatively, it can be boned, stuffed and roasted.

- CHUMP:

The thick part of the rump in front of the back legs. This may be sold cut into chops to grill (broil) or fry (sauté), or as one large joint connected to the leg, called a baron of lamb (excellent for roasting for a large party centrepiece).

- LEG:

Sold whole or in two smaller joints, the fillet and the knuckle end. Both are best roasted, braised or pot-roasted. Whole legs are also available part-boned.

- LEG STEAKS:

Cut from the fillet end, these can be grilled (broiled), fried (sautéed) or roast.

- LOIN:

The two loins connected make a saddle of lamb. Loin is sold on the bone, boned and rolled (often round the kidney) or as chops. Roast whole loin; grill (broil) or fry (sauté) chops.

- MIDDLE AND SCRAG END OF NECK:

These bony parts of the neck are usually stewed or cooked slowly in a hot-pot.

- NECK FILLET:

This is cut from the eye of the best end of neck. Roast it whole (serve thickly sliced), or cut into thin steaks, beat flat and fry (sauté), or cube for kebabs.

- SHOULDER:

On the bone or boned and rolled, this cut can be roasted, pot-roasted or diced for kebabs, stews or casseroles.

Traditional accompaniments for lamb

* ROAST, GRILLED (BROILED) AND FRIED (SAUTÉED) LAMB:

Mint sauce (page 263) or redcurrant jelly (clear conserve).

* ROAST OR BOILED MUTTON:

Onion sauce (page 264) or caper sauce (page 259).

Pork

A rich, well-flavoured meat that should always be well cooked, never served pink. It used to be known as a fatty meat, but nowadays pigs are bred to produce a much higher ratio of lean meat to fat.

Choosing pork

The flesh should be a glistening, pale pink with dense, white fat. The rind should be coarse, yellow to orange in colour with no sign of wetness. There should be no strong smell.

Cuts of pork

* BELLY PORK:

The fatty underside of the pig, this cut can be boned and roasted with a stuffing, or the rashers (slices) can be grilled (broiled) or fried (sautéed). However, it is best cut into pieces for rich stews and casseroles with pulses, cabbage and/or potatoes to offset the rich fattiness.

* BLADE: *see* SHOULDER

* CHUMP END (BUTTERFLY CHOPS):

Sold whole, chump can be roasted; cut into chops, it can be grilled (broiled) or fried (sautéed).

* FILLET: *see* LEG and TENDERLOIN

* HAND AND SPRING:

A large foreleg joint, often cut into small pieces for stewing. The whole boned hand also makes an economical large roast. It is best stuffed.

* LEG:

Whole or in joints, from the fillet end and the shank end, leg is sold either with the bone in or boned and rolled. It is best for roasting. Steaks cut from the leg are often called fillets. Grill (broil) or fry (sauté).

- LOIN:

Sweet and succulent, loin is sold whole, either on the bone, or boned and rolled, or cut into chops. Roast whole joints, stuffed if boned and rolled; grill (broil) or fry (sauté) chops. Two loins tied together can also make a pork guard of honour (see Cuts of lamb, page 97).

- SHOULDER OR BLADE:

A rich, strongly-flavoured cut that can be casseroled, braised or roasted.

- SPARE RIBS, CHINESE:

Cut from the lower part of the rib, these have very little meat. They are usually boiled first, then barbecued or grilled (broiled) with sweet and sour sauce (page 265), chilli sauce (page 260) or barbecue sauce (page 262).

- SPARE RIB CHOPS:

Cut from behind the shoulder, these are best grilled (broiled), fried (sautéed) or braised. They have a stronger flavour than cuts from the hindquarter.

- SPARE RIB RACK:

Cut from the upper end of the rib cage, these are often roasted in a rack and served with barbecue sauce (page 262), or two racks are sandwiched together with a stuffing before roasting.

- TENDERLOIN OR FILLET:

Cut from the eye of the loin, this is the most tender cut of pork. It can be cut into small steaks and fried (sautéed) or grilled (broiled), or stuffed and roasted whole, or beaten flat into escalopes, then coated in egg and breadcrumbs and fried. See also Leg.

Traditional accompaniments for pork

- ROAST, GRILLED (BROILED) AND FRIED (SAUTÉED):

Sage and onion stuffing (page 275), apple sauce (page 259).

Cooking methods for all types of meat

To grill (broil) meat

1 Brush with a little oil or dot with butter or margarine. Season lightly.
2 Place under a preheated grill (broiler) and cook until done to your liking. The time will depend on the thickness of the chops or steak (see Cook's tips for meat, page 103).

To fry (sauté) meat

1 Heat a little oil or butter and oil in a frying pan (skillet).
2 Season the steak or chops and brown quickly on both sides.
3 Reduce the heat and continue to cook, turning once, until cooked to your liking. The cooking time will depend on the thickness (see Cook's tips for meat, page 103).

To roast meat

1 Spread the meat with stuffing, roll up and tie with string, if appropriate. Place the joint in a roasting tin (pan) on a rack, if pork.
2 Brush beef or lamb with a little oil. Season lightly. For pork, score the rind and rub with oil and salt.
3 Roast in a preheated oven at 220°C/425°F/gas mark 7 for 10 minutes, then reduce the heat to 190°C/375°F/gas mark 5 for the remaining cooking time. For rare meat (beef only), allow 15 minutes per 450 g/1 lb plus 15 minutes over. For medium, i.e. slightly pink in the centre (for beef or lamb), allow 20 minutes per lb plus 20 minutes over. For well-done meat (beef, lamb or pork), allow 30 minutes per lb plus 30 minutes over.

To braise or casserole meat

1 Dip the meat, in thick slices or diced, in seasoned flour, if liked.
2 Brown in a little hot oil or butter or margarine. Lift out with a draining spoon.
3 Add diced vegetables and toss quickly in the hot fat.
4 Replace the meat and add stock or stock and wine. Bring to the boil, then cover and transfer to a preheated oven at 160°C/325°F/gas mark 3 for 1½–2½ hours.

To pot-roast meat

1 Prepare as for braising but use a whole joint of meat.
2 Cover and cook on the top of the stove or in a preheated oven at 160°C/325°F/gas mark 3 for 40 minutes per 450 g/1 lb.

To boil or stew meat

1 Place the joint or cubes of meat in a pan with vegetables and other flavourings of your choice. Cover with stock or water.
2 Bring to the boil, skim the surface, reduce the heat and cook at a very gentle simmer for up to 1 hour per 450 g/1 lb meat.

Offal

Offal is much less popular nowadays and so delicacies such as sweetbreads, tripe, brains and oxtail are not as widely available as they used to be. However, liver, kidneys and heart are still quite easy to buy and are highly nutritious. Heart needs long, slow cooking to tenderise it, but liver and kidneys can be either cooked very quickly or braised in a rich sauce. Tongue is also a treat although probably only for dedicated cooks as preparing it is a lengthy process. I haven't given you recipes for tongue here but you can buy it ready-cooked, either canned or fresh from the delicatessen counter if you wish.

To prepare liver

1 Pull off the thin membrane that covers the liver.
2 Trim away any fat or gristle that is still attached.
3 Cut into thin slices, if appropriate.

To prepare kidneys

1 Peel away any outer casing of fat (this will already have been done if you buy them from a supermarket).
2 Pull off the thin membrane surrounding the kidney.
3 Cut in half and snip out the central core with scissors.
4 Cut into neat pieces, if appropriate.

To prepare heart

1 Snip out the pipes and tendons from the top of the heart with scissors.
2 Trim any visible fat.
3 Either soak in cold water for 1 hour to remove the blood, or cut up and rinse under cold, running water.

To fry (sauté) liver or kidneys

1 Toss in seasoned flour.
2 Heat a little sunflower or olive oil and butter in a frying pan (skillet).
3 Add the liver or kidneys and fry until golden brown underneath.
4 Turn over and fry again, just until beads of juice appear on the surface.

To grill (broil) liver or kidneys

1 Brush with sunflower or olive oil or melted butter and season lightly.
2 Place on foil on a grill (broiler) rack and cook until golden brown. Turn over, brush again, and cook just until brown. If you overcook, the meat will be very hard.

To braise or casserole liver, kidneys or heart

1 Prepare the offal and cut into bite-sized pieces, or stuff lamb's hearts (see stuffing recipes, pages 274–5).
2 Brown in a little butter or margarine or sunflower or olive oil, then add your choice of vegetables, herbs and spices and enough stock, tomato juice or wine and stock mixed to cover.
3 Bring to the boil, cover and transfer to a preheated oven at 160°C/325°F/gas mark 3 for 1–3 hours or until the meat is really tender. Season and thicken the juices as liked.
● Lambs' and pigs' liver and kidneys will take 1–2 hours. Lambs' hearts and beef offal will take longer.

Recipes
Rich Country Beef Casserole   Serves 4

700 g/1½ lb braising steak, cubed, discarding any fat or gristle
60 ml/4 tbsp plain (all-purpose) flour
Salt and freshly ground black pepper
45 ml/3 tbsp sunflower oil
2 onions, sliced
2 carrots, diced
600 ml/1 pt/2½ cups beef stock, made with 1 stock cube
A little gravy block or browning
1 bay leaf
Jacket-baked potatoes and a green vegetable, to serve

1 Put the meat in a plastic bag with the flour and a little salt and pepper. Shake well to coat.
2 Heat the oil in a flameproof casserole (Dutch oven). Add the onions and carrots and fry (sauté), stirring, for 2 minutes. Remove from the pan.
3 Add the beef and fry, stirring, until browned on all sides.
4 Add any flour left in the bag and stir in with the onions and carrots.
5 Pour on the stock, stirring, and bring to the boil. Add a little gravy block or browning, a little more seasoning and the bay leaf.
6 Cover and cook in a preheated oven at 160°C/325°F/gas mark 3 for 2–2½ hours until really tender. Taste and adjust the seasoning, if necessary. Discard the bay leaf.
7 Serve with jacket-baked potatoes and a green vegetable.

Cook's tips for meat

- Always make sure you brush steaks or chops with oil or melted butter before grilling (broiling) or the surface will harden.

- To test whether a steak and chop is cooked to your liking, try pressing on it, once browned on both sides. If it still feels very flexible (wobbly), it will be very rare. If firmer but still with a little 'give', it will be medium-rare. If it feels firm to the touch it will be well done. If it is hard, it will be dry and overcooked!

- Snip the rind of pork chops before grilling (broiling) to prevent them curling at the edges.

- Don't keep prodding with a knife or fork during cooking. The juices will all run out.

- If you are serving small Yorkshire puddings with roast beef, it is best to roast the beef, then remove it from the oven to rest while you raise the temperature to cook the Yorkshires. Of course, if you are from Yorkshire, you may disagree, since traditionally a large Yorkshire pudding should be baked under the meat, so the juices drip down into it.

- If you are still daunted by making Yorkshires, cheat and buy them ready-made (but do try my recipe on page 43 first – I think it's foolproof!).

- Prime cuts of young lamb are delicious cooked until just pink and juicy in the centre. Older lamb or mutton is better cooked through.

- Lamb tends to spit in the oven when being roasted, so a roaster baster – a covered roasting tin (pan) – is a good idea.

- To get your pork crackling really crisp, score in narrow strips with a sharp knife, rub well with oil, then salt. Always stand the joint on a rack in the roasting tin.

- If your crackling is soggy, remove and place it under a preheated grill (broiler) for a few minutes to puff up. Turn once and take care it does not burn. Alternatively, wrap in greaseproof (waxed) paper and cook in the microwave for a minute or two until it stops making a crackling sound.

Brewer's Beef
Serves 4

Prepare as for Rich country beef casserole (page 102) but use a 330 ml can of brown ale or bitter beer and 250 ml/8 fl oz/1 cup beef stock, made with 1 stock cube instead of the stock in the recipe.

• •

Beef in Red Wine with Mushrooms
Serves 4

Prepare as for Rich country beef casserole (page 102), but use half red wine and half stock (made with 1 stock cube). Omit the gravy block or browning and add 100 g/4 oz button mushrooms, 15 ml/1 tbsp tomato purée (paste) and 2.5 ml/½ tsp caster (superfine) sugar.

• •

Creamy Peppered Steaks
Serves 4

4 fillet steaks
40 g/1½ oz/3 tbsp butter or margarine
15 ml/1 tbsp olive oil
30 ml/2 tbsp pickled green peppercorns
30 ml/2 tbsp brandy
150 ml/¼ pt/⅔ cup double (heavy) cream or crème fraîche
Salt and freshly ground black pepper
Plain rice and broccoli, to serve

1 Fry (sauté) the steaks in the butter or margarine and oil in a frying pan (skillet) until golden brown on both sides.
2 Reduce the heat and continue to cook for 4–10 minutes, depending on thickness and how well you like your steaks done, turning once or twice. To test whether they are ready, see Cook's tips for meat, page 103.
3 Remove from the pan and keep warm.
4 Add the peppercorns and brandy and ignite. Shake the pan until the flames subside.
5 Stir in the cream or crème fraîche and boil until slightly thickening. Season to taste. Spoon over the steaks and serve with rice and broccoli.

• •

Sumptuous Beef Pockets

Serves 2–4

The quantities are not vital for this dish. Use as little or as much beef and mushrooms as you like or make up with extra salad. Those with very large appetites will eat more pitta breads.

1 large onion, finely chopped
8 or more button mushrooms, sliced
25 g/1 oz/2 tbsp butter or margarine
100–175 g/4–6 oz/1–1½ cups leftover roast beef, cut into very thin strips
60 ml/4 tbsp Worcestershire sauce
5 ml/1 tsp lemon juice
15 ml/1 tbsp water
Salt and freshly ground black pepper
4 pitta breads
Shredded lettuce, sliced tomatoes and sliced cucumber, to garnish

1 Fry (sauté) the onions and mushrooms gently in the butter or margarine, stirring for 3–4 minutes until soft but not too brown.
2 Add the beef and toss over a gentle heat until just hot through.
3 Add the Worcestershire sauce, lemon juice, water and a little salt and pepper and simmer, stirring, until the meat is bathed in the juices.
4 Meanwhile, warm the pitta breads in a toaster, under the grill (broiler) or in the microwave. Cut in half widthways and gently open into pockets.
5 Spoon in the beef and fill with shredded lettuce, tomato and cucumber. Serve straight away.

• •

Beef Pot with Water Chestnuts

Serves 4

A really quick recipe – use canned carrots for extra speed!

3 large potatoes, scrubbed and sliced
Salt
2 × 420 g/2 × 15 oz/2 large cans of stewed steak in gravy
225 g/8 oz/1 small can of water chestnuts, drained and sliced
295 g/10½ oz/1 medium can of condensed mushroom soup
Freshly ground black pepper
Carrots, to serve

1 Cook the potatoes in boiling, lightly salted water for 3–4 minutes until almost tender but still holding their shape. Drain.
2 Spoon the stewed steak and its gravy into an ovenproof dish. Gently fold in the water chestnuts.
3 Spoon half the soup over.
4 Arrange the potatoes in overlapping slices on top.
5 Mix the remaining soup with 45 ml/3 tbsp water so that you can just pour it. Spread over the surface of the potato.
6 Bake in a preheated oven at 190°C/375°F/gas mark 5 for about 40 minutes until golden brown on top.
7 Serve hot with carrots.

· ·

Greek-style Lamb   Serves 4

½ leg of lamb, about 1 kg/2¼ lb
1 large garlic clove, cut into slivers
2.5 ml/½ tsp dried oregano
Salt and freshly ground black pepper
8 large potatoes, peeled and halved
450 ml/¾ pt/2 cups lamb or chicken stock, made with 1 stock cube
30 ml/2 tbsp chopped fresh parsley, to garnish
Warm pitta breads and a village salad (page 158), to serve

1 Put the lamb in a fairly large, flameproof casserole dish (Dutch oven). Lay the garlic slivers over and sprinkle with the oregano and a little salt and pepper.
2 Arrange the halved potatoes around and season lightly.
3 Pour in the stock.
4 Cover and cook in a preheated oven at 160°C/325°F/gas mark 3 for 3½ hours or until meltingly tender.
5 Transfer the meat and potatoes to a carving dish. Boil the liquid rapidly until slightly reduced.
6 Cut all the meat off the bone (it will fall away) and cut into neat pieces. Transfer to warm plates with the potatoes. Spoon the juices over and sprinkle with parsley. Serve with pitta breads and a village salad.

· ·

Lamb Paprikash
Serves 4

700 g/1½ lb diced lamb, trimmed of excess fat
1 large onion, chopped
15 ml/1 tbsp sunflower oil
15 ml/1 tbsp paprika
190 g/6¾ oz/1 small can of pimientos, drained and cut into strips
150 ml/¼ pt/⅔ cup lamb or chicken stock, made with ½ stock cube
Salt and freshly ground black pepper
5 ml/1 tsp caster (superfine) sugar
30 ml/2 tbsp plain (all-purpose) flour
30 ml/2 tbsp water
45 ml/3 tbsp crème fraîche
1 hard-boiled (hard-cooked) egg, chopped
15 ml/1 tbsp chopped fresh parsley
Ribbon noodles and a green salad with French dressing (page 268), to serve

1 Brown the lamb and onion in the oil in a saucepan for 3 minutes, stirring.
2 Add the paprika and cook for 30 seconds.
3 Stir in the pimientos, stock, a little salt and pepper and the sugar.
4 Bring to the boil, cover, reduce the heat and simmer very gently for 1 hour or until the lamb is really tender.
5 Blend the flour with the water until smooth. Stir into the pan and cook, stirring, for 2 minutes.
6 Stir in the crème fraîche. Spoon on to warm plates, sprinkle with the egg and parsley and serve with noodles and a green salad with French dressing.

· ·

Barbecued Lamb Spare Ribs
Serves 4

1.25 kg/2½ lb whole breast of lamb, trimmed of fat
60 ml/4 tbsp red wine vinegar
45 ml/3 tbsp clear honey
30 ml/2 tbsp tomato ketchup (catsup)
15 ml/1 tbsp tomato purée (paste)
30 ml/2 tbsp Worcestershire sauce
1 garlic clove, crushed
5 ml/1 tsp Dijon mustard
Egg fried rice (page 172) and an Oriental salad (page 159), to serve

1 With a sharp knife, cut between the bones to separate the lamb into ribs.
2 Place in a saucepan and cover with water. Add half the vinegar. Bring to the boil, cover, reduce the heat and simmer for 1 hour. Drain.
3 Mix the remaining vinegar with the remaining ingredients in a roasting tin (pan). Add the lamb and turn to coat with the sauce.
4 Place in a preheated oven at 200°C/400°F/gas mark 6 for 35 minutes until sticky and brown.
5 Serve with egg fried rice and an Oriental salad.

Easy Italian Lamb   Serves 4

Make this extra special by adding a 425 g/15 oz/large can of drained artichoke hearts, halved, to the lamb for the last 10 minutes of cooking time.

    4 lamb chump chops
    1 onion
    15 ml/1 tbsp olive oil
    295 g/10½ oz/1 medium can of condensed tomato soup
    2.5 ml/½ tsp dried basil
    Salt and freshly ground black pepper
    Tagliatelle and a green salad, to serve

1 Brown the chops and onion in the oil in a flameproof casserole (Dutch oven).
2 Spoon the soup over and sprinkle with the basil and a little salt and pepper.
3 Cover and cook in a preheated oven at 160°C/325°F/gas mark 3 for 1½ hours or until the chops are tender and bathed in sauce.
4 Spoon over tagliatelle and serve with a green salad.

Saucy Lamb Crunch   Serves 4

    75 g/3 oz/⅓ cup butter or margarine
    2 thick slices of bread, cut into cubes
    4 courgettes (zucchini), diced
    175 g/6 oz/1½ cups cooked lamb, diced, discarding any fat
    30 ml/2 tbsp capers, chopped
    15 ml/1 tbsp vinegar from the jar of capers

Salt and freshly ground black pepper
30 ml/2 tbsp plain (all-purpose) flour
300 ml/½ pt/1¼ cups lamb or chicken stock, made with 1 stock cube
2 eggs, beaten
30 ml/2 tbsp chopped fresh parsley
Middle Eastern coleslaw (page 160), to serve

1 Melt half the butter or margarine in a saucepan. Remove from the heat. Add the bread and toss to coat completely. Remove from the pan and reserve.
2 Melt the remaining butter or margarine in the same pan. Stir in the courgettes. Cover and cook gently for 3 minutes, shaking occasionally.
3 Add the lamb, capers, vinegar and a little salt and pepper. Cover and continue to cook for 5 minutes until the lamb is tender.
4 Stir in the flour and cook for 1 minute. Blend in the stock, bring to the boil and simmer, stirring, for 2 minutes.
5 Add the beaten eggs and parsley and heat through, stirring until slightly thickened but do not allow to boil. Taste and adjust the seasoning.
6 Turn into four individual flameproof dishes and top with the buttered bread cubes. Place under a preheated grill (broiler) until the top is golden brown. Serve hot with Middle Eastern coleslaw.

Lamb Steakwich

Serves 1

2.5 cm/1 in piece of cucumber
2.5 ml/½ tsp dried mint
30 ml/2 tbsp plain yoghurt
Salt and freshly ground black pepper
1 frozen minced (ground) lamb steak
1 small baguette
A little crisp lettuce, shredded
Tomato, corn and onion salad (page 161), to serve

1 Grate the cucumber and squeeze out the juice. Mix with the mint, yoghurt and a little salt and pepper and leave to stand while cooking the meat.
2 Grill (broil) the lamb steak on both sides until cooked through. Cut in half.
3 Split the baguette, spread with the yoghurt mixture and some shredded lettuce, then add the meat. Serve with a tomato, corn and onion salad.

Rustic Pan-fried Pork Steaks   Serves 4

4 pork loin steaks
25 g/1 oz/2 tbsp butter or margarine
Salt and freshly ground black pepper
100 g/4 oz chestnut mushrooms, sliced
150 ml/¼ pt/⅔ cup chicken stock, made with ½ stock cube
2 garlic cloves, finely chopped
30 ml/2 tbsp chopped fresh parsley
Sauté potatoes (page 137) and French (green) beans, to serve

1 Brown the pork in the butter or margarine in a frying pan (skillet) for
   2 minutes on each side. Season. Reduce the heat and fry (sauté) for about
   8 minutes until cooked through but still juicy. Remove from the pan.
2 Add the mushrooms and fry for 2 minutes, stirring. Add the stock and
   bring to the boil.
3 Return the pork to the pan, sprinkle the garlic and parsley over, cover and
   cook gently for 5 minutes.
4 Transfer the pork and mushrooms to warm plates. Taste the liquid and
   adjust the seasoning. Bring back to the boil and boil rapidly for 30 seconds.
5 Spoon over the pork and serve with sauté potatoes and French beans.

Pork, Oyster Mushroom and Green Pepper Stir-fry with Oyster Sauce   Serves 4

450 g/1 lb pork stir-fry meat
45 ml/3 tbsp cornflour (cornstarch)
Salt and freshly ground black pepper
45 ml/3 tbsp sunflower oil
1 bunch of spring onions (scallions), cut into 2.5 cm/1 in diagonal slices
1 green (bell) pepper, cut into thin strips
50 g/2 oz oyster mushrooms, sliced
30 ml/2 tbsp medium-dry sherry
300 ml/½ pt /1¼ cups pork or chicken stock, made with 1 stock cube
15 ml/1 tbsp oyster sauce
A pinch of dried sage
Chinese egg noodles, to serve

1 Toss the pork in the cornflour, seasoned with a little salt and pepper.
2 Heat the oil in a wok or large frying pan (skillet). Add the spring onions, pepper and mushrooms and stir-fry for 3 minutes. Remove from the pan with a draining spoon.
3 Add the pork and stir-fry until browned.
4 Return the vegetables to the pan and add the remaining ingredients. Simmer for 8 minutes, stirring occasionally until the pork is tender.
5 Serve hot on a bed of Chinese egg noodles.

Pork and Bean Hot-pot

Serves 4

225 g/8 oz/1⅓ cups dried haricot (navy) beans, soaked in cold water overnight
450 ml/¾ pt/2 cups water
1 pork stock cube
15 ml/1 tbsp olive oil
6 rashers (slices) of belly pork, rind and bone removed and cut into cubes
1 large onion, chopped
2 carrots, diced
225 g/8 oz/1 small can of chopped tomatoes
15 ml/1 tbsp black treacle (molasses)
1 bouquet garni sachet
Salt and freshly ground black pepper
30 ml/2 tbsp snipped fresh chives, to garnish
Crusty bread and a green salad, to serve

1 Drain the beans and place in a large, flameproof casserole (Dutch oven) with the water. Bring to the boil and boil rapidly for 10 minutes. Crumble in the stock cube and stir until dissolved.
2 Meanwhile, heat the oil in a frying pan (skillet). Brown the pork, onion and carrots.
3 Add to the beans with the remaining ingredients. Bring back to the boil.
4 Cover and place in a preheated oven at 150°C/300°F/gas mark 2 for 4 hours or until the beans are really tender and bathed in a rich sauce.
5 Remove the bouquet garni, taste and adjust the seasoning, if necessary. Sprinkle with chives and serve with crusty bread and a green salad.

Pork and Apricot Kebabs   Serves 4

350 g/12 oz pork fillet, cut into cubes
100 g/4 oz ready-to-eat dried apricots
1 red and 1 green (bell) pepper, cut into large dice
45 ml/3 tbsp olive oil
15 ml/1 tbsp lemon juice
1 garlic clove, crushed
5 ml/1 tsp dried oregano
Salt and freshly ground black pepper
Minted yoghurt and cucumber (page 269) and plain rice, to serve

1 Put the pork, apricots and peppers in a large, shallow dish.
2 Whisk together the oil, lemon juice, garlic, oregano and some salt and pepper. Pour over the meat mixture and toss well to coat completely. Leave to marinate for at least 2 hours, tossing occasionally.
3 Thread on four kebab skewers. Place on foil on a grill (broiler) rack. Grill (broil) for about 8 minutes, turning occasionally and brushing with any remaining marinade until golden and cooked through.
4 Serve with minted yoghurt and cucumber and plain rice.

Sweet and Sour Pork Balls   Serves 4

100 g/4 oz/1 cup self-raising (self-rising) flour
5 ml/1 tsp salt
150 ml/¼ pt/⅔ cup cold water
175 g/6 oz piece of roast pork, cut into small cubes
Oil, for deep-frying
Sweet and sour sauce (page 265) and egg fried rice (page 172), to serve

1 Mix the flour and salt in a bowl. Gradually stir in the water to form a smooth, coating batter. Add the pork and stir in.
2 Heat the oil for deep-frying until a cube of day-old bread browns in 30 seconds. Use a small spoon to drop each coated cube of meat into the hot oil. Cook the cubes for 3–4 minutes, turning occasionally until golden brown, puffy and crisp.
3 Remove from the oil with a draining spoon and drain on kitchen paper (paper towels). Keep warm while cooking the remainder.

4 Heat the sweet and sour sauce. Pour over the pork balls and serve with egg fried rice.

· ·

Pork Tiffin

Serves 4

425 g/15 oz/1 large can of pease pudding
20 ml/1½ tbsp curry paste
30 ml/2 tbsp sultanas (golden raisins)
2 large naan breads
60 ml/4 tbsp mango chutney
4 thin slices of delicatessen roast pork
30 ml/2 tbsp desiccated (shredded) coconut
A little lemon juice
A large mixed salad, to serve

1 Empty the pease pudding into a saucepan and stir in the curry paste and sultanas. Heat through, stirring gently.
2 Cut the naan breads into halves and put on the grill (broiler) rack. Spread each with a little of the mango chutney, then top with a slice of pork.
3 Grill (broil) until the pork is sizzling.
4 Spread the pease pudding mixture over and sprinkle with coconut and lemon juice. Fold over and serve hot with a large, mixed salad.

· ·

Hearty Country Casserole

Serves 4

4 lambs' hearts
1 small swede (rutabaga), cut into small chunks
1 large onion, halved and sliced
2 large carrots, thickly sliced
450 g/1 lb baby potatoes, scrubbed but left whole
10 ml/2 tsp tomato purée (paste)
2.5 ml/½ tsp caster (superfine) sugar
600 ml/1 pt/2½ cups beef stock, made with 1 stock cube
Salt and freshly ground black pepper
2.5 ml/½ tsp dried mixed herbs

1 Remove any pipes from the hearts and cut into halves, then into thick slices. Place in a flameproof casserole (Dutch oven) with the swede, onion, carrots and potatoes.
2 Blend the tomato purée with the sugar and stock. Pour into the casserole and add a little salt and pepper and the herbs.
3 Bring to the boil and transfer to a preheated oven at 160°C/325°F/gas mark 3. Cook for 3½ hours.
4 Ladle into warm bowls and serve piping hot.

Liver and Onion Hot-pot   Serves 4

450 g/1 lb pigs' liver, cut into bite-sized pieces
30 ml/2 tbsp milk
40 g/1½ oz/3 tbsp butter or margarine
3 large onions, sliced
1 eating (dessert) apple, sliced
15 ml/1 tbsp plain (all-purpose) flour
450 ml/¾ pt/2 cups chicken stock, made with 1 stock cube
5 ml/1 tsp dried sage
A little gravy block or browning
Salt and freshly ground black pepper
450 g/1 lb potatoes, scrubbed and sliced
Broad (fava) beans and baby carrots, to serve

1 Soak the liver in the milk for 15 minutes. Drain.
2 Heat 25 g/1 oz/2 tbsp of the butter or margarine in a flameproof casserole (Dutch oven). Fry (sauté) the onions for 3 minutes until lightly golden.
3 Add the liver and fry for 2 minutes.
4 Stir in the apple, flour, stock and sage. Bring to the boil, stirring. Add a little gravy block or browning, if liked, and season to taste.
5 Top with the potatoes and dot with the remaining butter or margarine.
6 Cover with a lid or foil and bake in a preheated oven at 190°C/375°F/gas mark 5 for 30 minutes. Remove the lid and cook for a further 30 minutes until cooked through and the top is turning golden brown.
7 Serve hot with broad beans and baby carrots.

Peppered Liver
Serves 4

15 ml/1 tbsp plain (all-purpose) flour
30 ml/2 tbsp coarsely crushed black peppercorns
350 g/12 oz lambs' liver, cut into very thin slices
25 g/1 oz/2 tbsp butter or margarine
30 ml/2 tbsp olive oil
150 ml/¼ pt/⅔ cup red wine
15 ml/1 tbsp tomato purée (paste)
5 ml/1 tsp caster (superfine) sugar
Salt
Creamed potatoes (page 138) and broccoli, to serve

1 Mix the flour and peppercorns together on a plate. Dip the liver in to coat on both sides.
2 Heat the butter and oil in a large frying pan (skillet). Fry (sauté) the liver on one side to brown. Turn over and cook just until droplets of juice appear on the surface. Remove from the pan and keep warm.
3 Stir in the wine, tomato purée, sugar and a little salt. Cook, stirring, until bubbling. Thin with a little water if necessary.
4 Transfer the liver to warm plates. Spoon the juices over and serve hot with creamed potatoes and broccoli.

Devilled Kidneys
Serves 4

8 lambs' kidneys
50 g/2 oz/¼ cup butter or margarine
4 rashers (slices) of streaky bacon, rinded and diced
5 ml/1 tsp curry paste
5 ml/1 tsp made English mustard
30 ml/2 tbsp tomato purée (paste)
15 ml/1 tbsp light brown sugar
15 ml/1 tbsp Worcestershire sauce
15 ml/1 tbsp water
Plain rice and French (green) beans, to serve

1 Cut the kidneys in half, snip out the cores with scissors and cut into bite-sized pieces, discarding the skin, if necessary.
2 Heat the butter or margarine in a large frying pan (skillet). Add the kidneys and bacon and fry (sauté), stirring, for 3 minutes.
3 Add the remaining ingredients and cook, stirring, for about 4 minutes until the kidneys are cooked through and bathed in sauce.
4 Serve on a bed of rice with French beans.

Sherried Kidneys with Fresh Sage   Serves 4

4 pigs' kidneys
25 g/1 oz/2 tbsp butter or margarine
2 large onions, halved and sliced
100 g/4 oz button mushrooms, sliced
10 ml/2 tsp chopped fresh sage
45 ml/3 tbsp crème fraîche
15 ml/1 tbsp medium-dry sherry
Salt and freshly ground black pepper
4 fresh sage leaves and 4 black olives, to garnish
New potatoes and spinach, to serve

1 Halve the kidneys, peel off the skin and snip out the cores. Cut into bite-sized pieces.
2 Melt the butter in a frying pan (skillet). Add the onions and mushrooms and fry (sauté) for 3 minutes.
3 Add the kidneys and fry for 2 minutes, stirring, to brown.
4 Cover with a lid or foil and cook over a very gentle heat for 8 minutes until the kidneys are tender.
5 Stir in the sage, crème fraîche and sherry and allow to bubble for 1 minute. Season to taste.
6 Spoon on to warm plates, garnish each with a sage leaf and an olive and serve with new potatoes and spinach.

cured meats and sausages

There is a whole range of cured meats and sausages to choose from in the supermarket or delicatessen. They are predominantly pork products but beef, poultry and sometimes mutton and game are also used. When people killed their own meat for consumption, selected cuts – like the offal – were eaten fresh and the remainder was cured to preserve it for the long winter months. Sausages were also made from the pieces left over, so nothing was wasted. Now, of course, we can enjoy fresh joints and cured meats from all over the world, all year round. But in these health-conscious days, we are not advised to eat cured meats too often as they have a high salt and fat content.

Bacon

Bacon is salted and cured pork. It is available smoked and unsmoked (green).

Types of bacon

- FAT BACON:

A variety of versions is available from different countries, each with its own particular flavour: pancetta, from Italy; tocino, from Spain; speck from Germany; lard de poitrine and poitrine fumé from France. They can be bought sliced or in a whole piece.

- JOINTS:

Joints are available in countries where whole pigs are cured, as they are in Britain. Collar, which is cut into prime, middle and end joints, and forehock, cut into the butt, foreslipper and small hock, can be boiled and/or roasted.

- RASHERS (SLICES):

The leanest bacon rashers come from the back. There is oyster cut, from the hind end of the back; short back; long back; and middle, which is a mixture of short back and streaky bacon. Streaky rashers, which are cut from the flank or belly, are cheaper and the best buy if you like your bacon crisp. Choose it cut thinly, then the streaks of fat will quickly melt and the whole thing become brown and crunchy. Extra-lean varieties are now available and you can choose to buy your rashers with or without rind.

● STEAKS AND CHOPS:

These, too, come from whole cured pigs and are cut like the fresh ones but are usually sold off the bone. They are usually grilled (broiled) or fried (sautéed).

Ham

Traditionally, ham is the cured hind leg of the pig but the loin, shoulder and forehock (top of the foreleg) are also cured in the same way. There are two sorts of ham: boiling ham, which is bought either raw to cook at home or ready-cooked as boiled ham; and cured ham, to be eaten raw.

Boiling and boiled ham

Traditionally cooked ham has no added water, but many of the commercially produced, precooked and sliced varieties will have an added water content, which should be clearly stated on the packet. Also watch for words like 'made from shaped pieces of meat'. This is not true ham but reconstituted 'bits' that will lack real texture and flavour but will, of course, be cheaper. (Economy bacon steaks are manufactured in the same way). Here are some of the most famous varieties.

● GAMMON OR WILTSHIRE HAM:

This is cut from the whole cured pig and divided into the corner, middle and hock. It is also sold in steaks and cooked and sliced.

● JAMBON DE PARIS:

A sweet-cured ham from France.

● KAISERFLEISCH:

This is an Austrian smoked, cured loin.

● KASSLER:

This is a smoked, cured loin from Germany, Denmark and Poland.

● PRAGUE HAM:

A sweet-cured ham, smoked over beech wood.

- VIRGINIA HAM:

This American country ham is smoked over hickory and apple wood.

- YORK HAM:

A dry-salted and oak-smoked ham.

Raw cured ham

There are several varieties available from all over Europe. Each has its own traditional cure, which distinguishes it from the others. They can be eaten on their own with crusty bread and butter, or with fresh fruits such as melon or figs, or diced and added to speciality dishes such as pastas, risottos and pizzas, or used as a stuffing or wrap for fish, pork and poultry dishes. The best-known are Parma, coppa and culatello from Italy; Black Forest, Westphalian and lachsschinken from Germany; jamón serrano, from Spain; jambon de campagne from France; and jambon de grisons from Switzerland.

Salt pork

Salt pork differs from ham or bacon in that it is not completely cured, just soaked in brine. British pickled pork is salted belly pork. It is traditionally boiled with root vegetables and served with pease pudding. Bath chaps (jowls) are cured pigs' cheeks. The British eat them with mustard, the Americans with black-eyed peas. American salt pork (snowbelly) is salted very fat belly, traditionally used for Boston baked beans and chowders. The French petit salé is lightly salted flank, belly or collar. It is traditionally cooked in potée (a thick cabbage soup made with other cured meats and vegetables), or served with braised cabbage, puréed peas or beans. Scandinavian stylte is also pickled belly, boned and rolled with crushed mustard seeds and black peppercorns. It is served cold, thinly sliced.

Beef

After pork, the next most popular meat for curing is beef. Again, there are those that are to be served cooked and those to be served raw.

Cured dried beef

These are lean cuts of beef, salted with added spices and then air-dried until rich and dark. There are two varieties easily available: bresaola, from Italy, usually served with a lemon, olive oil and parsley dressing; and bündenerfleisch from Switzerland, eaten in thinly scraped slivers with a vinaigrette dressing.

Salted beef

Salt beef is brined rather like salt pork but with the addition of saltpetre, which turns it pinky red. Brisket and silverside are usually treated in this way. They are then traditionally boiled with onions, carrots, potatoes and dumplings and served with mustard or mustard sauce. Alternatively, they can be pressed and served cold, thinly sliced. Corned beef is a variety of salt beef (corning is the original term for salting) and in America it means the traditional salt beef used for corned beef hash but in Europe it refers to pressed, flaked, salt beef available in cans or sliced on the delicatessen counter. Pastrami is smoked salt beef seasoned liberally with black peppercorns. It is cooked and pressed and sold either in one piece or sliced. It is good served hot or cold with rye bread.

Cook's tips for bacon and ham

- Raw bacon, ham, salt pork or beef joints for home cooking may need soaking before use. If pre-packaged, follow the packet instructions. If not, soak in cold water for at least 2 hours or even overnight before cooking. Drain and cook as required.

- Even if the joint is labelled 'ready-to-cook', I would advise you to cover it with cold water, bring it to the boil and then throw the water away before starting to cook: this will ensure the end result is not too salty.

- Look out for ham and bacon pieces at your delicatessen. They are just the off-cuts from whole joints and are ideal for dicing and cooking, at a fraction of the normal price.

- When grilling (broiling) gammon or bacon steaks, snip all round the edges with kitchen scissors to prevent them curling when cooking.

Other cured meats

Most of these are not so well known or widely available. They include smoked mutton, venison and reindeer, all of which have strong, highly concentrated flavours and are very much an acquired taste! They can all be eaten raw with bread and unsalted (sweet) butter. Smoked mutton is good braised with root vegetables.

Smoked poultry and game

Smoked chicken and turkey breast is now available everywhere. They have a sweet, subtle flavour and are particularly good in salads and sandwiches.

Smoked guinea fowl, quail, duck and goose are all wonderful delicacies and worth trying for special occasions.

Sausages

This generic term covers an enormous variety of types that can be divided into several main groups.

Fresh sausages

This group includes all the varieties of British banger and American sausage, made from basic pork, beef, or a mixture of pork and beef. Fresh sausages named after particular regions tend to have much better flavours and textures but all are different, using different herbs and spices to give their distinctive taste. The best are pure meat, but most have some rusk added. They are sold by weight and separated by the casing being twisted between each sausage. English Cumberland sausage is sold in a continuous spiral. Sausagemeat, made without the casing, can be shaped into balls, for stuffings and for sausage rolls. There are also the varieties of French sausage, including the regional varieties, known as saucisses de campagne, which have exciting added flavourings, such as truffles or pistachio nuts. The Italians and Spanish varieties tend to be hot and spicy. Turkey sausages are now becoming popular too, as are vegetarian ones, made from soya protein or Quorn.

Cook's tips for fresh sausages

- To reduce the fat content, either grill (broil) or dry-fry sausages and drain well on kitchen paper (paper towels) before serving.

- You can choose extra-lean varieties but the flavours are not as good as the regional specialities.

Preserved cooking sausages

Some sausages are lightly smoked and already cooked and just need reheating; others have been smoked and salted but need to be fully cooked before eating. The most common is the frankfurter. Others include bockwurst, knackwurst, the Polish smoked pork rings, the French saucisson-cervelas and its English equivalent, the saveloy.

> ## Cook's tips for preserved sausages
>
> - Canned frankfurters (or hot dog sausages) are flabby and fairly tasteless. The vacuum-packed ones are better. Best of all are those bought fresh on the delicatessen counter.
>
> - All the preserved cooking sausages taste excellent served with cabbage or sauerkraut and potatoes and mustard. They are good in dried pea, bean or lentil stews and can be served cold in salads.

Pudding sausages

These all contain larger amounts of cereal than fresh sausages and tend to include blood and offal. The best known are black and white puddings and the German blutwurst (blood sausage). Scottish haggis is sometimes known as a glorified sausage but it is really a delicacy in its own right. Faggots, too, made of liver, lights, cereals and salt pork, could be considered as round sausages and are another cheap, tasty dish worth trying.

> ## Cook's tips for pudding sausages
>
> - For grilling (broiling) or frying (sautéing), cut blood sausages thickly or they will fall apart.
>
> - Most haggis is best steamed. Make sure it is piping hot before serving with the traditional mashed tatties – potatoes – and neeps – turnip or swede (rutabaga) – and a good, rich gravy (pages 263 and 266).
>
> - Faggots should be baked in the oven and served with potatoes, peas and a well-flavoured gravy. Pour any juices from the cooked faggots into the gravy before serving.

Salamis

There are literally thousands of these wonderful, firm, flavoursome sausages. They are all matured for anything from a few weeks to several months to become dense with an intense flavour. Most are a mixture of pork meat and fat, some have beef or veal added. They are flavoured with wines, peppercorns, garlic, chilli or paprika and each has its own distinctive texture and taste. Some are smoked too. Look out for pink Danish salami; rich, Italian varieties from Naples and Milan; the various saucissons secs of France; peppery German and Hungarian salamis; chorizo and salsicha from Spain; and the smaller, kabanos, peperoni, peperami and landjäger from Europe.

Cook's tips for salami

- As a general rule, the harder a salami, the thinner you should slice it.

- If adding some to a cooked dish, use sparingly as the taste is very strong and can overpower any other flavours.

- Remove the outer rind before serving – it's inedible.

Slicing sausages

The most widely found are mortadella from Italy; bierwurst, brawn and the cervelats from Germany and Hungary; and all the pâté-style sausages such as German, French and Danish liver sausages. Most can be sliced, but a few are so soft that they are best spread.

Cook's tips for slicing sausages

- If serving as a starter, choose a selection of slicing sausages and salamis and serve with crusty bread and butter.

- When buying from a delicatessen counter, ask for them to be medium sliced if serving on a platter, as you will get neat, whole slices.

- Remove any rind before serving as it will probably be plastic!

Recipes

Nectarine and Serrano Ham Crostini

Serves 4

2 nectarines, skinned, halved and stoned (pitted)
8 slices of ciabatta bread
30 ml/2 tbsp olive oil
4 wafer-thin slices of serrano ham, halved widthways
175 g/6 oz Bel Paese, Port Salut or other semi-soft cheese, rinded if necessary and sliced
Lollo rosso leaves
French dressing (page 268)

1 Cut each of the nectarine halves into four slices. Grill (broil) for 4 minutes, turning once, until turning slightly golden. Remove and keep warm.

2 Drizzle both sides of the slices of bread with the olive oil. Toast on both sides, then top each with a slice of serrano ham, then the cheese. Cook until the cheese is beginning to melt. Top each with two slices of nectarine.
3 Transfer to plates and add a garnish of lollo rosso leaves with a little French dressing spooned over.

Chorizo with Churrasco Salsa

Serves 4

350 g/12 oz chorizo sausages
60 ml/4 tbsp olive oil
30 ml/2 tbsp sweet sherry
20 ml/4 tsp white wine vinegar
5 ml/1 tsp lemon juice
1 shallot, very finely chopped
1 garlic clove, crushed
30 ml/2 tbsp finely chopped fresh parsley
10 ml/2 tsp chopped fresh oregano
A good pinch of chilli powder
Freshly ground black pepper
Salt
Fresh, crusty bread, to serve

1 Brush the sausages with a little of the olive oil ready for grilling (broiling).
2 Whisk all the remaining ingredients well together, cover and leave to allow the flavours to develop.
3 Grill the sausages for 2–3 minutes on each side until hot through and sizzling.
4 Cut into chunks, pour the salsa over and serve with lots of crusty bread to mop up the juices.

Hot Pastrami on Rye

Serves 4

8 slices of dark rye bread
100 g/4 oz/½ cup cream cheese
15 ml/1 tbsp horseradish cream
8 slices of pastrami
15 ml/1 tbsp sunflower oil
Freshly ground black pepper
8 gherkins (cornichons), halved lengthways

1 Toast the slices of bread on one side.
2 Mash the cheese and horseradish together and spread over the untoasted side. Place the slices of bread on plates.
3 Place the pastrami on foil on the grill (broiler) rack. Brush with oil and grill (broil) until just beginning to sizzle.
4 Quickly place on top of the cheese, sprinkle with pepper and top each with a halved gherkin. Serve straight away.

Savoury Sausage Rolls

Makes 8

350 g/12 oz shortcrust pastry (page 181)
Tomato, corn or chilli relish or sweet pickle
450 g/1 lb pork sausagemeat
1 egg, beaten

1 Roll out the pastry (paste) to a 46 × 18 cm/18 × 7 in rectangle.
2 Spread with the relish or pickle to within 2.5 cm/1 in of the long edge and right up to the shorter sides.
3 Shape the sausagemeat into a roll, 46 cm/18 in long. Place on the pastry.
4 Brush the edges of the pastry with water and fold over the filling, pressing the edges together to seal.
5 Knock up and flute with the back of a knife. Cut into eight pieces.
6 Transfer to a baking (cookie) sheet and brush with beaten egg.
7 Bake in a preheated oven at 200°C/400°F/gas mark 6 for about 30 minutes until golden and cooked through. Serve hot or cold.

Sausage, Sage and Apple Burgers

Serves 4

1 cooking (tart) apple, sliced
1 small onion, finely chopped
2.5 ml/½ tsp dried sage
Sugar, to taste
450 g/1 lb pork sausagemeat
15 ml/1 tbsp sunflower oil
A little mayonnaise
Sliced tomato, cucumber and shredded lettuce
4 burger buns

1 Put the apple, onion, sage and 5 ml/1 tsp sugar in a non-stick saucepan. Cook gently, stirring until the apple is pulpy. Sweeten to taste, then cool.
2 Divide the sausagemeat into eight pieces. Flatten four pieces and spoon the apple mixture in the centre (do not spread out to the edges). Top with the remaining sausagemeat and press the edges well together to seal.
3 Brush with oil and grill (broil) for about 4–5 minutes on each side until cooked through, or fry (sauté) in the oil. Drain on kitchen paper.
4 Put a little mayonnaise and salad in the burger buns and add the burgers. Serve hot.

Toad in the Hole

Serves 4

45 ml/3 tbsp sunflower oil
450 g/1 lb pork sausages
1 quantity of Yorkshire pudding batter (page 43)
A good pinch of dried sage
Plain potatoes, a green vegetable and gravy (pages 263 and 266) or onion sauce (page 264), to serve

1 Put the oil and sausages in a shallow 28 × 18 cm/11 × 7 in baking tin (pan).
2 Place in a preheated oven at 220°C/425°F/gas mark 7 for about 5 minutes or until sizzling.
3 Pour in the Yorkshire pudding batter and sprinkle with the sage.
4 Cook near the top of the oven for about 35 minutes until risen, crisp and golden. Serve hot with potatoes, vegetables and gravy or onion sauce.

Ham, Broccoli and Tomato Gratin   Serves 4

450 g/1 lb broccoli, cut into 8 florets
8 thin slices of ham
150 ml/¼ pt/⅔ cup passata (sieved tomatoes)
2.5 ml/½ tsp dried basil
1 quantity of cheese sauce (page 260)
25 g/1 oz/¼ cup Cheddar cheese, grated
30 ml/2 tbsp cornflakes, crushed

1 Cook the broccoli florets in lightly salted boiling water for about 5 minutes until just tender. Drain.
2 Wrap a slice of ham round each floret and arrange in a flameproof serving dish.
3 Spoon the passata over and sprinkle with the basil.
4 Pour over the cheese sauce and sprinkle with the cheese and cornflakes.
5 Place under a preheated grill (broiler) until the top is golden and bubbling. Serve hot.

Swiss Gammon Grill   Serves 4

4 gammon steaks
225 g/8 oz/1 small can of peach slices, drained
30 ml/2 tbsp chopped gherkins (cornichons)
4 slices of Emmental (Swiss) cheese
1 tomato, sliced
Sauté potatoes (page 137) and peas, to serve

1 Snip the edges of the gammon with scissors. Place on foil on a grill (broiler) rack.
2 Grill (broil) the gammon for 4 minutes on each side.
3 Top each with slices of peach and some chopped gherkins. Lay a slice of cheese on top, then a slice of tomato.
4 Grill until the cheese melts and bubbles and the fruit is hot. Serve with sauté potatoes and peas.

Polish Supper   Serves 4

45 ml/3 tbsp olive oil
1 large leek, halved and chopped
1 large garlic clove, crushed
1 large onion, chopped
1 small green cabbage, shredded
1 smoked pork ring, sliced
300 ml/½ pt/1¼ cups pork or chicken stock, made with 1 stock cube
2 large potatoes, cut into small pieces
5 ml/1 tsp dried thyme
Salt and freshly ground black pepper
10 ml/2 tsp poppy seeds
Rye bread, to serve

1 Heat the oil in a large saucepan.
2 Add the leek, garlic and onion and fry (sauté), stirring, for 3 minutes.
3 Stir in the cabbage and cook for 2 minutes until beginning to soften.
4 Add all the remaining ingredients, stir well, cover and cook over a gentle
   heat for 30 minutes until everything is tender.
5 Taste and adjust the seasoning, if necessary. Ladle into warm bowls and
   serve with lots of rye bread.

....

Bratwurst with Chunky Tomato and Herb Sauce   Serves 4

400 g/14 oz/1 large can of chopped tomatoes
1 large garlic clove, crushed
5 ml/1 tsp dried rosemary
5 ml/1 tsp dried oregano
2.5 ml/½ tsp German mustard
Salt and freshly ground black pepper
5 ml/1 tsp light brown sugar
450 g/1 lb bratwurst
Crusty bread, to serve

1 Put the tomatoes, garlic, herbs, mustard, a little salt and pepper and the sugar in a saucepan. Bring to the boil and simmer for 5 minutes, stirring until pulpy.
2 Lay the bratwurst on foil on a grill (broiler) rack. Brush with a little of this mixture.
3 Grill (broil) for 15 minutes, turning and brushing with the sauce mixture, until golden and cooked through.
4 Heat the remaining sauce until boiling and serve with the sausages with lots of crusty bread.

Antipasto Speciality

Serves 6

12 medium slices of salami Milano
6 thin slices of Parma ham
6 medium slices of mortadella
12 thin slices of bresaola
6 fresh figs
1 small galia or ogen melon
12 black and 12 green olives
45 ml/3 tbsp olive oil
Freshly ground black pepper
1 lemon, cut into small wedges
Focaccia with sun-dried tomatoes, to serve

1 Arrange the meats attractively on plates.
2 Quarter the figs and arrange in a starburst pattern in the centre of each plate.
3 Halve the melon and remove the seeds. Cut each half into six slices. Cut off the rind.
4 Cut the slices into chunks and arrange around the edge of each plate.
5 Scatter the olives over, drizzle with olive oil and add some freshly ground black pepper. Put a lemon wedge on each plate and serve with focaccia with sun-dried tomatoes.

Roast Cidered Gammon with Seeded Potatoes

Serves 4–6

700 g/1½ lb smallish potatoes, halved
30 ml/2 tbsp olive oil
Salt
30 ml/2 tbsp sesame seeds
700 g/1½ lb gammon joint, soaked if necessary
300 ml/½ pt/1¼ cups medium-sweet cider
300 ml/½ pt/1¼ cups water
1 bay leaf
15 ml/1 tbsp clear honey
15 ml/1 tbsp wholegrain mustard
30 ml/2 tbsp cornflour (cornstarch)
French (green) beans and redcurrant jelly (clear conserve), to serve

1 Put the potatoes in a roasting tin (pan). Drizzle with the oil and toss with a little salt and the sesame seeds until evenly coated.
2 Place in the top of a preheated oven at 190°C/375°F/gas mark 5.
3 Put the gammon in a small roasting tin (pan). Pour the cider and water around and add the bay leaf.
4 Cover with foil and place below the potatoes. Cook for 45 minutes. Turn the potatoes over.
5 Remove the foil and discard any rind from the gammon. Spread the surface with the honey and mustard. Return to the oven and roast for a further 15 minutes or until cooked through. Transfer to a carving dish.
6 Blend the cornflour with 30 ml/2 tbsp water and stir into the cooking juices. Bring to the boil and cook for 1 minute, stirring. Discard the bay leaf.
7 Carve the gammon and serve with the sauce, seeded potatoes, French beans and redcurrant jelly.

vegetables, pulses and herbs

If you still think of vegetables as being soggy cabbage and boiled spuds, then think again. There is a whole world of exciting, colourful vegetables for you to enjoy. They can be served, obviously, as accompaniments to meat or fish, but they are also excellent on their own as a starter or in a whole variety of dishes as a main course. Vegetables provide a variety of essential vitamins, minerals and fibre and should be eaten in abundance by everyone, every day. In this chapter I shall explain how to choose the best buys, how to prepare fresh vegetables and how to use frozen and canned varieties too.

Vegetables can be divided into several categories.

Brassicas

These include all the varieties that form a head – green, white (sometimes called Dutch), red, spring and Savoy cabbages, white and purple cauliflower, broccoli, purple and white sprouting broccoli, Brussels sprouts.

To prepare and boil brassicas

1 Remove any damaged or discoloured leaves.
2 Cut cabbages in half and remove the thick central core. Shred the leaves. Separate cauliflower or broccoli into small florets, discarding any thick stump. Small heads, such as sprouting broccoli and Brussels sprouts, may be left whole.
3 Put about 2.5 cm/1 in water in a saucepan with a pinch of salt. Put the pan over a high heat until it is boiling rapidly.

4 Add the brassicas and boil over a high heat until they are just tender but still with some texture. This will take about 3–5 minutes.

5 Strain in a colander in the sink or over a bowl if you want the cooking water for gravy.

To prepare and steam brassicas

1 Prepare as for boiling.

2 Place in a steamer or colander over a pan of simmering water.

3 Cover and cook until just tender.

• NOTE:

Red cabbage is best casseroled (see Sweet and sour red or white cabbage, page 150) or pickled.

Greens

This includes all the leafy green vegetables like spinach, spring (collard) greens, kale and curly kale, young Swiss chard and pak soi (a dark green oriental leaf with a thick, white stem). It also includes wild leaves such as sorrel, dandelions and nettles.

To prepare and boil greens

1 Remove any damaged or discoloured leaves. Separate the leaves to be cooked, discarding any thick stalks.

2 Rinse in cold water and drain.

3 Cut or tear the leaves into pieces or thin shreds as appropriate.

4 Cook as for brassicas, pushing down in the boiling water as they soften.

• NOTE:

For spinach, wash well but add no water to the pan while cooking.

To steam greens

1 Prepare as for boiling.

2 Steam as for brassicas.

3 Cover and cook until just tender.

Mushrooms and other fungi

These are not technically vegetables but used in the same way. Unless you know what you are doing, I don't recommend picking your own. There is now a huge variety of different fungi available in supermarkets, from the humble cultivated button and cup mushrooms to richer-flavoured open mushrooms which resemble their wild counterpart, the field mushroom. There are also the nuttier flavoured chestnut mushrooms, strong, meaty ceps (porcini in Italy) and morel varieties, delicate, apricot-scented chanterelles (which take a long time to cook), well-flavoured, delicately coloured oyster mushrooms and the slightly acid shiitake or Japanese tree mushrooms – to name just a few! The key here is to experiment and see which you like. The flavours vary considerably but they are all virtually interchangeable in recipes.

Quorn, the vegetarian protein, is also manufactured from a fungus. It is bland but versatile and available minced (ground) and in chunks and steaks. It can be substituted for meat in any dish. It needs extra fat or oil when frying (sautéing) and grilling (broiling).

Black and white truffles, too, come under this category. A tiny sliver of a black truffle can transform a humble omelette into a masterpiece or make a simple roast chicken stuffing out of this world. But as fresh truffles are staggeringly expensive (if you can get hold of them) and canned ones are not worth bothering about, no more mention need be made.

To fry (sauté) mushrooms and other fungi

1 Wipe clean and trim stalks.
2 Peel only the large, flat varieties.
3 Heat a little butter or oil in a frying pan (skillet) and fry (sauté) until golden and just tender.

To stew mushrooms or other fungi

1 Prepare as for frying (sautéing).
2 Place in a saucepan with a little stock or water.
3 Cover and bring to the boil. Reduce the heat and cook gently for about 5 minutes until just tender. Season as required.

The onion family

Red, yellow, white and Spanish onions, shallots, button (pearl) onions, spring onions (scallions), leeks and garlic are all part of this group. This is one of the oldest families of vegetables, used for centuries for their medicinal properties as well as being indispensable for flavouring many savoury dishes and excellent as vegetables in their own right.

To chop an onion

1 Cut the point off the top of the onion. Pull off all the outer skin, leaving the root intact (this will help stop you crying). Cut the onion in half lengthways through the root.
2 Hold each half, one at a time, between your thumb and fingers, flat side down on a board, and cut from the root end to the tip at intervals.
3 Now cut across the first set of cuts. Discard the root end. To chop finely, make all the cuts close together. To chop coarsely, make the cuts wider.

To slice an onion

1 Don't peel the onion. Hold it firmly between your thumb and middle finger, with the root end in your hand. Cut into fairly thin slices, starting at the tip end. When you get to the root end, discard it.
2 Peel off the brown, outer layer and the next layer, if it seems tough, from each slice.
3 Separate the slices into rings.

Pods and cobs

These include all the fresh peas and beans – garden peas, mangetout (snow peas), sugar snap peas, runner beans, the many varieties of thin, green beans, broad (fava) beans, flat beans, okra (ladies' fingers) and whole sweetcorn (corn), both large and baby cobs.

To prepare and boil pods and cobs

1 Trim baby corn cobs, top and tail okra, beans and mangetout. Shell broad beans and peas. String and cut runner beans in thin, diagonal slices. Cut thin, green, flat beans and okra into pieces as required.
2 Cook as for brassicas until just tender – about 3 minutes for mangetout and baby corn cobs, 5–6 minutes for beans or peas, depending on age. Corn-on-the-cob should be cooked until a kernel will come away from the husk easily – about 20 minutes.

To steam pods and cobs

1 Prepare as for boiling.
2 Place in an layer in a steamer or colander over a pan of simmering water.
3 Cook until just tender.

Tips for vegetable shopping

- Choose clean vegetables (you pay for the clods of earth!).
- Look for firmness and a bright colour.
- Avoid any with flabby skin or skin that wrinkles when pushed gently.
- The skin of a fresh, new potato should peel easily if scraped with a finger.
- Avoid any that look discoloured or bruised.
- Avoid wet vegetables or ones that feel very cold with translucent patches – they have been stored at too low a temperature and are frosted.
- Loose vegetables tend to be cheaper than pre-packed and it's easier to select the ones you want. The exception is old potatoes, where large bags are cheaper than small quantities and will keep well.
- Buy in quantities that can be used quickly. Green vegetables, in particular, don't keep well, but pulses, being dried, can be stored for ages in a cool, dark place.
- If buying pre-packed, choose the longest sell-by date on offer.

Roots and tubers

Roots and tubers are the stalwarts of the vegetable kingdom; they are earthy, rustic and simple but amongst the most useful of all. They include the many varieties of potato, which can be divided into two basic groups: old or main crop varieties, with tough skins that can be stored in a cool dark place, and new, young crop potatoes, which do not keep well and should be scraped or scrubbed to remove the thin skin, or simply rinsed and cooked with the skin on.

New potatoes are often imported – Cyprus and Egyptian new potatoes are particularly good – but the ones with the most delicious, earthy flavour are Jersey Royals. Old potatoes can be very different in colour and texture. Some are good all-rounders, for cooking in every way; of these, the most famous are milky King Edwards and red-skinned, yellow-fleshed Desiree but we can also include those now simply labelled Whites or Reds in the supermarket. Others, like Charlotte and Anna, are fairly small and waxy, ideal for boiling whole, layering in potato dishes and for salads; and there are also floury varieties, like Majestic, which are suitable for mashing, roasting and jacket-baking.

Yams, sweet potatoes and cassava are also included in this group of vegetables, along with carrots, parsnips, salsify, celeriac (celery root), swede (rutabaga), turnip, kohlrabi, Jerusalem artichoke and beetroot (red beet). Finally, we mustn't forget the mouli, or large winter radish, and the varieties of small summer radish, mostly used for salads.

To dice root vegetables

1 Peel thinly with a potato peeler or sharp knife, if necessary.
2 Cut in half lengthways.
3 Hold between your thumb and middle finger and cut into strips.
4 Turn the vegetable, still holding it firmly, and cut at right angles to the first cuts. For large dice, make the cuts wide apart. For smaller dice, make them closer together.

To prepare and boil root vegetables

1 Peel, thinly, with a potato peeler or sharp vegetable knife, or scrape or scrub, as necessary.
2 Cut into even-sized pieces (large chunks for potatoes, slices or sticks for carrots, chunky wedges for parsnips, for instance). Leave baby new potatoes or carrots whole.
3 Place in a pan with just enough cold water to cover and add a very little salt.

4 Cover with a lid and bring up to the boil over a high heat. When bubbling, turn the heat down to moderate and let the vegetables boil gently until they feel tender when a knife is inserted in them. This could be 5 –15 minutes, depending on the size of the pieces and the type of vegetable, so test at intervals.

5 Tip into a colander in the sink to drain. (If you want the cooking water for making gravy then put the colander over a mixing bowl).

- NOTE:

To cook beetroot (red beet), wash, then boil whole, without peeling or removing the top or the root. This will prevent them from 'bleeding' into the water.

To make chips (fries) or sauté potatoes

1 Wash or scrub the potatoes (leave the skins on unless you really object to them – they add extra texture and fibre). Cut each one into thick slices, then cut the slices into strips to make chips or into cubes. Wrap in a clean tea towel (dish cloth) to dry.

2 Pour about 2.5 cm/1 in oil into a frying pan (skillet) and heat until your hand feels hot when held 5 cm/2 in above the surface.

3 Use a fish slice to slide the chips or diced potatoes down into the pan and allow to fry (sauté) until golden, gently turning them occasionally. Drain on kitchen paper (paper towels).

- NOTE:

If you have a deep-fat fryer, follow the manufacturer's instructions.

To prepare and cook scalloped potatoes

1 Wash or scrub the potatoes (don't peel unless you want to). Cut into thin slices. Wrap in a clean tea towel (dish cloth) to dry.

2 Heat the oil as for chips (fries) or sauté potatoes (above). Slide in the potato slices and cook until golden brown, turning once if necessary. Drain on kitchen paper (paper towels).

To prepare and cook mashed root vegetables

1 Prepare and boil as above, then drain and return to the saucepan.

2 Mash well, with a fork or potato masher, adding a knob of butter or margarine, some salt and pepper and a little milk.

3 Once mashed, give the mixture a good beat with a potato masher or a wooden spoon to make it smooth and fluffy.

To prepare and cook creamed potatoes

1 Prepare and cook as for mashed root vegetables (page 137) but use single (light) cream instead of milk. An egg yolk can also be beaten in to enrich the vegetable.

To prepare and roast root vegetables

1 Prepare as for boiling (page 136) but boil for 3 minutes only. Drain.
2 For potatoes, put a lid on the pan and shake vigorously to roughen the surface.
3 Heat just enough oil to cover the base of a roasting tin (pan). When sizzling, add the vegetables. Turn to coat in the hot oil.
4 Roast near the top of a preheated oven at 190°C/375°F/gas mark 5 for about 1 hour, turning once or twice, until golden brown and cooked through.

To prepare and cook jacket-baked potatoes

● TO BAKE IN THE OVEN:
1 Choose large, even-sized potatoes. Scrub, then prick the skins all over with a fork.
2 Rub the skin with oil and salt, if liked.
3 Place on a baking (cookie) sheet or directly on the middle oven shelf and cook in a preheated oven at 180°C/350°F/gas mark 4 for about 1½ hours until really tender when squeezed. The time and oven temperature are not vital: cook for longer in a slow oven for longer or more quickly in a faster one. However, the flavour is best when cooked slowly.

● TO MICROWAVE:
1 Scrub, prick with a fork and wrap each one in kitchen paper (paper towels).
2 Microwave on High (100 per cent power) for about 4 minutes per potato, depending on size and the output of your microwave (check manufacturer's instructions).

● JACKET-BAKED POTATO TOPPINGS:
Minted yoghurt and cucumber (page 269)
Soured (dairy sour) cream and snipped fresh chives or chopped spring onion (scallion)
Baked beans and grated cheese
Tuna, sweetcorn and mayonnaise
Prawns in rosy dressing (page 270)

Cream cheese (plain or with garlic and herbs)
Cottage cheese (plain or flavoured)
Crisp, crumbled bacon, chopped tomato and mayonnaise
Grated Mozzarella cheese, chopped sun-dried tomatoes and olives

Stalks and shoots

Asparagus, Florence fennel, globe artichokes, celery, bamboo shoots and palm hearts are the best known in this group. Thick stalks of full-grown Swiss chard can also be included in this category as the stalks may be cooked and eaten like asparagus.

To prepare and boil asparagus and Swiss chard stalks

1 Tie asparagus in a bundle and trim off the ends of the woody stalks, if necessary. For Swiss chard, cut off the green part (this can be cooked separately) and trim the stalks. Tie in a bundle.
2 Bring a pan of water to the boil. Add a pinch of salt, if liked. Stand the bundle in the pan with the asparagus spears upright.
3 Cover with a lid (or foil if the stems are too tall). Cook thin stalks for 5 minutes, and thick stalks for 10 minutes. Turn off the heat and leave to stand for a further 5 minutes until the stalks are just tender but the heads of asparagus are still intact.
4 Drain and use as required. They may be eaten with the fingers if served as a starter.

To steam asparagus or Swiss chard

1 Prepare as for boiling (above) but do not tie in a bundle.
2 Lay the stems in an even layer in a steamer or colander over a pan of simmering water.
3 Cover and cook until the stems are just tender but the heads of asparagus are still intact.

To prepare and boil globe artichokes

1 Trim off the points of the leaves, if liked.
2 Twist off the stalks.
3 Bring a large pan of water to the boil. Add 15 ml/1 tbsp lemon juice and a pinch of salt, if liked.

4   Drop in the artichokes and boil for about 20 minutes until a leaf pulls away easily. Drain.
5   To eat, pull off one leaf at a time and dip the fleshy part in melted butter or other dipping sauce. Draw the leaf between the teeth to scrape off the fleshy part at the base. When all the large leaves are eaten, pull off all the inner leaves at the top and cut off the hairy choke. Eat the fleshy base with a knife and fork.

To prepare and boil fennel or celery

1   Trim the base and separate into sticks. Scrub and discard any coarse strings, cut into short lengths or cut into slices across the stalks.
2   Cook in boiling, lightly salted water or stock for about 15 minutes until tender. Drain.

Tips for storing vegetables

- Green vegetables will keep best in the fridge.

- Roots and tubers should be stored in a cool, dark place.

- Store mushrooms and other fungi in the fridge in a paper, not plastic, bag.

- All vegetables are best removed from plastic packaging before storing as plastic does not 'breathe' so moisture forms, which will rot them.

Vegetable fruits

This is a huge, colourful group including all the Mediterranean favourites like red, green, yellow, orange and purple (bell) peppers, aubergines (eggplants), chillies, courgettes (zucchini), all the different marrows (squashes), pumpkins, tomatoes, avocados, green and black olives and cucumbers. They are called vegetable fruits because they all contain the seeds that grow into the future generation of the plant. Many are eaten raw in salads as well as cooked in a whole variety of dishes.

To prepare and fry (sauté) vegetable fruits

1   Halve, peel, remove the seeds and any stalks, as appropriate.
2   Cut into slices.
3   Heat a little oil in a frying pan (skillet) or wok.
4   Fry, stirring or turning, until just tender, lightly golden and cooked through.
5   Drain on kitchen paper (paper towels), unless part of a stir-fry.

To boil vegetable fruits

1 Prepare as for frying (sautéing).
2 Drop into boiling, lightly salted water and cook until just tender. Do not overcook. As they have a high water content, they cook quite quickly.

To steam vegetable fruits

1 Prepare as for frying (sautéing).
2 Place in a steamer or colander over a pan of simmering water.
3 Cover and cook until just tender.

To grill (broil) vegetable fruits

Prepare as for frying (sautéing) but leave in halves if more suitable. Place on foil on a grill (broiler) rack and brush with oil. Cook under a hot grill until cooked through. Aubergines (eggplants) and (bell) peppers can be grilled (broiled) until the skin blackens; the skin should be peeled off before use.

Cook's tips for vegetables

- To preserve maximum goodness, prepare vegetables just before cooking.

- Use the cooking water where possible for a sauce or gravy as water-soluble vitamins will be lost otherwise.

- To speed up cooking any vegetable, cut it into smaller pieces if appropriate. For suitable vegetables, like roots or courgettes (zucchini), pare them with a potato peeler. They will cook almost instantly into beautiful ribbons, when plunged for 1–2 minutes in boiling water.

- Jacket potatoes can be baked in the oven more quickly by threading them on metal skewers. The heat will be conducted through to the centre more quickly and reduce the cooking time by about a third.

- To heat canned vegetables when you are using the oven, remove the paper label. Open the can and stand it on the oven shelf. When ready to serve, drain off the cooking liquid (no extra fuel or washing up!).

- Frozen vegetables cook well in the microwave in their bag. Snip the corner of the bag and place in the oven. Flatten out evenly. Microwave for 2 minutes, then flex the bag to rearrange the vegetables. Cook for a few more minutes until piping hot. Remove with oven-gloved hands as the bag will get soft and very hot. Drain off any liquid before serving.

Tips for freezing vegetables

- Most vegetables (except potatoes) can be home-frozen very successfully. As a general guide, prepare in your usual way. Blanch in boiling water (pages 131–2) for 1 minute. Drain and plunge immediately in ice-cold water. Drain thoroughly, pack in freezer bags, label and freeze.

- (Bell) peppers can be put in a bag and frozen whole for speed. They can be cut up while still frozen.

- Bags or plastic containers of herbs can be popped in the freezer, then chopped as required from frozen.

Commercially frozen and canned vegetables and pulses

Frozen vegetables are just as nutritious as fresh, and canned and dried veg will make very useful additions to your storecupboard. Ideally, choose varieties canned in water rather than brine and without sugar or added colourings. The 'naturally sweet' ranges are excellent, having less sugar and calories in them. When cooking frozen vegetables, always follow the instructions on the packet. Most are best cooked from frozen, without being thawed first. On the whole, I am not keen on dried vegetables (except pulses and mushrooms) although they can be a useful standby, and I must admit I could not live without sun-dried tomatoes! So it is always worth having some cans, frozen and dried vegetables to hand for convenience and the following list gives those I recommend.

Cans

- Asparagus
- Baked beans
- Carrots
- Chick peas (garbanzos)
- Haricot (navy), flageolet or other beans
- Mixed pulses
- Mushrooms
- Ratatouille
- Red kidney beans
- Sauerkraut
- Sweetcorn (corn)
- Tomatoes

Frozen

- Broad and French (green) beans
- Broccoli and cauliflower mix
- Herbs
- Peas
- Spinach

Dried

- Chillies
- Herbs
- Minced (ground) onion and garlic
- Peppers (bell)
- Pulses
- Speciality mushrooms, e.g. chanterelles and shiitake
- Sun-dried tomatoes, dried and/or in oil

Pulses

This group includes all the colourful dried peas, beans and lentils. They form an essential part of any vegetarian diet but should not be considered as fit only for cranks – they are versatile, tasty, and full of protein and fibre. Varieties include green, yellow and marrowfat peas, split red, green and brown lentils, dhals, chick peas (garbanzos) and all the beans – large white, flat butter (lima) beans, black beans, black-eyed beans, red and white kidney beans, haricot (navy), broad (fava), mung, soya and borlotti beans and the pale green flageolets, to name but a few!

Soya protein (TVP) is a meat substitute made from soya beans. It is available in chunks or minced (ground) and must be reconstituted before use.

To boil dried pulses

1 All dried pulses except split red lentils need soaking before use. Place in either boiling water for 2–3 hours or cold water overnight. Drain.
2 Place in a saucepan with enough water just to cover. Bring to the boil.
3 Boil rapidly for 10 minutes to destroy any toxins, then simmer gently until tender – it will take from 40 minutes to 3 hours, depending on the type. Top up with boiling water as necessary during cooking.
4 Season with salt after cooking, if liked.
5 Drain and use as required.

::: Cook's tips for pulses

- 100 g/4 oz/⅔ cup pulses is equal to a drained 425 g/15 oz/large can.

- To speed up soaking, cover with boiling water and soak for 2–3 hours.

- It is vital to boil all pulses rapidly (except for red lentils) for 10 minutes before simmering until tender. This destroys any toxins in them.

- Don't add salt to pulses during cooking, it toughens the skins.

- All dried beans are interchangeable in recipes.

- Red lentils make a good thickening agent as well as adding extra nourishment. Add them to stews and casseroles at the beginning of the cooking time, and they will become pulpy in the liquid.

- Use canned pulses to 'stretch' meat dishes. A casserole for four people, for instance, will serve an extra one or two people if you add a drained 425 g/15 oz/large can.

- Canned pulses, if drained and rinsed, make great salads, tossed in French dressing. Add other salad stuffs for perfect one-bowl meals.

Herbs

Herbs are fragrant leaves, used to add flavour and colour to dishes.

Fresh herbs are widely available in supermarkets, both ready-cut in packets, and growing in pots. Keep one or two pots of your favourites on the windowsill (but remember to water them!). Packets of fresh herbs can be frozen and then used in cooked dishes. They won't be suitable for garnishing, however, as they go limp once thawed. You can now buy ready-prepared herbs already frozen, and these are excellent, too.

Dried herbs should be stored in a cool, dark place. They should be used within six months or they will fade and lose their flavour, so don't buy them in large quantities. Dried herbs are a lot more pungent than fresh. If substituting them for fresh in any recipe, use very sparingly (less than half the given quantity for fresh) or they will dominate rather than enhance your food. Add just a pinch at a time, taste, then add some more if necessary.

Using the right herb

Here's a rough guide to the most common combinations of herbs and foods.

- BASIL:

Tomato-based dishes, poultry, cheese, salads.

- CORIANDER (CILANTRO):

Poultry, seafood, lamb, pork, spicy dishes, salads.

- MINT:

Lamb, vegetables, fruit.

- OREGANO/MARJORAM:

Beef, lamb, pork, poultry, cheese and tomato-based dishes.

- PARSLEY:

Almost any savoury food.

- ROSEMARY:

Lamb, chicken and other poultry and dried fruit.

- SAGE:

Pork, duck, cheese, offal.

- THYME:

Poultry, fish, offal, vegetables.

Cook's tips for herbs

- The easiest way to chop fresh herbs is to place the leaves in a teacup and snip with kitchen scissors.

- Fresh herbs, particularly parsley, coriander (cilantro) and basil, are often added towards the end of cooking for maximum flavour.

- You can dry herbs yourself. Either tie fresh sprigs in bundles and hang in a warm, airy place for several weeks, or lay the sprigs on a baking (cookie) sheet and bake in the oven at 180°C/350°F/gas mark 4 until they are crisp and crumble easily when squeezed. You can also lay them in a single layer on kitchen paper (paper towels) in the microwave, place a small cup of water to one side (to absorb some of the microwaves) and microwave on High (100 per cent power), checking every minute, until discoloured and crumbly. Strip from the stalks, crush and place in clean, airtight containers. Label and store in a cool, dark place.

Recipes

Corn Fritters

Serves 4–6

Try these with garlic mayonnaise as a starter, with a large mixed salad as a main course, or as an accompaniment to Chicken Maryland (page 86).

100 g/4 oz/1 cup plain (all-purpose) flour
1 small onion, grated
1 egg
150 ml/¼ pt/⅔ cup milk
350 g/12 oz/1 medium can of sweetcorn (corn), drained
Salt and freshly ground black pepper
45 ml/3 tbsp sunflower oil

1 Sift the flour into a bowl. Add the onion.
2 Make a well in the centre and add the egg. Gradually beat in the milk to form a thick batter. Stir in the corn and some salt and pepper.
3 Heat the oil in a frying pan (skillet), add spoonfuls of the corn mixture and fry (sauté) for about 2 minutes on each side until golden brown.
4 Drain on kitchen paper (paper towels) and keep warm while cooking the remainder. Serve hot.

• •

Cauliflower or Broccoli Cheese

Serves 4

1 cauliflower or large head of broccoli
2 quantities of cheese sauce (page 260)
5 ml/1 tsp made English mustard
50 g/2 oz/½ cup Cheddar cheese, grated
25 g/1 oz/½ cup cornflakes, crushed
3 tomatoes, sliced

1 Cut the cauliflower or broccoli into small florets. Cook in boiling, lightly salted water for 4–5 minutes until just tender.
2 Drain and place in a flameproof serving dish.
3 Stir the mustard into the sauce and spoon over the vegetables.
4 Scatter the cheese and cornflakes over and arrange the sliced tomatoes round the edge.

5 Place under a preheated grill (broiler) until the top is golden and bubbling. Alternatively, place in a preheated oven at 190°C/375°F/gas mark 5 for about 30 minutes.

....

Curried Cabbage

Serves 4

1 small cabbage, shredded, discarding the central stump
1 vegetable or chicken stock cube
50 g/2 oz/¼ cup butter or margarine
10 ml/2 tsp mango chutney, chopped, if necessary
5 ml/1 tsp curry paste
15 ml/1 tbsp lemon juice
Salt and freshly ground black pepper
45 ml/3 tbsp desiccated (shredded) coconut, toasted

1 Cook the cabbage in 2.5 cm/1 in boiling water to which the stock cube has been added in a large saucepan until just tender. Drain (use the stock for soup) and return to the pan.
2 Add all the remaining ingredients except the coconut and toss over a gentle heat until well blended.
3 Pile into a serving dish and sprinkle the toasted coconut over.

....

French-style Peas

Serves 4

1 onion, finely chopped
50 g/2 oz/¼ cup butter or margarine
225 g/8 oz frozen peas
5 ml/1 tsp dried mint
Salt and freshly ground black pepper
½ small round lettuce, shredded

1 Put the onion and butter or margarine in a saucepan. Cover and cook gently for 3 minutes, stirring once or twice.
2 Add all the remaining ingredients, toss gently, cover and cook for about 8 minutes until tender, tossing from time to time. Serve hot.

....

Ratatouille

Serves 4

1 aubergine (eggplant), sliced
1 red onion, sliced
1 each of green, red and yellow (bell) peppers, sliced
1 large courgette (zucchini), sliced
4 ripe tomatoes, quartered
30 ml/2 tbsp olive oil
15 ml/1 tbsp tomato purée (paste)
30 ml/2 tbsp red wine or water
2.5 ml/½ tsp dried mixed herbs
A pinch of caster (superfine) sugar
Salt and freshly ground black pepper

1 Place the aubergine in a colander and sprinkle with salt. Leave to stand for 30 minutes. Rinse thoroughly and drain.
2 Place in a large saucepan with all the remaining vegetables and the oil.
3 Cook over a moderate heat, stirring, until the vegetables begin to soften.
4 Add the tomato purée, wine or water, herbs, sugar and a little salt and pepper. Bring to the boil, cover, reduce the heat and cook gently for 20 minutes until tender, stirring occasionally.
5 Serve hot or leave until cold, then chill before serving.

....

Dutch Roast Onions

Serves 4

These are particularly good with roast chicken or pork or can be served on their own with crusty bread for a light meal.

4 Spanish onions
Salt and freshly ground black pepper
50 g/2 oz/¼ cup butter or margarine
10 ml/2 tsp chopped fresh sage
75 g/3 oz/¾ cup Gouda cheese, grated

1 Cut the root end off each onion but do not peel. Cut a slice off each top, sprinkle with salt and pepper, then put the tops back in position. Line a small roasting tin (pan) with foil and spread with a little of the butter or margarine. Stand the onions in the tin.

2 Roast in a preheated oven at 180°C/350°F/gas mark 4 for 2 hours or until the onions feel tender when a knife is inserted in them.
3 Discard the 'lids' and use a knife and fork to peel off the skins. Top with the butter, sage and cheese. Return to the oven for 5 minutes or until the cheese melts.
4 Transfer to warm plates and spoon the juices over.

Pommes Dauphinoise
Serves 4

700 g/1½ lb potatoes, thinly sliced
1 garlic clove, crushed
225 g/8 oz/2 cups Gruyère or Emmental (Swiss) cheese, grated
Salt and freshly ground black pepper
2 eggs
150 ml/¼ pt/⅔ cup crème fraîche
150 ml/¼ pt/⅔ cup milk

1 Cook the sliced potatoes in boiling water for 2 minutes. Drain and rinse with cold water.
2 Layer in a 1.2 litre/2 pt/5 cup ovenproof serving dish with the garlic, 175 g/6 oz/1½ cups of the cheese and a little salt and pepper.
3 Beat the eggs, crème fraîche and milk together and pour over. Cover with the remaining cheese.
4 Bake in a preheated oven at 180°C/350°F/gas mark 4 for about 1–1¼ hours until the potatoes are tender and the top is golden brown.

Broad Beans with Oyster Mushrooms
Serves 4

100 g/4 oz mixed oyster mushrooms, sliced
225 g/8 oz shelled fresh or frozen broad (fava) beans
15 g/½ oz/1 tbsp butter or margarine
15 ml/1 tbsp chopped fresh parsley
1 bouquet garni sachet
5 ml/1 tsp lemon juice
Salt and freshly ground black pepper

150 ml/¼ pt/⅔ cup vegetable or chicken stock, made with ½ stock cube
15 ml/1 tbsp cornflour (cornstarch)
15 ml/1 tbsp water
30 ml/2 tbsp double (heavy) cream (optional)

1 Put the mushrooms and broad beans in a flameproof casserole (Dutch oven).
2 Dot with the butter or margarine, add the parsley, bouquet garni and lemon juice and season lightly.
3 Pour on the stock and bring to the boil. Cover and cook in a preheated oven at 180°C/350°F/gas mark 4 for 45–60 minutes or until tender. Discard the bouquet garni sachet.
4 Blend the cornflour with the water and stir in. Bring to the boil on top of the stove and cook for 1 minute, stirring.
5 Stir in the cream, if using. Taste and adjust the seasoning, if necessary, before serving.

Sweet and Sour Red or White Cabbage

Serves 6

450 g/1 lb red or white cabbage, shredded, discarding the stump
1 onion, thinly sliced
1 cooking (tart) apple, chopped
50 g/2 oz/½ cup raisins
30 ml/2 tbsp red or white wine vinegar
30 ml/2 tbsp water
30 ml/2 tbsp light brown sugar
Salt and freshly ground black pepper
25 g/1 oz/2 tbsp butter or margarine
30 ml/2 tbsp snipped fresh chives, to garnish

1 Layer the cabbage, onion, apple and raisins in a casserole (Dutch oven).
2 Mix all the remaining ingredients except the butter or margarine together and pour over. Dot with the butter or margarine.
3 Cover and cook in a preheated oven at 160°C/325°F/gas mark 3 for 1¼ hours until tender. Stir well, then serve sprinkled with snipped chives.

Creamy Baked Garlic Mushrooms   Serves 4

8–12 large, flat mushrooms
25 g/1 oz/2 tbsp butter or margarine
2 large garlic cloves, very finely chopped
Salt and freshly ground black pepper
1 wineglass of dry white wine
150 ml/¼ pt/⅔ cup double (heavy) cream
30 ml/2 tbsp chopped fresh parsley
Hot French bread, to serve

1 Peel the mushrooms, cut off the stalks, and chop them.
2 Grease a large, shallow baking tin (pan) with the butter or margarine. Place the mushrooms in it and sprinkle the chopped stalks over.
3 Sprinkle the garlic over and season lightly.
4 Pour in the wine. Cover with foil and bake in a preheated oven at 190°C/375°F/gas mark 5 for 20 minutes.
5 Carefully transfer the mushrooms to warm plates. Stir the cream into the juices and bring just to the boil. Taste and adjust the seasoning. Pour over the mushrooms and sprinkle with parsley. Serve with hot French bread.

Spring Vegetable Pot   Serves 4

1 large onion, cut into chunks
15 g/½ oz/1 tbsp butter or margarine
2 large potatoes, cut into chunks
3 large carrots, cut into chunks
1 turnip, cut into chunks
2 leeks, cut into chunks
425 g/15 oz/1 large can of haricot (navy) beans, drained
400 g/14 oz/1 large can of chopped tomatoes
600 ml/1 pt/2½ cups vegetable stock, made with 2 stock cubes
1 bay leaf
Salt and freshly ground black pepper

100 g/4 oz baby sweetcorn (corn) cobs
100 g/4 oz okra (ladies' fingers), trimmed
½ small green cabbage, shredded
Grated Cheddar cheese and crusty bread, to serve

1 Fry (sauté) the onion in the butter or margarine in a large flameproof casserole (Dutch oven) for 2 minutes, stirring.
2 Add everything up to, but not including, the sweetcorn cobs. Bring to the boil, cover, reduce the heat and simmer gently for 30 minutes.
3 Add the sweetcorn, okra and cabbage and stir gently. Cover and cook for a further 20 minutes or until everything is really tender.
4 Remove the bay leaf and serve in large, warm bowls, with grated cheese to sprinkle over and crusty bread.

....

Chick Pea Goulash   Serves 4

Add two sliced peperami sticks or a smoked pork ring to this dish for non-veggies, if you like.

225 g/8 oz/1⅓ cups chick peas (garbanzos), soaked overnight in cold water
1.2 litres/2 pts/5 cups vegetable stock, made with 2 stock cubes
1 onion, chopped
1 garlic clove, crushed
30 ml/2 tbsp olive oil
2 large carrots, diced
1 celery stick, chopped
2 leeks, chopped
100 g/4 oz button mushrooms, sliced
190 g/6¾ oz/1 small can of pimiento caps, drained and diced
15 ml/1 tbsp sweet pimenton or paprika
2.5 ml/½ tsp dried oregano
30 ml/2 tbsp tomato purée (paste)
15 ml/1 tbsp Worcestershire sauce
5 ml/1 tsp light brown sugar
Salt and freshly ground black pepper
60 ml/4 tbsp crème fraîche and 15 ml/1 tbsp caraway seeds, to garnish

1 Drain the chick peas and place in a large saucepan with the stock. Bring to the boil and boil rapidly for 10 minutes.
2 Meanwhile, fry (sauté) the onion and garlic in the olive oil in a large flameproof casserole (Dutch oven) for 2 minutes. Add all the remaining ingredients including the pan of chick peas and stock. Bring to the boil, stirring.
3 Cover and place in a preheated oven at 160°C/325°F/gas mark 3 for 3½ hours until the chick peas are really tender and bathed in a rich sauce.
4 Ladle into warm bowls and serve topped with a spoonful of crème fraîche and a sprinkling of caraway seeds.

Vegetarian Cottage Pie

Serves 4

450 g/1 lb potatoes, cut into chunks
A knob of butter or margarine
15 ml/1 tbsp milk
350 g/12 oz/3 cups leftover cooked vegetables, finely chopped
2 slices of wholemeal bread, chopped
400 g/14 oz/1 large can of baked beans
10 ml/2 tsp Marmite or Vegemite
30 ml/2 tbsp boiling water
2.5 ml/½ tsp dried mixed herbs
Salt and freshly ground black pepper
50 g/2 oz/½ cup Cheddar cheese, grated
3 tomatoes, sliced

1 Cook the potatoes in plenty of boiling, lightly salted water until tender. Drain and mash with the butter or margarine and the milk.
2 Mix the vegetables with the bread and beans in a 1.2 litre/2 pt/5 cup ovenproof serving dish.
3 Blend the Marmite or Vegemite with the water and stir in, adding herbs and seasoning to taste. Stir into the dish until thoroughly mixed.
4 Top with the mashed potato, then the cheese. Arrange the tomatoes round the edge.
5 Bake in a preheated oven at 200°C/400°F/gas mark 6 for about 35 minutes until golden brown and piping hot.

salads

There's more to a salad than half a tomato and a limp lettuce leaf. A salad can be a masterpiece of colour, texture and flavours, and can be served warm or cold, as an accompaniment, a starter or a main dish. Almost any ingredient can be used – vegetables cooked, blanched (pages 131–2) or raw; pasta; rice; meat; fish; cheese; eggs; nuts; fruit or pulses – the combinations are endless. Salads can make perfectly balanced meals, especially if you use raw vegetables, so they have the maximum vitamin and mineral content. This chapter tells you about all the salad leaves and how to choose them and at the end you'll find some of my favourite salad recipes. But try experimenting with your own combinations, using the different dressings given on pages 266–71 to give them an extra-special lift.

Types of salad leaves

The basis of many salads is made up of raw, edible leaves, which contain mostly water but also supply minerals, including iron, some vitamins and fibre. Here is a guide to the most common varieties.

- CHICORY (BELGIAN ENDIVE):

Small, white and pale green or yellow spear-shaped heads with white, fleshy stalks.

- CHINESE LEAVES (STEM LETTUCE):

Large heads with crinkled leaves and fleshy stems.

- COS (ROMAINE):

A long lettuce with tall, pointed leaves.

- CURLY ENDIVE (FRISÉE):

Large, flat-topped heads with frizzy leaves and slightly bitter stems.

- HERBS:

Rocket, coriander (cilantro), flat-leaf parsley, sorrel and basil and fresh herbs are particularly good added to other salad leaves.

- ICEBERG AND WEBB'S WONDERFUL:

Hearty lettuces with crisp, juicy leaves.

- LAMBS' LETTUCE (CORN SALAD):

Small, green, oval sprigs of leaves with a nutty taste.

- LITTLE GEM:

Small and hearty with crinkled leaves.

- LOLLO ROSSO AND LOLLO BIONDO:

Soft, curvy leaves with a red or white tinge respectively.

- OAKLEAF AND RED OAKLEAF:

Green or red-tinged leaves, resembling oak leaves.

- RADICCHIO:

Small oval heads with red, fleshy leaves and a slightly bitter taste.

- ROUND:

Loosely packed, with green, soft leaves.

- SALAD CRESS, MUSTARD AND CRESS:

The familiar seedlings of mustard and cress in a box.

- SPROUTED SHOOTS:

Loosely packed bags of sprouted seeds such as mung beans.

- WATERCRESS:

Sprigs of dark-green, peppery, round leaves.

- YOUNG SPINACH:

Baby spinach leaves are delicious in salads – and are particularly good for you, having a high iron content.

Choosing salad leaves

- As with all greens, the heads should be firm, and fresh-looking, not limp.
- Avoid any that are discoloured or have slimy patches – they are rotting.
- They should have little or no smell. A strong, 'cabbagey' smell means they are way past their best.
- If buying ready-prepared salad, check there are no brown edges where the salad has been cut.

Cook's tips for salads

- Most leaves should be pulled apart and torn into pieces, not chopped. The exception is lettuce for use in any form of sandwich filling (from pittas to tortillas) or as a base for starters like prawn (shrimp) cocktail, which may be finely shredded with a knife.

- Prepare just before serving so the ingredients don't discolour, go limp or lose their nutrients.

- If buying ready-prepared salad leaves, always wash before use, even if the packet says it is ready to eat. Lambs' tongue lettuce and spinach in particular are notorious for being gritty, so wash in several changes of cold water before use.

- Chicory (Belgian endive) has a bitter core. Cut a cone shape out of the base, to remove the bitter part, before separating the leaves.

Recipes

Warm Potato Salad with Fragrant Herbs
Serves 4

450 g/1 lb waxy baby potatoes, scrubbed
Salt
75 ml/5 tbsp plain yoghurt
75 ml/5 tbsp mayonnaise
2.5 ml/½ tsp finely grated lemon rind
15 ml/1 tbsp chopped fresh parsley
15 ml/1 tbsp chopped fresh basil
15 ml/1 tbsp snipped fresh chives
Freshly ground black pepper

1 Cook the potatoes in lightly salted boiling water until just tender. Drain and leave to cool.
2 Mix all the remaining ingredients together in a salad bowl. Add the potatoes and toss to coat. Chill for at least 2 hours to allow the flavours to develop.

Salade Niçoise

Serves 4

8 baby new potatoes, boiled and halved
225 g/8 oz French (green) beans, boiled
3 hard-boiled (hard-cooked) eggs, quartered
8 cherry tomatoes, halved
5 cm/2 in piece of cucumber, diced
1 Little Gem lettuce, torn into bite-sized pieces
185 g/6½ oz/1 small can of tuna, drained
8 black olives
45 ml/3 tbsp olive oil
15 ml/1 tbsp white wine vinegar
2.5 ml/½ tsp dried mixed herbs
A good pinch of caster (superfine) sugar
2.5 ml/½ tsp Dijon mustard
Salt and freshly ground black pepper
1 small onion, thinly sliced
15 ml/1 tbsp chopped fresh parsley

1 Put the first eight ingredients into a salad bowl.
2 Whisk together the oil, vinegar, mixed herbs, sugar, mustard and some salt and pepper.
3 Pour over the salad and toss gently.
4 Scatter the onion rings on top and sprinkle with parsley.

··

Caesar Salad Sensation

Serves 4

1 garlic clove, halved
2 slices of white bread, cut into small dice
75 ml/5 tbsp olive oil
15 ml/1 tbsp white wine vinegar
15 ml/1 tbsp balsamic vinegar
2.5 ml/½ tsp dried tarragon
2.5 ml/½ tsp caster (superfine) sugar
Salt and freshly ground black pepper
15 g/½ oz/1 tbsp butter or margarine
1 egg

15 ml/1 tbsp milk or single (light) cream
1 cos (romaine) lettuce, torn into bite-sized pieces
50 g/2 oz/1 small can of anchovy fillets, drained and roughly chopped
50 g/2 oz Parmesan cheese, shaved with a potato peeler

1 Rub the garlic clove all round a salad bowl and discard.
2 Fry (sauté) the bread in 30 ml/2 tbsp of the oil until golden brown. Drain on kitchen paper (paper towels).
3 Whisk the remaining oil with the vinegars, tarragon, sugar and seasoning.
4 Melt the butter or margarine in a small saucepan. Beat the egg and milk or cream together and add to the butter. Cook very gently, stirring until lightly scrambled. Put the base of the pan into cold water immediately, to prevent further cooking.
5 Put the lettuce in the salad bowl. Add the dressing, egg mixture and anchovy fillets and toss gently.
6 Add the Parmesan cheese and croûtons. Toss and serve straight away.

Village Salad

Serves 4

¼ small white cabbage, shredded
¼ iceberg lettuce, shredded
2 beefsteak tomatoes, quartered and sliced
5 cm/2 in piece of cucumber, diced
12 black olives
1 small onion, sliced and separated into rings
100 g/4 oz/1 cup Feta cheese, crumbled into pieces
2.5 ml/½ tsp dried oregano
15 ml/1 tbsp chopped fresh parsley
Salt and freshly ground black pepper
45 ml/3 tbsp olive oil
15 ml/1 tbsp red wine vinegar

1 Put the cabbage and lettuce on a shallow platter.
2 Scatter the tomatoes, cucumber, olives, onion and cheese over.
3 Sprinkle with the oregano, parsley and some salt and pepper.
4 Drizzle with the oil and vinegar and leave to stand for 30 minutes before serving.

Seafood Pasta Salad   Serves 4

175 g/6 oz conchiglie (pasta shells)
Salt
225 g/8 oz frozen seafood cocktail, thawed
1 small onion, finely chopped
1 green (bell) pepper, finely chopped
60 ml/4 tbsp olive oil
30 ml/2 tbsp lemon juice
5 ml/1 tsp caster (superfine) sugar
1 garlic clove, crushed
Freshly ground black pepper
Lettuce leaves

1 Cook the pasta in boiling, lightly salted water, according to the packet directions. Drain, rinse with cold water and drain again. Place in a bowl.
2 Drain the thawed seafood and add to the pasta with the onion and green pepper.
3 Whisk the oil and lemon juice together with the sugar, garlic and a little salt and pepper.
4 Pour over the salad, toss and chill until ready to serve on a bed of lettuce.

....

Oriental Salad   Serves 4

225 g/8 oz/1 small can of pineapple rings, drained, reserving the juice
1 green (bell) pepper, diced
2 spring onions (scallions), chopped
175 g/6 oz beansprouts
15 ml/1 tbsp soy sauce
15 ml/1 tbsp sunflower oil
A pinch of ground ginger

1 Cut the pineapple into small pieces and mix with the pepper, spring onions and beansprouts.
2 Whisk together all the remaining ingredients with 15 ml/1 tbsp of the pineapple juice.
3 Pour over the salad, toss and serve.

....

Middle Eastern Coleslaw

Serves 4

½ small white cabbage, coarsely grated
2 carrots, coarsely grated
30 ml/2 tbsp raisins
Salt and freshly ground black pepper
45 ml/3 tbsp olive oil
30 ml/2 tbsp sliced green olives
30 ml/2 tbsp black mustard seeds
15 ml/1 tbsp lemon juice

1 Mix the cabbage, carrots, raisins and olives in a salad bowl. Season lightly.
2 Heat the oil in a frying pan (skillet). Add the mustard seeds and fry (sauté) until they start to 'pop'.
3 Add the lemon juice, stir, pour over the salad, toss and serve.

Tabbouleh

Serves 4

225 g/8 oz/2 cups bulgar (cracked wheat)
4 spring onions (scallions), chopped
1 garlic clove, crushed
30 ml/2 tbsp chopped fresh parsley
15 ml/1 tbsp chopped fresh mint
30 ml/2 tbsp lemon juice
60 ml/4 tbsp olive oil
Salt and freshly ground black pepper
¼ cucumber, finely chopped
4 ripe tomatoes, cut into small pieces

1 Put the bulgar in a large bowl. Cover with boiling water and leave to stand for 30 minutes. Toss well with a fork.
2 Add the spring onions, garlic, herbs, lemon juice and olive oil. Toss well and leave until cold.
3 Stir in the cucumber and tomatoes and serve.

Tomato, Corn and Onion Salad   Serves 4

6 tomatoes, cut into small wedges
200 g/7 oz/1 small can of sweetcorn (corn), drained
4 spring onions (scallions), cut into short lengths
15 ml/1 tbsp apple juice
10 ml/2 tsp lemon juice
45 ml/3 tbsp olive oil
Salt and freshly ground black pepper
Lettuce leaves

1 Mix the tomatoes, corn and spring onions together.
2 Whisk the apple juice, lemon juice and oil together with a little salt and pepper. Pour over the salad and toss.
3 Spoon on to a bed of lettuce and serve.

Summer Chicken Salad   Serves 4

175 g/6 oz/¾ cup long-grain rice
50 g/2 oz frozen peas
Salt
225 g/8 oz/1 small can of pineapple rings, drained, reserving the juice, and cut into small pieces
2 tomatoes, cut into chunks
5 cm/2 in piece of cucumber, cut into chunks
1 small green (bell) pepper, diced
175 g/6 oz/1½ cups diced cooked chicken
45 ml/3 tbsp mayonnaise
Freshly ground black pepper
Lettuce leaves

1 Cook the rice in boiling salted water for 10 minutes, adding the peas halfway through cooking. Drain, rinse with cold water and drain again.
2 Place in a bowl and add all the remaining ingredients except the lettuce. Toss gently, adding a little pineapple juice to thin, if necessary.
3 Pile on to lettuce leaves and serve.

Salamagundi

Serves as many as you want

Quantities are not important: just create a beautiful salad from whatever you have available, making it delicious and colourful.

Shredded lettuce
Cooked, roast meat (beef, lamb, pork, chicken, turkey or ham), cut into
    thin strips
Hard-boiled (hard-cooked) eggs, cut into quarters
Cooked potatoes, cut into neat pieces, tossed in a little mayonnaise
Cooked peas and carrots, tossed in a little mayonnaise
Cooked French (green) beans
Pickled beetroot (red beets), diced
Pickled baby (pearl) onions
Tomatoes, cut into wedges
Cucumber, sliced and tossed in vinegar and freshly ground black pepper
Canned, drained sweetcorn (corn)
Canned pimientos, drained and cut into thin strips
Olives
Olive oil
White wine vinegar
Salt
Chopped fresh parsley
Mayonnaise, to serve

1   Put a bed of shredded lettuce on a large meat platter.
2   Arrange the meat and your selection of other ingredients in neat piles over
    the lettuce.
3   Drizzle lightly with oil and vinegar and season with a little salt and freshly
    ground black pepper.
4   Sprinkle with chopped, fresh parsley. Serve with mayonnaise.

Mixed Bean Salad

Serves 4

An easy salad to put together from storecupboard ingredients.

425 g/15 oz/1 large can of mixed pulses, drained, rinsed and drained
  again
1 onion, chopped
190 g/6¾ oz/1 small can of pimiento caps, drained and sliced
4 gherkins (cornichons), chopped
30 ml/2 tbsp olive oil
15 ml/1 tbsp red wine vinegar
A pinch of caster (superfine) sugar
Salt and freshly ground black pepper
5 ml/1 tsp dried chives

1 Mix the pulses with the onion, pimientos and gherkins.
2 Whisk all the remaining ingredients together and pour over the salad. Toss
   and chill for at least 1 hour to allow the flavours to develop.

pasta and rice

Pasta and rice are two of the staple foods of the world and both provide vital carbohydrates for energy. Not only that, they are delicious vehicles for a whole variety of meat, fish, egg, cheese and vegetable dishes – and some desserts too.

Pasta varieties

There are over 600 different pasta shapes made in Italy alone, both fresh and dried. They are made in a variety of colours and flavours, including standard durum wheat (pale and creamy); egg pasta (more golden); green spinach; rustic wholewheat; sun-dried tomato (orange); black mushroom or squid ink; and speckled olive-flavoured. There are also noodles from the Far East and from German-speaking countries. All pasta can be divided into five main types.

- RIBBON NOODLES:

These are cut from flat pasta of varying widths and lengths, including tagliatelle and fettuccine (about 5 mm/¼ in wide); pappardelle (about 2 cm/¾ in wide) and lasagne (wide sheets used for layering with sauce).

- SHAPES:

There are literally dozens to choose from including conchiglie (shells); farfalle (bows); rotelli (spirals) and ruote (wheels).

- STRANDS:

These types include spaghetti; vermicelli (very thin strands); fusilli (twisted strands); Chinese egg noodles; Chinese and Japanese wheat noodles; cellophane noodles and soba (buckwheat noodles).

- STUFFED SHAPES AND DUMPLINGS:

These may be made of pasta or other ingredients. They include ravioli (little cushions); tortellini (stuffed crescents joined into rings); cappelletti (stuffed hat shapes); gnocchi (Italian dumplings made from flour, semolina – cream of wheat – or potato); wonton (Oriental ravioli) and dim sum (Chinese dumplings).

- TUBES:

There are many varieties, both short and long, including bucatini (thick spaghetti with a hole in the middle); cannelloni (large fat tubes, served stuffed); short-cut macaroni; penne and rigatoni.

Pasta quantities

The amount required per person depends on appetites, but a good guide is about 75 g/3 oz pasta per portion.

Cooking pasta

All pasta should be cooked in a large pan so that there is plenty of room for it to circulate. The aim is an 'al dente' texture: just tender but still with a slight bite to it. Keep testing so that you don't overcook it and allow it to go soggy.

To cook fresh pasta

Bought or home-made fresh pasta cooks much more quickly than dried so it is particularly important not to overcook it.

1 Bring a large pan of water to the boil and add a pinch of salt.
2 Drop in the pasta and return the pan to the boil for 2–4 minutes.

To cook spaghetti and other long strands

1 Bring a large pan of water to the boil and add a pinch of salt.
2 Hold the pasta firmly and gently feed it into the pan. It will soften in the water and curl around the pan. Don't push too hard or it will break.
3 When completely submerged, stir gently to separate the strands and cook according to the packet directions, usually about 10 minutes.

To cook pasta shapes

1 Bring a large pan of water to the boil and add a pinch of salt.
2 Add the pasta all at once, stir well to separate, bring back to the boil and cook for 5–15 minutes, depending on the type of pasta.

To cook Chinese egg noodles

These are very quick to cook.

1 Place the blocks or nests in a pan and cover with boiling water.
2 Bring back to the boil and simmer for 3–5 minutes, according to the packet directions. Drain and use as required.

Cook's tips for pasta

- Don't cover the pan with a lid or the pasta will boil over.

- Add 15 ml/1 tbsp olive oil to the pan when cooking pasta to prevent it boiling over and to help keep the pieces separate.

- If you intend to spoon a sauce over the pasta after cooking, don't rinse it. The sauce will adhere to the strands better, for easier eating.

- If you keep cooked pasta warm, it will stick together in a knotted mass. To separate, pour boiling water over it and loosen gently with a fork.

- To test pasta is cooked, lift out a strand or piece. Either taste or pinch between your finger and thumb: there should be just a faint resistance.

- If you've made a pasta sauce and extra people turn up for supper, simply increase the amount of pasta and toss in the sauce rather than spooning the sauce over the pasta. Add a little extra oil or butter, if necessary, to moisten.

Milk pudding grains

Milk puddings, once a favourite in every British nursery, are made from semolina (cream of wheat), tapioca and sago, as well as rice (see below). Semolina, like pasta, is made from durum wheat. It is used to make gnocchi (see Tuna and celery gnocchi, page 176) as well as milk puddings. All the grains are simmered in milk until cooked and creamy, and sweetened to taste. After the initial cooking, they can be turned into a buttered ovenproof dish and baked until the top is golden brown. Flavourings such as grated lemon or orange rind, raisins or nutmeg may also be added.

Rice varieties

Over a third of the world's population eats rice as its staple food. There are many varieties with different flavours, colours and cooking properties. Here are the most common ones you'll come across.

- BROWN LONG-GRAIN RICE:

Brown rice is higher in B-vitamins and fibre than white varieties. It is brown because it has not been polished to remove the outer bran. It also takes longer to cook and benefits from being soaked first. It has a nutty texture and makes a good basis for a pilaf or salad.

- FLAKED AND GROUND RICE, RICE FLOUR:

Flaked and ground rice can be simmered in milk and sweetened as milk puddings; rice flour is used for thickening.

- RISOTTO RICE:

Arborio is the most common, although you will see other varieties. The short, round grains can absorb a great deal of liquid over a fairly long period without becoming too soft. This produces the grainy but 'creamy' result expected of good risottos, paellas and jambalayas.

- SHORT-GRAIN (PUDDING) RICE:

The grains are pearly and round and become very soft when cooked, absorbing a lot of liquid to a creamy mass. It is ideal for milk puddings.

- WHITE LONG-GRAIN RICE:

Varieties include patna, American, basmati, Thai fragrant and many more. They are ideal for pilafs, salads, stuffings and all 'dry' rice dishes. I use basmati, which has a delicious, delicate flavour, for most rice dishes but you may prefer the more bland American or patna varieties. There are also easy-cook varieties, which must be cooked according to the packet directions.

- WILD RICE:

This is not strictly rice at all but an aquatic grass, related to the rice family. It has a distinctive nutty flavour and is more expensive than rice. You can now buy it in a mixture that contains long-grain and wild rice.

Cooking rice

Long-grain rice should be just cooked with the grains remaining separate. It should be soft but not mushy. As a rough guide, for savoury dishes, allow 25 g/1 oz/2 tbsp uncooked brown rice per portion and up to 50 g /2 oz/¼ cup uncooked white.

To boil plain long-grain rice

1 Bring a large pan of water to the boil and add a pinch of salt.
2 Add the rinsed rice. Stir well. Bring back to the boil and boil rapidly until the grains are just tender but still with some texture. To test, lift out a few grains and either taste or pinch between the finger and thumb: there

should be a slight resistance. Cooking time depends on the brand, but is usually about 10 minutes (check the packet directions) for white long-grain varieties. Brown rice takes between 30–40 minutes.

To cook rice pudding

1 Put 50 g/2 oz/¼ cup round-grain (pudding) rice in an ovenproof dish and add 25 g/1 oz/2 tbsp caster (superfine) sugar.
2 Add a 400 g/14 oz/large can of evaporated milk, made up 600 ml/1 pt/ 2½ cups with water. Alternatively, add plain milk. Stir well.
3 Sprinkle with grated nutmeg and add a knob of butter or margarine. Bake in a preheated oven at 160°C/325°F/gas mark 3 for 2 hours.

Cook's tips for rice

- All long-grain varieties should be washed well to remove excess starch before use.

- Don't overcook or the grains will become a sticky mass.

- Rinse plain-cooked rice well with boiling water after cooking, if serving hot, or with cold water if serving cold. Drain thoroughly before use.

- Don't cover the pan when boiling or it will boil over, due to the large amount of water. However, the pan must be covered when cooking in a measured amount of water because the grains need to continue to cook in the steam when the water is absorbed.

- Rice pudding benefits from long, slow cooking in the oven but it can be cooked on top of the stove, if required. Use the quantities in the recipe above. Simmer the rice in a little water until absorbed, then drain and cook with the remaining ingredients in a non-stick saucepan, stirring frequently, for about 40 minutes, until the rice is tender.

Canned favourites

- Canned vegetable ravioli in tomato sauce can quickly be made into a tasty meal. Heat it in a pan, then tip into a flameproof dish and smother with loads of grated cheese mixed with a handful of crushed cornflakes. Grill (broil) until the cheese melts.
- Creamed rice pudding is delicious. Use on its own or as a condé (served cold in layers with fresh or canned fruits).

Recipes
Spaghetti Bolognese
Serves 4

350 g/12 oz extra-lean minced (ground) beef
1 large onion, finely chopped
1 carrot, finely chopped
1 garlic clove, crushed
400 g/14 oz/1 large can of chopped tomatoes
30 ml/2 tbsp tomato purée (paste)
45 ml/3 tbsp red wine or water
5 ml/1 tsp caster (superfine) sugar
5 ml/1 tsp dried oregano
Salt and freshly ground black pepper
350 g/12 oz spaghetti
Grated Parmesan cheese
Garlic and herb bread (page 245) and a mixed green salad, to serve

1 Put the beef, onion, carrot and garlic in a saucepan and cook, stirring, over a moderate heat, for about 5 minutes until the meat is brown and all the grains are separate.
2 Add the tomatoes, tomato purée, wine or water, sugar and oregano. Season well. Bring to the boil, stirring. Part-cover, reduce the heat and simmer gently for 30 minutes until tender and the meat is bathed in a rich sauce.
3 Meanwhile, cook the spaghetti as on page 165 or according to packet directions. Drain.
4 Pile the spaghetti on to warm plates. Top with the Bolognese sauce and sprinkle with Parmesan before serving with garlic bread and a mixed green salad.

Cannelloni al Forno
Serves 4

1 Prepare as for Lasagne al forno (page 170), but spoon the meat mixture into no-need-to-precook cannelloni tubes.
2 Place in a shallow, ovenproof dish, top with the cheese sauce and bake and serve as above.

Lasagne al Forno

Serves 4

Prepare the cheese sauce while the Bolognese sauce is cooking. If you like lots of sauce, make double the quantity of cheese sauce for the top.

Bolognese sauce (as for Spaghetti Bolognese, page 169)
6–8 sheets of no-need-to-precook lasagne
1 quantity of cheese sauce (page 260)
Garlic and herb bread (page 245) and a mixed green salad, to serve

1 Spoon just a little of the meat sauce in a shallow ovenproof dish, then cover with a layer of sheets of the lasagne.
2 Layer the meat thinly with the remaining lasagne sheets until all the meat is used, finishing with a layer of lasagne.
3 Spoon the cheese sauce over.
4 Bake in a preheated oven at 190°C/375°F/gas mark 5 for 35 minutes or until golden brown and bubbling and the lasagne feels tender when a knife is inserted down through the centre. Serve hot with garlic bread and a mixed green salad.

Vermicelli with Smoked Salmon and Broccoli

Serves 4

This sounds grand but smoked salmon trimmings are very inexpensive.

225 g/8 oz vermicelli
175 g/6 oz broccoli, cut into tiny florets
Salt
175 g/6 oz smoked salmon trimmings
150 ml/¼ pt/⅔ cup single (light) cream
2 eggs
Freshly ground black pepper
30 ml/2 tbsp chopped fresh parsley
A little lemon juice
Grated Parmesan cheese, to garnish

1 Cook the vermicelli and broccoli together in a large pan of boiling, lightly salted water until just tender. Drain well and return to the saucepan.
2 Separate the salmon trimmings and add to the pan.
3 Beat the cream and eggs with some salt and lots of pepper. Add to the pan.
4 Cook, stirring gently, over a low heat until the mixture is piping hot. Do not allow to boil or the mixture will curdle.
5 Stir in the parsley and add lemon juice and a little more salt and pepper to taste.
6 Pile on to warm plates and serve sprinkled with grated Parmesan cheese.

Chicken and Corn Pasta Bake

Serves 4

This tasty supper dish is a great way to use up leftover chicken.

225 g/8 oz pasta shapes
1 quantity of tomato sauce (page 265)
175 g/6 oz/1½ cups cooked chicken, roughly cut up
200 g/7 oz/1 small can of sweetcorn (corn), drained
225 g/8 oz frozen spinach, thawed (optional)
50 g/2 oz/½ cup Cheddar cheese, grated

1 Cook the pasta according to the packet directions. Drain.
2 Meanwhile, make the tomato sauce. Stir into the pasta with the chicken.
3 Spoon half into an ovenproof serving dish. Add the corn and spinach, if using, top with the remaining pasta and sprinkle with the cheese.
4 Bake in a preheated oven at 190°C/375°F/gas mark 5 for about 30 minutes or until bubbling and turning golden.

Neapolitan Tortellini

Serves 2–4

250 g/9 oz/1 packet of dried tortellini, stuffed with cheese or mushrooms
Salt
500 ml/17 fl oz/2¼ cups passata (sieved tomatoes)
5 ml/1 tsp dried basil
Freshly ground black pepper
Grated Parmesan cheese, to garnish
A mixed salad, to serve

1 Cook the tortellini according to the packet directions. Drain and return to the pan.
2 Add the passata and basil and a good grinding of pepper. Heat through, stirring until bubbling and the tortellini is bathed in the sauce.
3 Spoon into warm bowls, sprinkle with Parmesan cheese and serve with a mixed salad.

••

Egg Fried Rice   Serves 4

175 g/6 oz/¾ cup long-grain rice
Salt
50 g/2 oz frozen peas
30 ml/2 tbsp sunflower oil
1–2 eggs, beaten
A pinch of Chinese five spice powder
5 ml/1 tsp soy sauce

1 Cook the rice in plenty of boiling, lightly salted water for 10 minutes or until just tender. Add the peas halfway through cooking. Drain, rinse with cold water and drain again thoroughly.
2 Heat the oil in a frying pan (skillet).
3 Add the rice and peas and toss for 2 minutes.
4 Push the rice to one side and tilt the pan. Pour in a beaten egg.
5 Cook the egg, stirring, then gradually draw in the rice until it is filled with tiny strands of egg. Add a pinch of Chinese five spice powder and a sprinkling of soy sauce. Toss and serve.

••

Special Egg Fried Rice   Serves 4

Prepare as for egg fried rice (above), but add 50 g/2 oz/½ cup finely chopped, cooked chicken with the peas and 50 g/2 oz cooked, peeled prawns (shrimp), thawed if frozen. Then continue as before.

••

Quick Pilau Rice

Serves 4

175 g/6 oz/¾ cup basmati rice
Salt
5 ml/1 tsp ground turmeric
4–6 split cardamom pods
2.5 cm/1 in piece of cinnamon stick
1 onion, finely chopped
15 ml/1 tbsp sunflower oil

1 Bring a pan of lightly salted water to the boil. Add the rice and spices. Bring back to the boil, stir and cook for 10 minutes or until the rice is just tender. Drain.
2 Meanwhile, cook the onion in the oil until golden brown and soft. Fork through the rice before serving. Remove the spices, if preferred.

....

Oven Pilaf

Serves 4–6

100 g/4 oz/⅔ cup dried fruit salad, soaked overnight in cold water
1 onion, finely chopped
25 g/1 oz/2 tbsp butter or margarine
225 g/8 oz/1 cup long-grain rice, well-washed and drained
600 ml/1 pt/2½ cups chicken stock
Salt and freshly ground black pepper

1 Put the fruit and its soaking water in saucepan, bring to the boil and simmer for 10 minutes or until tender. Leave to cool. Drain, then roughly chop the fruit, discarding any stones (pits).
2 Fry (sauté) the onion in the butter or margarine for 2 minutes in a flameproof casserole (Dutch oven).
3 Stir in the rice until coated in the fat. Pour in the stock and add a little seasoning. Bring to the boil, cover and transfer to a low shelf in a preheated oven at 200°C/400°F/gas mark 6. Cook for 12 minutes.
4 Add the chopped fruit and fork through. Cover with foil and a lid, and return to the oven for a further 10 minutes until the rice is cooked and has absorbed all the liquid. Fluff up and serve.

....

Ham and Mushroom Risotto   Serves 4–6

Try oyster, chestnut or chanterelle mushrooms for a more exotic flavour.

25 g/1 oz/2 tbsp butter or margarine
30 ml/2 tbsp olive oil
1 onion, finely chopped
100 g/4 oz button mushrooms, sliced
450 g/1 lb/2 cups risotto rice
1.2 litres/2 pts/5 cups hot chicken stock, made with 1 stock cube
Salt and freshly ground black pepper
100 g/4 oz/1 cup cooked ham, diced
150 ml/¼ pt/⅔ cup single (light) cream
30 ml/2 tbsp chopped fresh parsley
Grated Parmesan cheese, to serve

1 Melt the butter or margarine with the oil in a large, flameproof casserole (Dutch oven).
2 Add the onion and mushrooms and fry (sauté) gently, stirring, for 2 minutes.
3 Add the rice and cook, stirring, for 1 minute, until glistening.
4 Pour on about 300 ml/½ pt/1¼ cups of the stock and simmer, stirring occasionally, until the liquid is absorbed. Repeat in this way until all the liquid is used and the rice is tender.
5 Stir in the ham and cream and heat through, stirring. Do not boil.
6 Pile the creamy mixture on to warm plates, sprinkle with parsley and serve with grated Parmesan cheese.

Shanghai Rice   Serves 4

350 g/12 oz/1½ cups long-grain rice
30 ml/2 tbsp sunflower oil
4 eggs, beaten
100 g/4 oz/1 cup cooked chicken, diced
175 g/6 oz/1½ cups cooked vegetables, chopped
5 cm/2 in piece of cucumber, diced
4 spring onions (scallions) or 1 small onion, chopped
15 ml/1 tbsp soy sauce
Salt and freshly ground black pepper

1 Cook the rice in plenty of boiling, lightly salted water for 10 minutes or until just tender. Drain, rinse with cold water and drain again.
2 Heat half the oil in a large frying pan (skillet) or wok. Add half the beaten eggs and fry (sauté), stirring, until just beginning to set. Add the rice, chicken, vegetables, cucumber and onion and cook, tossing and stirring, until piping hot. Sprinkle in the soy sauce and toss gently.
3 Meanwhile, heat the remaining oil in a separate, small frying pan. Pour in the remaining egg, season with salt and pepper and cook until the underside is set, lifting gently, to allow the uncooked egg to run underneath.
4 Slide out of the pan, then turn over and tip back in to cook the underside. Roll up the omelette and cut into shreds.
5 Spoon the rice on to warm plates and scatter the omelette on top.

Vegetable Dolmas

Serves 4

8 large outer cabbage leaves
425 g/15 oz/1 large can of ratatouille
60 ml/4 tbsp cooked long-grain rice
300 ml/½ pt/1¼ cups vegetable or chicken stock, made with 1 stock cube
30 ml/2 tbsp tomato purée (paste)
Salt and freshly ground black pepper
Grated Cheddar cheese and crusty bread, to serve

1 Cut out the thick central base to the stalk of the leaves in a 'V' shape.
2 Bring a pan of water to the boil. Drop in the leaves and blanch for 3 minutes. Drain, rinse with cold water and drain again. Dry on kitchen paper (paper towels).
3 Mix the ratatouille with the rice.
4 Lay one leaf on a board, overlapping the two points where the stalk was to close the gap. Put an eighth of the filling on top. Fold in the sides, roll up and place in a flameproof casserole (Dutch oven).
5 Repeat with the remaining cabbage leaves and filling.
6 Mix the stock and tomato purée together and pour around the cabbage rolls. Season lightly.
7 Bring to the boil, cover, reduce the heat and simmer gently for 20 minutes until the cabbage is really tender. Lift on to warm plates and spoon any juices over. Sprinkle with grated cheese, and serve hot, with crusty bread.

One-pot Kedgeree

Serves 4

3 eggs, scrubbed under cold water
225 g/8 oz/1 cup long-grain rice
Salt and freshly ground black pepper
5 ml/1 tsp ground turmeric or curry powder (optional)
225 g/8 oz smoked haddock fillet, skinned
100 g/4 oz frozen peas
45 ml/3 tbsp chopped fresh parsley
45 ml/3 tbsp single (light) cream
Grated nutmeg, to taste

1　Put the eggs in a large saucepan of water. Bring to the boil.
2　Add the rice, a pinch of salt and the turmeric or curry powder, if using. Stir, then cook for 5 minutes. Add the fish and peas and cook for a further 5 minutes or until the rice and fish are tender.
3　Lift out the eggs and fish. Put the eggs in a bowl of cold water. Drain the rice thoroughly and return to the pan.
4　Remove the skin from the fish and break into chunks. Add to the rice.
5　Shell the eggs and cut into chunks. Add to the rice.
6　Add the parsley, cream, lots of pepper and nutmeg to taste. Toss over a gentle heat until piping hot. Pile on to warm plates and serve.

Tuna and Celery Gnocchi

Serves 4

600 ml/1 pt/2½ cups milk
7.5 ml/1½ tsp salt
Freshly ground black pepper
1 bouquet garni sachet
1.5 ml/¼ tsp grated nutmeg
150 g/5 oz/scant 1 cup semolina (cream of wheat)
2 eggs
100 g/4 oz/1 cup Cheddar cheese, grated
Oil, for greasing
185 g/6½ oz/1 small can of tuna, drained
2 celery sticks, finely chopped
295 g/10½ oz/1 medium can of condensed celery soup
15 ml/1 tbsp chopped fresh parsley
15 g/½ oz/1 tbsp butter or margarine, melted

1 Put the milk, salt, a little pepper, the bouquet garni and nutmeg in a non-stick pan. Stir in the semolina. Bring to the boil and cook for 10 minutes, stirring all the time, until really thick. Remove the bouquet garni.
2 Beat in the eggs and 75 g/3 oz/¾ cup of the cheese. Turn into an oiled baking tin (pan) and smooth out with a wet palette knife to a square about 2 cm/¾ in thick. Leave to cool, then chill for at least 1 hour.
3 Meanwhile, mix the tuna with the celery, soup and parsley in a 1.2 litre/2 pt/5 cup ovenproof dish.
4 Cut the gnocchi into 4 cm/1½ in squares and arrange round the top, slightly overlapping. Brush with the melted butter or margarine and sprinkle with the remaining cheese.
5 Bake in a preheated oven at 200°C/400°F/gas mark 6 for about 30 minutes until golden brown.

Caramel Chocolate Creamed Rice Pudding

Serves 4

300 ml/½ pt/1¼ cups milk
50 g/2 oz/½ cup plain (semi-sweet) chocolate, grated
15 g/½ oz/1 tbsp butter or margarine
50 g/2 oz/¼ cup round-grain (pudding) rice
300 ml/½ pt/1¼ cups single (light) cream
Light brown sugar
2.5 ml/½ tsp vanilla essence (extract)

1 Put the milk in a saucepan and add the chocolate. Heat, stirring, until the chocolate melts.
2 Grease a 900 ml/1½ pt/3¾ cup ovenproof dish with butter or margarine.
3 Add the chocolate milk and the rice and leave to stand for 30 minutes.
4 Stir in the cream, 30 ml/2 tbsp light brown sugar and the vanilla.
5 Bake in a preheated oven at 160°C/325°F/gas mark 3 for 2½ hours, stirring twice during the first hour.
6 Sprinkle the top liberally with brown sugar and place under a preheated grill (broiler) until melted and bubbling. Serve hot.

pastries, pies and pizzas

There are several types of pastry (paste) but in general they are all used in the same way: as a crisp, golden shell to encase sweet and savoury fillings. Some, like shortcrust (basic pie crust) and choux pastry, are very easy to make yourself at home. Others, like puff and filo pastry, are best bought ready-made because the time and effort needed to make them is enormous and the results, unless you are highly skilled, might be disappointing. The exception to the rule is suet crust pastry, which is very simple to make. It is used for dumplings, and substantial savoury and sweet steamed delights such as traditional steak and kidney pudding and the buttery, lemony Sussex Pond pudding (page 193).

Most pastries are high in fat, so should be eaten in moderation. If you are watching your weight or your fat intake, filo is the lowest in fat; and, if you are making your own pastry, you can use a reduced-fat spread, suitable for baking, instead of the more usual lard and hard margarine or butter.

Types of pastry

Biscuit (cookie) crust

This is mostly used for sweet flan cases (pie shells). Use 50 g/2 oz/¼ cup fat to 200 g/7 oz biscuits (cookies). Crush the biscuits into crumbs, then mix with the melted butter or margarine. A little sugar may be added for a crisper, sweeter crust, if liked. Press the mixture into the base and sides of a flan dish (pie pan) or flan ring set on a baking (cookie) sheet, and chill for at least 2 hours to harden. Ring the changes with different biscuits. Plain or chocolate digestives, gingernuts, rich tea or Nice biscuits are all suitable.

Choux

This is the crisp, puffy pastry that profiteroles, éclairs and gougères are made of and it is not nearly as difficult to make as you may think. The quantities are 50 g/2 oz/¼ cup butter or margarine, 150 ml/¼ pt/⅔ cup water, 65 g/ 2½ oz/generous ½ cup plain (all-purpose) flour and a pinch of well-sifted salt. Heat the fat and water in a saucepan until the fat melts. Then add the flour and salt all in one go and beat the mixture with a wooden spoon until it is smooth and leavees the sides of the pan clean. Add 2 beaten eggs a little at a time until the mixture is smooth and glossy but still holds its shape. It can be spooned or piped into shapes for baking. You cannot make more than double the given quantities at one time.

Enriched shortcrust (basic pie crust)

This is a savoury or sweet pastry with a crisp texture. The method is the same as for shortcrust (page 181), but you use 175–225 g/6–8 oz/1½–2 cups flour, and add an egg yolk with a little cold water. For sweet shortcrust pastry, simply stir in 15 g/½ oz/1 tbsp caster (superfine) or icing (confectioners') sugar before adding the egg yolk and water.

Filo

This is also known as strudel dough. It is a lengthy business to make it at home and so I think it is much easier to buy fresh or frozen. Always keep the sheets covered until ready to use as they dry out very quickly.

Flaky

Rub one quarter of the fat into the flour and mix to a dough. Divide the remaining fat into thirds. Roll the dough to an oblong and dot one third of the fat in flakes over the surface. Fold the dough, seal, turn and roll again as for rough puff (page 180), then repeat the procedure twice more before wrapping and leaving to rest. The quantities are the same as for rough puff.

Flavoured

- You can add herbs, onion powder, spices or grated orange or lemon rind to any home-made pastry without changing the basic quantities.
- To make cheese pastry, use enriched shortcrust, but substitute half the fat with grated Cheddar cheese and add a pinch of cayenne.
- To make chocolate pastry, use the sweet, enriched shortcrust but substitute 15 g/½ oz/2 tbsp of the flour with cocoa (unsweetened chocolate) powder.

French flan

The classic, crisp, thin, buttery, sweet pastry of all French pâtisserie and other elaborate flans and tarts. The usual quantities are 100 g/4 oz/1 cup plain (all-purpose) flour, 50 g/2 oz/¼ cup softened butter, 50 g/2 oz/¼ up caster (superfine) sugar and 2 egg yolks. Sift the flour and salt on to a work surface and make a well in the centre. Add the caster sugar, softened butter and egg yolks and draw the flour gradually in with your fingers from round the edge until a soft dough is formed. Wrap and chill the dough before using.

Hot water crust

This is traditionally used for raised pies, like pork pie. It is fun to work with but you are unlikely to use it often. Always prepare your filling first. Heat 100 g/4 oz/½ cup lard with 150 ml/¼ pt/⅔ cup water or milk and water until the fat melts and bring to the boil. Add 350 g/12 oz/3 cups sifted plain (all-purpose) flour and a good pinch of salt and beat the mixture until a smooth paste is formed. When cool enough to handle, knead it on a lightly floured surface. It must then be used quickly while still warm or it will set hard.

Puff

Only large quantities can be made successfully and the process is very lengthy and complicated. I suggest you buy it fresh or frozen and use at your leisure!

Quick mix

This is the best method if you are using soft, reduced-fat spread rather than hard fat. The quantities are 65 g/2½ oz/generous ¼ cup reduced-fat spread or soft margarine and 15 ml/1 tbsp water to 100 g/4 oz/1 cup flour and a pinch of salt. Mix the soft spread or margarine with a quarter of the flour and the measured water to a paste with a fork. Then work in the rest of the flour to form a soft dough. Wrap and chill for 30 minutes before using.

Rough puff

This is a cross between shortcrust and puff pastry, creating crisp, flaking layers. The usual quantities are three-quarters fat to flour and 2–3 tsp ice-cold water per 25 g/1 oz/¼ cup flour. The fat must be very cold. Cut it into cubes and add to the flour. Mix in the iced water, with a squeeze of lemon juice added, to form a lumpy paste. Flatten the dough slightly with a rolling pin into a narrow oblong on a floured surface. Fold up the bottom third of the dough and fold the top third over the top. Press the edges together with a rolling pin. Give the dough a quarter-turn and repeat the rolling and folding and turning twice more. Wrap and leave to rest in a cool place before rolling out.

Shortcrust (basic pie crust)

This is the most versatile pastry; it has a crumbly, melting texture and is used for all types of flan, tart and double crust pie. The usual quantities are half the amount of fat to flour. Rub the fat into the flour with a pinch of salt until the mixture resembles fine breadcrumbs. Sir in cold water to form a firm dough. It should be wrapped and chilled, if time allows, before using.

To make 350 g/12 oz of shortcrust, use 225 g/8 oz/2 cups of plain (all-purpose) flour, 50 g/2 oz/¼ cup each of butter or margarine and lard (shortening) and 30–45 ml/3–4 tbsp of cold water.

Suet crust

This soft, spongy pastry should be light to eat, yet filling. It can be steamed, boiled or baked. Generally, use half the amount of shredded (chopped) suet to flour. For dumplings, reduce the quantity of suet to one-third.

Mix the shredded beef or vegetable suet (I prefer vegetable) with self-raising (self-rising) flour, a little added baking powder and a pinch of salt. Mix with cold water to form a soft but not sticky dough, then knead briefly and leave to rest while preparing the filling – no longer. Dumplings should be used as soon as the water is added.

Cooking and decorating pastry

To bake pastry blind

This method is used to precook a pastry case (pie shell) before filling. Traditionally the pastry case was lined with a circle of greaseproof (waxed) paper, then filled with baking beans but this is fiddly and crumpled foil or greaseproof paper works just as well (step 3). The aim is just to stop the pastry rising, to give a flat-bottomed case.

1 Roll out the pastry and use to line a flan dish (pie pan) or flan ring set on a baking (cookie) sheet, pressing the pastry well into the corners.
2 Trim the edges and prick the base with a fork.
3 Crumple up foil or greaseproof paper and place in the flan to prevent the pastry rising up.
4 Bake in a preheated oven at 200°C/400°F/gas mark 6 for 10 minutes. Remove the foil or paper and return the flan to the oven for a further 5 minutes to dry out.

Cook's tips for pastry

- The art of making good pastry for rolling out is to keep the ingredients cool, work quickly and handle as little as possible.

- A marble slab is the best surface to roll out your pastry on.

- If you haven't got a rolling pin, a clean milk or wine bottle will do.

- Always roll pastry away from you in one direction only. Lift and turn the pastry, not your rolling pin: that way you will avoid stretching the dough, which would subsequently shrink again on cooking.

- Always use a sharp knife to trim pastry to avoid tearing or pulling it.

- To prevent fillings making the pastry soggy, brush the base of the pastry with egg white before adding the filling. If using raw fruit in a double crust pie, dust it with a little cornflour to thicken the juices as they cook.

- If pies are in danger of over-browning before being fully cooked, lay a sheet of foil lightly over the top.

- When steaming puddings or rolls, make sure they are well wrapped so that moisture cannot get into the pastry or it will become soggy.

- When steaming, keep the water topped up, so it does not boil dry.

Pastry decorations

To make decorations, collect all the trimmings, gently re-knead and roll out.

- LATTICE:

Cut the rolled trimmings into thin strips and lay these in a criss-cross pattern over the tart or flan to give a lattice pattern.

- LEAVES:

Cut trimmings into strips about 2 cm/¾ in wide. Cut the strips diagonally at about 2.5 cm/1 in intervals to make diamond shapes. Mark on the 'veins' with the point of a knife.

- ROSES:

Simpler than you'd think! Cut a strip of pastry as wide as the height you want your rose to be. Roll it up and pinch the base to hold together. Then gently pinch and pull back the layers slightly at the top, at intervals, to resemble petals.

- SHAPES:

There are numerous little biscuit (cookie) or petit four cutters available to cut out attractive shapes to stick on top of the pie.

- TASSELS:

Cut a strip of pastry as for a rose. Make cuts at even intervals along the length of the strip, to form a fringe. Roll up.

To glaze pastry

Use any of the following to brush over a pie to give it a shiny, golden appearance after cooking: whole beaten egg; egg yolk, beaten with a little water; egg white, lightly beaten; milk; single (light) cream; plain yoghurt.

Types of pie

Pies can be made in all different shapes and sizes with all sorts of different pastry. Here are the basic ones you will come across.

Deep double crust pies

These are deep-filled sweet or savoury pies, with the base and the covering made with shortcrust pastry, enriched shortcrust or quick-mix pastry.

Flans (pies), quiches and gougères

Flans are deep shells of pastry; they may be baked blind, filled and then served cold, or simply filled and baked. Quiches are flans filled with a mixture of egg and milk or cream and other ingredients, and then baked. Gougères are rings of choux pastry baked with a filling (usually savoury) in the centre.

Pasties, turnovers, buns

Shortcrust, quick mix, rough puff and puff pastry can all be used for pasties or turnovers. The differences lie in the shape. Pasties are cut from a circle of dough, filled and the pastry folded over the filling and sealed either along the top or round the base. They are decorated by crimping, then glazed and baked. Pasties are usually savoury. Turnovers are usually made from squares of dough, topped with a filling, then folded over diagonally to form triangles. The edges are sealed and decorated, and the pastry glazed and baked. Buns are made from choux pastry, spooned into rounds or oblongs on a greased baking (cookie) sheet. They can be as small or large as you like. Buns are baked and then filled before serving.

Raised pies

These are usually made with hot water crust pastry but can be made with shortcrust. The pastry is moulded in a loose-bottomed or springform tin (pan) and filled with a mixture of meat, poultry or vegetables and flavourings – such as minced (ground) pork and spices for a traditional pork pie – and topped with a lid of pastry. The pie is glazed and baked until crisp and cooked through and left to cool, then the tin carefully removed to leave the 'raised' pie. When using hot water crust pastry, the dough can be moulded round jam jars and left to set firm. The jars are then removed and the pies filled, covered with pastry lids, glazed and baked.

Steamed and baked rolls and puddings

For steamed and baked rolls, suet crust pastry is rolled out and laid on a double thickness of greased greaseproof (waxed) paper or foil, or a floured pudding cloth. A sweet or savoury filling is then spread on, not quite to the edges. The dough is rolled up with the help of the paper, foil or cloth, and tied securely. It is either steamed over a pan of simmering water, boiled in a pan of simmering water, or baked in the oven.

* NOTE:
A pudding cloth is not suitable for baking in the oven.

For steamed suet puddings, three-quarters of the quantity of pastry is used to line a greased pudding basin and then filled with a sweet or savoury filling. The remaining pastry is rolled out, brushed with water and pressed into place as a lid. The top is covered with a double thickness of greased greaseproof paper or foil with a pleat in the centre to allow the dough to rise, twisting and folding under the rim to secure. The pudding is then placed either in a steamer over a pan of simmering water or on an upturned saucer in a covered pan of simmering water, with the water coming halfway up the sides of the basin.

Strudels

These are made with strudel dough or filo pastry. Layers of filo are brushed with melted butter or oil, spread with a sweet or savoury mixture and rolled up. They can be made in large or individual sizes. They are then brushed with more fat and baked. The rolls can also be deep-fried (Chinese-style spring rolls, for example). Filo is also used for many Middle Eastern sweet and savoury pastries.

Tarts, open and closed

Shortcrust, enriched shortcrust, quick mix and French flan pastry are usually used for tarts. For open tarts, the pastry is used to line a pie plate or individual tartlet tins (patty pans) and then the filling put on top, leaving an edge of crust. For closed tarts, the procedure is the same but the filling is topped with a layer of pastry. Rough puff, flaky or puff pastry may be used instead of the shortcrust varieties for the top crust to give a different texture and appearance.

Top crust pies

These sweet or savoury pies may be made with shortcrust, enriched shortcrust, quick mix, rough puff, flaky or puff pastry. The pastry is simply laid over the filling. A pie funnel is often used to prevent the pastry sinking into the filling.

Pizzas

A pizza is just a variation on a pie, the difference being in the dough: for pizzas, bread or scone (biscuit) doughs are used to hold the filling rather than pastry dough. Originally from Italy, pizzas are now popular all over the world in many different guises. In Italy, you can still buy pizzas by the metre from street sellers or enjoy a traditional stone-baked, thin-crust Neapolitan version, bathed in olive oil, fragrant with fresh basil and sun-ripe tomatoes and oozing with real Mozzarella cheese. Or perhaps you'd prefer a deep-pan American speciality – the selection of fillings is almost endless. Just look in any supermarket chiller or freezer cabinet and you'll see the fast food array of thin crust, thick crust, stuffed crust and even no crust at all! There are also stuffed pizzas and calzones (pizza pasties). Pizzas are very easy to make at home, using either a basic bread dough or scone dough. To make things even simpler, you can buy packets of pizza base and bread mix.

Cook's tips for pizzas

- If you like your cheese really gooey, sprinkle it on the pizza for just the last 10 minutes of cooking time.

- If time is short, buy frozen cheese and tomato (Marguerita) Italian stoneground pizzas and add your own individual toppings, finally sprinkling with extra Mozzarella cheese before baking.

Recipes
Traditional Apple Pie

Serves 6

For a change, substitute 2 apples with 2 oranges, all rind and pith removed, then segmented, and serve with hot orange sauce (page 272).

225 g/8 oz/2 cups plain (all-purpose) flour
A pinch of baking powder
A pinch of salt
100 g/4 oz/½ cup hard block margarine, diced
Cold water, to mix
10 ml/2 tsp cornflour (cornstarch)
4 large cooking (tart) apples, sliced
45 ml/3 tbsp granulated sugar
2 cloves (optional)
Milk, to glaze
Caster (superfine) sugar, for dusting
Cream or custard, to serve

1 Sift the flour, baking powder and salt into a bowl.
2 Add the margarine and rub in with your fingertips until the mixture resembles fine breadcrumbs.
3 Mix with enough cold water to form a firm dough.
4 Knead gently on a lightly floured surface. Cut in half.
5 Roll out one half and use to line a pie plate. Dust with the cornflour.
6 Top with the apples, sprinkle over the sugar and add the cloves, well apart, if using.
7 Brush the edge of the pastry (paste) with water.
8 Roll out the remaining pastry. Lay on top and press the edges well together to seal. Trim, knock up and crimp between finger and thumb.
9 Make a hole in the centre to allow steam to escape. Make leaves out of pastry trimmings and use to decorate the pie.
10 Brush with milk and sprinkle with a little caster sugar. Place on a baking (cookie) sheet. Bake in a preheated oven at 200°C/400°F/gas mark 6 for 40 minutes until golden and cooked through. Sprinkle with a little more caster sugar and serve warm or cold with cream or custard.

Tarte Tatin

Serves 4

175 g/6 oz/1½ cups plain (all-purpose) flour
150 g/5 oz/⅔ cup unsalted (sweet) butter
120 ml/8 tbsp caster (superfine) sugar
1 egg yolk
Cold water
700 g/1½ lb cooking (tart) apples, peeled, quartered and cored

1 Sift the flour into a bowl.
2 Add 90 g/3½ oz/scant 1 cup of the butter and rub in with your fingertips.
3 Stir in 15 ml/1 tbsp of the sugar. Mix with the egg yolk and enough cold water to form a firm dough.
4 Wrap in clingfilm (plastic wrap) and chill for 30 minutes.
5 Meanwhile, butter a deep pie dish with 15 g/½ oz/1 tbsp of the remaining butter.
6 Cover the base with about 75 ml/5 tbsp of the sugar.
7 Top with the quartered apples. Sprinkle with the remaining sugar and dot with the last of the butter.
8 Roll out the pastry (paste) and use to cover the apples. Trim to fit. Place the dish on a baking (cookie) sheet.
9 Bake in a preheated oven at 190°C/375°F/gas mark 5 for about 30 minutes until cooked through and the sugar has caramelised. Carefully turn out on to a serving plate and serve hot.

....

Classic Syrup Tart

Serves 6

225 g/8 oz/2 cups plain (all-purpose) flour
A pinch of salt
100 g/4 oz/½ cup hard block margarine
Cold water, to mix
75 g/3 oz/1½ cups fresh white breadcrumbs
90 ml/6 tbsp golden (light corn) syrup
Finely grated rind and juice of 1 small lemon
Cream or ice cream, to serve

1 Sift the flour and salt into a bowl.
2 Add the margarine, cut into small pieces and rub in with your fingertips until the mixture resembles fine breadcrumbs.
3 Mix with enough cold water to form a firm dough. Knead gently on a lightly floured surface. Roll out and use to line a 23 cm/9 in deep pie plate. Trim with a sharp knife.
4 Spread the breadcrumbs in the pastry case (pie shell). Drizzle the syrup over and sprinkle with the lemon rind and juice.
5 Make a lattice out of the trimmings, if liked, and lay over the tart.
6 Bake in a preheated oven at 220°C/425°F/gas mark 7 for about 30 minutes until golden. Serve warm or cold with cream or ice cream.

Curried Lamb Turnovers

Serves 4–6

1 onion, finely chopped
1 eating (dessert) apple, finely chopped
15 ml/1 tbsp sunflower oil
175 g/6 oz minced (ground) lamb
30 ml/2 tbsp raisins
15 ml/1 tbsp desiccated (shredded) coconut
15 ml/1 tbsp curry paste
15 ml/1 tbsp water
350 g/12 oz puff pastry (paste), thawed if frozen
A little yoghurt or milk, to glaze

1 Fry (sauté) the onion and apple in the oil for 2 minutes, stirring.
2 Add the lamb and cook, stirring, until all the grains are separate and no longer pink.
3 Stir in the raisins, coconut and curry paste and moisten with the water.
4 Roll out the pastry (paste) and cut into eight squares.
5 Divide the curry mixture between the squares. Brush the edges with water. Fold over each to form a triangle. Knock up and flute with the back of a knife. Make a slit in the top of each to allow steam to escape.
6 Transfer to a dampened baking (cookie) sheet. Glaze with yoghurt or milk.
7 Bake in a preheated oven at 220°C/425°F/gas mark 7 for about 20 minutes until puffy and golden brown. Serve hot or cold.

Christmas Peach Parcels

Makes about 8

8 sheets of filo pastry (paste)
75 g/3 oz/⅓ cup butter or margarine, melted
410 g/14½ oz/1 large can of peach halves, drained, reserving the juice
450 g/1 lb/1 jar of mincemeat

1 For each parcel, brush a sheet of filo pastry with a little butter or margarine. Fold in half widthways and brush again.
2 Place a peach half in the centre and add a spoonful of mincemeat. Draw the filling up over the fruit to form a parcel.
3 Transfer to a greased baking (cookie) sheet. Brush with a little more butter or margarine. Repeat with the remaining peach halves.
4 Bake in a preheated oven at 200°C/400°F/gas mark 6 for about 15 minutes until golden brown. Serve hot or cold with a little of the reserved juice.

• •

Tomato Leek and Basil Gougère

Serves 4

4 leeks, sliced
4 tomatoes, chopped
75 g/3 oz/⅓ cup butter or margarine
15 ml/1 tbsp chopped fresh basil
A pinch of caster (superfine) sugar
Salt and freshly ground black pepper
65 g/2½ oz/good ½ cup plain (all-purpose) flour
150 ml/¼ pt/⅔ cup water
2 eggs, beaten
25 g/1 oz/¼ cup Parmesan cheese, grated

1 Cook the leeks and tomatoes in 25 g/1 oz/2 tbsp of the butter or margarine for 2 minutes, stirring.
2 Add the basil, sugar and a little salt and pepper, cover and cook gently for a further 4 minutes.
3 Meanwhile, sift the flour and a pinch of salt together.
4 Melt the remaining butter or margarine in the water in a small saucepan.
5 Add the flour all at once and beat with a wooden spoon until the mixture leaves the sides of the pan clean.

6 Beat in the eggs a little at a time, until the mixture is smooth and glossy but still holds its shape.
7 Spoon round the edge of a lightly greased 23 cm/ 9 in shallow baking dish.
8 Spoon the leek mixture in the centre and sprinkle all over with the Parmesan cheese. Bake in a preheated oven at 220°C/425°F/gas mark 7 for 30 minutes until puffy and golden brown. Serve hot.

Chocolate Éclairs

Makes about 9

65 g/2½ oz/good ½ cup plain (all-purpose) flour
A pinch of salt
150 ml/¼ pt/⅔ cup water
50 g/2 oz/¼ cup butter or margarine
2 eggs, beaten
150 ml/¼ pt/⅔ cup double (heavy) cream
10 ml/2 tsp caster (superfine) sugar
15 ml/1 tbsp cocoa (unsweetened chocolate) powder
100 g/4 oz/⅔ cup icing (confectioners') sugar
20 ml/4 tsp water

1 Sift the flour and salt on to a piece of kitchen paper (paper towel).
2 Heat the water and butter in a saucepan until the butter melts.
3 Add the flour all at once and beat with a wooden spoon until the mixture is smooth and leaves the sides of the pan clean.
4 Remove from the heat and cool slightly. Beat in the eggs, a little at a time, until the mixture is really smooth and glossy but still holds its shape.
5 Fill a piping bag fitted with a large plain tube (tip) and pipe the choux pastry (paste) in 7.5 cm/3 in lengths, well apart on a greased baking (cookie) sheet.
6 Cook in a preheated oven at 220°C/425°F/gas mark 7 for 15 minutes, then reduce the heat to 180°C/350°F/gas mark 4 and continue cooking for a further 10 minutes until crisp and golden.
7 Transfer to a wire rack, make a slit in the side of each one to allow steam to escape and leave to cool.
8 Whip the cream and sugar until peaking and use to fill the éclairs. Sift the icing sugar and cocoa together and mix with enough cold water to form a smooth paste. Spread over each éclair and leave until set.

Chocolate Profiteroles
Serves 4

1 Make as for chocolate éclairs (page 190) but spoon or pipe the mixture into small balls on the baking (cookie) sheet.
2 Bake in a preheated oven at 200°C/400°F/gas mark 6 for 15 –18 minutes until risen, crisp and golden.
3 Cool on a wire rack, fill with sweetened cream as for chocolate éclairs but pile up and top with instant chocolate sauce (page 273).

Mushroom and Onion Quiche
Serves 4

Use any savoury filling: try ham and tomato, or tuna and sweetcorn (corn).

175 g/6 oz/1½ cups plain (all-purpose) flour
A pinch of salt
75 g/3 oz/⅓ cup hard block margarine, cut into small pieces
Cold water, to mix
100 g/4 oz button mushrooms, sliced
1 onion, sliced
15 ml/1 tbsp sunflower oil
50 g/2 oz/½ cup Cheddar cheese, grated
Freshly ground black pepper
300 ml/½ pt/1¼ cups milk or milk and single (light) cream, mixed
1 egg

1 Sift the flour and salt in a bowl.
2 Add the margarine and rub in with your fingertips until the mixture resembles fine breadcrumbs.
3 Mix with enough cold water to form a firm dough.
4 Knead gently on a lightly floured surface. Roll out and use to line a 20 cm/8 in flan dish (pie pan). Prick the base with a fork. Place on a baking (cookie) sheet.
5 Fry (sauté) the mushrooms and onion in the oil for 3 minutes, stirring, until softened. Turn into the flan case (pie shell). Top with the cheese.
6 Beat the milk and egg together and season with some salt and pepper.
7 Pour into the flan and bake in a preheated oven at 190°C/375°F/gas mark 5 for about 30 minutes until the filling is set and golden brown.

Banoffee Pie
Serves 6

350 g/12 oz/1 large can of sweetened condensed milk
200 g/7 oz/1¾ cups plain biscuits (cookies), crushed
50 g/2 oz/¼ cup butter or margarine, melted
2 bananas
300 ml/½ pt/1¼ cups double (heavy) cream
30 ml/2 tbsp caster (superfine) sugar
15 ml/1 tbsp instant coffee powder
Drinking (sweetened) chocolate powder or grated chocolate, to decorate

1 Put the unopened can of condensed milk in a saucepan of boiling water and simmer for at least 3 hours, keeping the can submerged all the time. Allow to cool in the water (it's worth boiling a few cans at a time – store them in the cupboard until required).
2 Mix the biscuit crumbs with the butter or margarine and press into a 20 cm/8 in flan tin (pie pan). Chill until firm.
3 Spread the cold, caramelised milk on the base. Top with sliced bananas.
4 Whip the cream, sugar and coffee powder together. Spread over the top.
5 Sprinkle with chocolate powder or grated chocolate and chill until ready to serve.

Steak and Kidney Pudding
Serves 4–6

365 g/12½ oz/generous 3 cups self-raising (self-rising) flour
5 ml/1 tsp mustard powder
Salt
175 g/6 oz/1½ cups shredded (chopped) beef or vegetable suet
A little oil, for greasing
700 g/1½ lb stewing steak, trimmed of fat and gristle and cubed
175 g/6 oz beef kidney, sliced
Freshly ground black pepper
30 ml/2 tbsp chopped fresh parsley
300 ml/½ pt/1¼ cups beef stock, made with 1 stock cube
Carrots and extra gravy (pages 263 and 266), to serve

1 Sift all but 30 ml/2 tbsp of the flour with the mustard and 5 ml/1 tsp salt into a bowl. Stir in the suet.
2 Mix with enough cold water to form a firm dough.
3 Knead gently on a lightly floured surface. Cut off a quarter for a lid. Roll out the remainder and use to line a lightly greased 1.2 litre/2 pt/5 cup pudding basin.
4 Toss the meat and kidney in the remaining flour, seasoned with salt and pepper and the parsley.
5 Pack into the basin and pour in the stock. Roll out the remaining pastry (paste), dampen with water and place in position.
6 Cover with a double thickness of greased greaseproof (waxed) paper or foil, with a pleat in the centre, twisting and folding under the rim to secure.
7 Steam for 4 hours. Serve hot with carrots and gravy.

Sussex Pond Pudding
Serves 6

225 g/8 oz/2 cups self-raising (self-rising) flour
A pinch of salt
100 g/4 oz/1 cup shredded (chopped) beef or vegetable suet
100 g/4 oz/⅔ cup currants
150 g/5 oz/⅔ cup light brown sugar
Grated rind and juice of 1 lemon
Cold water, to mix
100 g/4 oz/½ cup butter or margarine, plus a little for greasing
Single (light) cream, to serve

1 Sift the flour and salt into a bowl.
2 Add the suet, currants and 25 g/1 oz/2 tbsp of the sugar.
3 Mix with the lemon juice and enough water to form a soft but not sticky dough.
4 Knead gently on a lightly floured surface. Cut off a quarter and roll out to a round large enough to use as a lid. Roll out the remaining dough and use to line a greased 900 ml/1½ pt/3¾ cup pudding basin.
5 Beat the remaining sugar, lemon rind and butter together until smooth.
6 Place in the basin, brush the edges of the dough with water and cover with the 'lid'. Press the edges well together to seal.

7 Cover with a double thickness of greased greaseproof (waxed) paper or foil with a pleat in the middle to allow for rising. Twist and fold under the rim of the basin to secure.

8 Steam for 2½ hours. Turn out and serve with single (light) cream.

Pork Pie   Serves 6

100 g/4 oz streaky bacon, rinded and diced
700 g/1½ lb diced pork
Freshly ground black pepper
1.5 ml/¼ tsp ground ginger
30 ml/2 tbsp chopped fresh parsley
350 g/12 oz/3 cups plain (all-purpose) flour
Salt
150 ml/¼ pt/⅔ cup water
100 g/4 oz/½ cup lard or white vegetable fat
1 egg, beaten, to glaze
10 ml/2 tsp powdered gelatine
300 ml/½ pt/1¼ cups chicken or pork stock, made with 1 stock cube

1 Mince (grind) the bacon and pork or chop in a food processor. Mix with some pepper, the ginger and parsley.

2 Sift the flour and a good pinch of salt into a bowl.

3 Melt the water and fat together in a saucepan. Pour into the flour and mix to form a dough. Knead gently until smooth.

4 Cut off a quarter of the dough, wrap and reserve. Mould the remainder into an 18 cm/7 in loose-bottomed cake tin (pan). Quickly fill with the meat mixture and add 30 ml/2 tbsp water.

5 Roll out the remaining dough to form a lid, dampen and place on top. Crimp the edges between your finger and thumb. Make a hole in the centre to allow steam to escape and make leaves out of any trimmings.

6 Brush with beaten egg to glaze. Place on a baking (cookie) sheet). Bake in a preheated oven at 180°C/350°F/gas mark 4 for 2½ hours. Remove from the oven and leave to cool.

7 Dissolve the gelatine in the stock. When on the point of setting, pour into the pie. Chill for several hours until the jelly has set. Serve cut into wedges.

Perfect Pizza Marguerita

Serves 4

You can add any pizza toppings you like before sprinkling with the cheese.

½ quantity of basic yeast bread dough (page 244)
Oil, for greasing
45 ml/3 tbsp tomato purée (paste)
2.5 ml/½ tsp dried oregano
4 ripe tomatoes, sliced
30 ml/2 tbsp olive oil
Freshly ground black pepper
100 g/4 oz Mozzarella cheese, sliced
8 fresh basil leaves, torn
A few black olives

1 Make the bread dough and leave in a warm place until doubled in bulk.
2 Knock back (punch down) and knead again. Roll out to a thin round, about 23 cm/9 in in diameter and place on an oiled baking (cookie) sheet.
3 Spread with the tomato purée and sprinkle with the oregano.
4 Top with the tomato slices and drizzle with half the oil. Add a good grinding of pepper.
5 Bake in a preheated oven at 220°C/425°F/gas mark 7 for 10 minutes. Top with the cheese, drizzle with the remaining oil and scatter the basil and olives over. Bake for a further 10 minutes or until the base is golden round the edges and the cheese has melted and is bubbling. Serve hot.

Quick Pan Pizza

Serves 1–2

100 g/4 oz/1 cup self-raising (self-rising) flour
A pinch of salt
45 ml/3 tbsp sunflower or olive oil
225 g/8 oz/1 small can of chopped tomatoes, drained
1.5 ml/¼ tsp dried oregano
50 g/2 oz/½ cup Cheddar cheese, grated

1 Mix the flour and salt in a bowl. Add 30 ml/2 tbsp of the oil and mix with enough cold water to form a soft but not sticky dough.
2 Knead gently on a lightly floured surface and roll out to a round the size of a medium frying pan (skillet).

3 Heat the remaining oil in the frying pan and add the round of dough. Cook for 3 minutes until golden brown underneath.

4 Turn over and top with the tomatoes, oregano and cheese. Cook for 2–3 minutes, then transfer the pan to a preheated grill (broiler) and cook for about 3 minutes or until the cheese melts and bubbles. Serve hot.

Calzone

Serves 4

400 g/14 oz/3½ cups strong plain (bread) flour
15 ml/1 tbsp light brown sugar
Salt and freshly ground black pepper
100 g/4 oz/½ cup butter or margarine
60 ml/4 tbsp olive oil, plus extra for greasing and brushing
1 sachet of easy-blend dried yeast
250 ml/8 fl oz/1 cup milk, hand-hot
2 spring onions (scallions), finely chopped
1 garlic clove, crushed
225 g/8 oz frozen chopped spinach, thawed and squeezed dry
350 g/12 oz/1½ cups ricotta cheese
1.5 ml/¼ tsp grated nutmeg
2 beefsteak tomatoes, skinned and chopped
15 ml/1 tbsp chopped fresh parsley

1 Mix the flour, sugar and 5 ml/1 tsp salt in a bowl.
2 Rub in the butter or margarine. Stir in half the oil and the yeast.
3 Mix with the milk to form a firm dough. Knead gently on a lightly floured surface until smooth and elastic. Place in an oiled plastic bag and leave in a warm place while preparing the filling.
4 Fry (sauté) the spring onions and garlic in the remaining oil for 2 minutes. Stir in all the remaining ingredients.
5 Knock back (punch down) the dough and quarter. Roll out to thin rounds.
6 Spread the filling over half of each round. Brush the edges with water.
7 Fold the dough over the filling and press to seal.
8 Transfer to a lightly oiled baking (cookie) sheet and brush with a little oil. Bake in a preheated oven at 200°C/400°F/gas mark 6 for 20 minutes or until golden and cooked through. Serve warm.

Cosa Nostra

Serves 2

1 packet of pizza base mix
2 tomatoes, chopped
1 canned pimiento cap, chopped
A few cooked French (green) beans, cut into small pieces
1 slice of ham, diced
5 ml/1 tsp capers
1.5 ml/¼ tsp dried oregano
30 ml/2 tbsp grated Mozzarella cheese
Salt and freshly ground black pepper
A little olive oil
200 ml/7 fl oz/scant 1 cup passata (sieved tomatoes)
A good pinch of dried basil
Grated Parmesan cheese

1 Make up the pizza base mix and knead into a ball.
2 Cut in half and roll out each half to a fairly thin round.
3 Divide the tomatoes, pimiento, beans, ham, capers, oregano and Mozzarella between the centres of the rounds. Season lightly.
4 Brush the edges with water and draw the dough up over the filling to cover completely. Press the edges together to seal.
5 Place the sealed sides down on a lightly oiled baking (cookie) sheet.
6 Brush with olive oil. Bake in a preheated oven at 200°C/400°F/gas mark 6 for about 20 minutes until golden brown and cooked through.
7 Meanwhile, warm the passata with the basil. Transfer the stuffed pizzas to warm plates. Spoon the sauce over the centre and sprinkle with Parmesan cheese before serving.

• •

Quick Cornish Pasties

Serves 4

1 carrot, finely chopped
¼ small swede (rutabaga), finely chopped
1 potato, finely chopped
1 small onion, finely chopped
100 g/4 oz cooked lamb or beef, finely chopped
Salt and freshly ground black pepper

350 g/12 oz shortcrust (basic pie crust) or puff pastry (paste)
Milk, to glaze
Baked beans and brown table sauce, to serve

1 Mix the prepared vegetables with the meat and some salt and pepper.
2 Roll out the pastry and cut into four 18 cm/7 in squares or circles.
3 Spoon the filling into the centre of each. Add 10 ml/2 tsp water to each. Brush the edges with water and draw up over the filling, pressing well together to seal, and crimp the edge between your finger and thumb.
4 Transfer to a baking (cookie) sheet, lightly greased if using shortcrust, or dampened if using puff pastry. Decorate with any trimmings and make a small hole in the top to allow steam to escape. Brush with milk to glaze.
5 Bake in a preheated oven at 200°C/400°F/gas mark 6 for 15 minutes, then reduce the heat to 180°C/350°F/ gas mark 4 and continue cooking for 30 minutes until the vegetables are tender and the pastry is golden brown.
6 Serve hot with baked beans and brown table sauce.

....

Chicken and Cranberry Pouches   Serves 4

Try this with a 295 g/10½ oz/medium can of condensed mushroom soup and about 175 g/6 oz/1½ cups cooked, diced chicken instead of the chicken in sauce.

4 sheets of frozen filo pastry (paste), thawed
50 g/2 oz/¼ cup butter or margarine, melted
425 g/15 oz/1 large can of chunky chicken in sauce
2.5 ml/½ tsp dried thyme
60 ml/4 tbsp cranberry sauce
Plain potatoes and French (green) beans, to serve

1 Lay the pastry sheets on a board and brush with some of the butter or margarine. Fold in half and brush again.
2 Spoon the chicken in the centres and sprinkle with the thyme. Top with the cranberry sauce.
3 Draw the pastry sheets up over the filling and pinch together to form pouches. Transfer to a greased baking (cookie) sheet.
4 Brush with the remaining butter or margarine and bake in a preheated oven at 200°C/400°F/gas mark 6 for about 10–15 minutes until golden brown. Transfer to warm plates and serve with potatoes and beans.

....

fruit, nuts and seeds

All fresh fruit contain vitamin C, small amounts of beta-carotene (vitamin A), other vitamins and minerals as well as fibre. The amount of vitamin C varies considerably. Blackcurrants are top of the league, with strawberries, kiwi fruit, citrus fruits and other soft fruits next in line. Canned fruits, too, contain moderate amounts of vitamin C and both fresh and canned contain natural sugar. There is probably not enough to cause tooth decay, but when the fruit is processed, into things like fruit juice, its composition changes and dental caries can result.

Fruit, like vegetables, can be divided into different categories.

Citrus fruit

All citrus fruits ripen on the tree. They all have an oily skin, or zest, with thick, white pith under the surface, encasing juicy, acidic flesh, separated by tough membranes. The most common are lemons, limes and oranges (the three best-known being thin-skinned Valencia and blood oranges, thicker-skinned Navel oranges and bitter Seville oranges). But there are also tangerines, mandarins, clementines, satsumas, pink and yellow grapefruit and the less well-known ortaniques, kumquats, ugli fruit, tangelos and minneolas (a cross between a tangerine and a grapefruit).

Preparing citrus fruit

• TO GRATE THE RIND AND SQUEEZE THE JUICE:
1 Rub the whole, unpeeled fruit all round on the fine side of a grater until all the coloured zest is grated, but not the white pith.
2 Cut the fruit in half widthways and squeeze the juice on a citrus squeezer. If you don't have a squeezer, hold the fruit firmly in one hand, with a fork in the other, over a bowl. Push the fork into the fruit while squeezing it, turning the fork to squash the flesh.

- TO PEEL FIRM-SKINNED CITRUS FRUIT TO EAT IN YOUR FINGERS:
1 Cut a slice off the top and bottom of the fruit.
2 Make a series of cuts down through the peel and pith all round the fruit, taking care not to cut through the flesh.
3 Gently ease off the sections of peel with the pith all round. (Small citrus like clementines and satsumas usually peel very easily, so there is no need to cut the skin first.)

- TO SEGMENT UNPEELED GRAPEFRUIT OR ORANGE HALVES:
1 Cut in half widthways and remove any pips.
2 Place in small serving dishes. Use a serrated-edged knife (preferably a curved, grapefruit one). Cut all the way round the fruit between the flesh and the white pith.
3 Cut down both sides of each membrane to loosen the segments. Remove the central white core, if preferred.

- TO SEGMENT PEELED CITRUS FRUIT:
1 Hold the fruit over a bowl to catch any juice.
2 Cut the peel and pith off the fruit, using a serrated-edged knife in a sawing motion, and cutting either down the fruit in sections or in a continuous circular motion round the fruit, like peeling an apple.
3 Hold the peeled fruit firmly and cut down both sides of each membrane to loosen the segments, gently sliding them out with the knife into the bowl.
4 Squeeze the membranes over the bowl to extract the last of the juice.

Cook's tips for citrus fruit

- Thin-skinned Valencia oranges are best for squeezing for juice.

- Seville oranges are best for marmalade.

- If you have citrus fruit you need to use up, finely grate the rind and squeeze the juice. Freeze the rind in an airtight container and the juice in ice cube trays, for flavouring cakes, puddings and sauces.

- You'll get more juice from a citrus fruit if you warm it briefly first in the microwave or in hot water.

- Where possible, add lemon or other citrus juice at the very end of the cooking time, to preserve as much vitamin C as possible.

Cooking citrus fruit

Citrus fruits are usually eaten raw, although the rind and juice are frequently used in cooked dishes. Grilled (broiled) oranges and grapefruit make a quick and simple starter, however, and, of course, citrus fruit of all kinds may be cooked to make marmalade and curds.

- TO GRILL GRAPEFRUIT OR ORANGES:

1 Prepare in halves, loosening the segments.
2 Place in flameproof dishes on the grill (broiler) rack or directly in the grill pan if the dishes are too deep.
3 Spoon a little port or liqueur over, if liked.
4 Sprinkle liberally with granulated or light brown sugar.
5 Place under the preheated grill until the sugar melts and bubbles. Serve straight away.

- MARMALADE:

Use 900 g/2 lb sugar and 1.2 litres/2 pts/6 cups water to every 450 g/1 lb fruit.

1 Scrub the fruit and simmer gently in the water for about 1½ hours until really tender.
2 Remove the fruit from the water. When cool enough to handle, slice, chop finely or shred. Put all the pips in the cooking water, boil rapidly for 15 minutes, then strain the water into a preserving pan.
3 Add the fruit and sugar. Stir until dissolved, then boil until setting point is reached. (Test by putting a little on a cold saucer and push with your finger. It will wrinkle if setting point is reached.)
4 Pot and label.

Core fruit

This group comprises apples and pears and other related fruits.

Apples

Apples are related to the rose family and can be divided into categories.

- COOKING (TART) APPLES:

These varieties, for example Bramley's Seedling, are only suitable for cooking.

- CRAB APPLES AND QUINCES:

These are also related to the rose family. They are small, sour and fragrant and most frequently used to make jelly (clear conserve), fruit cheeses, jams (conserves) and home-made wine. A few slices of quince added to an apple pie will give it a delicious, scented flavour.

- CRISP SWEET APPLES:

Varieties such as Cox's Orange Pippin, Worcester Pearmain, Empire and Golden Delicious are all suitable for eating and cooking. Some benefit from a drop of lemon juice to add tartness when cooking.

- GREEN, CRISP APPLES:

These are also suitable for both eating and cooking (Granny Smith is a good example) but will take longer to cook than other varieties.

- SOFT, SWEET APPLES:

Varieties of this type, such as Red Delicious, are not suitable for cooking as their flavour is too mild.

Pears

Pears do not keep as well as apples and can go from being rock hard to 'sleepy' (soft and pulpy) within days. There are many varieties, all suitable for cooking and eating. The most common are Comice pears (greeny-yellow), Conference pears (long-shaped, harder and the best variety for cooking) and William pears (yellow and juicy), which are perfect when just ripe but become overripe very quickly.

Preparing core fruit

1 Peel, if necessary, cut into quarters and remove the cores.
2 Slice if appropriate.

Cooking core fruit

- TO STEW APPLES:

1 Peel and core and cut into slices.
2 Place in a saucepan with 30–45 ml/2–3 tbsp water.
3 Bring to the boil, reduce the heat and simmer until pulpy.
4 Sweeten to taste.

- TO PURÉE APPLES:

1 Prepare and cook as for stewing.
2 Pass through a sieve (strainer) or purée in a blender or food processor until smooth.
3 Sweeten to taste.

Cook's tips for core fruit

- Apples discolour quickly when peeled. If slicing, put immediately in water with 15 ml/1 tbsp lemon juice added to prevent this. Drain thoroughly before use.

- Soft, cooking apples go pulpy very quickly when cooked. To help keep their shape, add sugar only at the end of cooking.

- To prevent apples from bursting when baking, make a cut round the centre through the skin.

- All pears can be poached but the riper they are, the shorter the cooking time – hard pears can take up to 1 hour. Hard ones will also have less flavour, so add cloves, cinnamon stick, port or ginger wine to the syrup to enhance it.

- TO BAKE APPLES:

1 Remove the cores from even-sized cooking (tart) apples.
2 Place in a roasting tin (pan).
3 Fill the centres with your chosen filling. Try brown sugar; dried fruit; jam (conserve); lemon or orange curd; golden (light corn) syrup.
4 Sprinkle the fruit with a little extra sugar, if liked, and add a dot of butter to each.
5 Bake in a preheated oven at 180°C/350°F/gas mark 4 for 30–40 minutes, basting occasionally with the juices, until tender but still holding their shape.

- TO POACH PEARS:

1 Peel and core, then halve or leave whole, as appropriate.
2 Make a sugar syrup. Put 300 ml/½ pt/1¼ cups water, wine, juice or a mixture in a saucepan or flameproof casserole. Add 50 g/2 oz/¼ cup white or brown sugar.
3 Heat, stirring until the sugar dissolves. Add the pears.

4 Bring to the boil, reduce the heat, cover and either simmer on top of the stove or in the oven at 160°C/325°F/gas mark 3 for 20–40 minutes until the pears are just tender but still hold their shape. Larger fruit should be turned once in the juice during cooking.
5 Taste the juice and add more sugar, if necessary.
6 If liked, the pears can then be removed from the juice and the liquid boiled until reduced and syrupy.
7 The pears can be served hot or cold.

Exotic fruit

From the tropics to the Mediterranean, there are now many exciting fruits available in the supermarkets for you to try. These include bananas and plantains (green cooking bananas); pineapples; mangoes; papayas or pawpaws; pomegranates; lychees; rambutans (like hairy lychees); physalis (cape gooseberries); persimmons; kiwi fruit; passion fruit; fresh figs and dates; custard apples; guavas and prickly pears (which vary from green to pink and are covered with prickles) and Asian pears (which taste like a cross between an apple and a pear).

Preparing and eating exotic fruit

● ASIAN PEARS:

Peel and core like core fruit (page 202) and eat the crisp, white, very juicy flesh. Delicious served with cheese or raw, cured ham.

● CUSTARD APPLES:

1 Cut a slice off the top and eat the flesh with a spoon.

● DATES (FRESH):

Serve as they are. Put the stones (pits) at the side of your plate when you eat them. Alternatively, cut into halves and remove the stones before serving.

● FIGS (FRESH):

To eat whole when ripe, make a cut in the stalk. Gently pull back the skin and eat off the flesh. If the skin is very soft, it may be eaten too. To serve with cheese or raw, cured ham, cut the figs into quarters.

● KIWI FRUIT:

Cut off the top and eat with a spoon. Alternatively, pull or cut the skin off and cut the flesh into slices.

- LYCHEES:

To eat individually, bite the skin and pull off the end between your teeth. Gently squeeze and suck, the lychee will pop in your mouth. Eat the fruit and discard the stone (pit).

To prepare for fruit salad, etc: Make a cut in the skin with a knife. Pull off the skin, cut the fruit in half and remove the stone.

- MANGOES:

Cut off the skin. Score the flesh in both directions right through to the large, hairy stone, then cut off the pieces. Alternatively, cut in slices all round and remove.

- PAPAYAS (PAW PAWS):

Peel, cut in half and scoop out the black seeds. Slice or dice as required.

- PASSION FRUIT:

Cut in half and scoop out the scented juicy seeds, which are delicious to eat. Use to flavour ice cream, fruit sauces or a fruit salad.

- PERSIMMONS:

Peel back the leathery orange or red skin and eat the jelly-like flesh.

- PHYSALIS:

Peel back the papery leaves and eat the round fruit straight off the stem. They can also be frosted (page 208) or dipped in fondant. They are often prepared and used to decorate other desserts.

- PINEAPPLES:

Cut off the green leafy end and the base. Cut off all the rind, then cut into slices. Remove the central core (not necessary for baby pineapples).

- POMEGRANATES:

Cut into quarters. Bend back the skin and gently remove the juicy seeds, or eat straight from the skin.

- PRICKLY PEARS:

Cut in half lengthways. Peel off the skin and eat the flesh plain or sprinkled with lemon or lime juice.

- RAMBUTANS:

Make a cut in the skin with a knife. Pull off the skin, cut the fruit in half and remove the stone.

Cooking exotic fruit

- TO PURÉE EXOTIC FRUIT:

1 Prepare the fruit (pages 204–5), place in a blender or food processor, and run the machine until smooth. Alternatively, rub through a sieve (strainer).
2 Sharpen with lemon or lime juice or sweeten with sugar as necessary.

- TO FLAMBÉ BANANAS OR PINEAPPLES:

1 Prepare the fruit and cut bananas into halves, pineapple into slices.
2 In a large frying pan (skillet), melt a knob of butter for each banana or slice of pineapple.
3 Add the fruit and fry (sauté) on each side until lightly browned but still firm.
4 Sprinkle liberally with light brown sugar and add 10 ml/2 tsp kirsch, rum or orange liqueur per banana or slice of pineapple.
5 Ignite and shake the pan until the flames subside.
6 Spoon on to warm plates and spoon the juices over.

Cook's tips for bananas

- Peel only when ready for use.
- Bananas discolour quickly once cut, so toss in a little lemon juice to prevent this.
- Overripe bananas are ideal for cooked desserts, cakes, breads and milkshakes.

Soft fruit

The soft fruit group includes all the berries – strawberries; raspberries; black, red and white currants; blackberries; loganberries; blueberries; gooseberries and cranberries. I have also included rhubarb, which is really a vegetable, in this section, as it cooks to a soft pulp with no central stones (pits) or pips. The sweeter varieties (strawberries, raspberries, blackberries, blueberries and loganberries) are delicious served fresh on their own, or with cream or ice-cream, or sprinkled over breakfast cereals. Others, like rhubarb and green gooseberries, must be cooked with sugar to make them palatable. They are also used to make jams (conserves) and jellies (clear conserves).

Preparing soft fruit

Remove any hulls and pull currants off their stalks. Top and tail gooseberries and cut rhubarb into short lengths, removing any leaves and trimming the base.

Cooking soft fruit

- TO STEW AND PURÉE HARDER VARIETIES:

1 Prepare the fruit (see above) and place in a saucepan with 150 ml/¼ pt/ ⅔ cup water, fruit juice or a mixture of wine and water.
2 Bring to the boil, reduce the heat and simmer very gently just until the fruit is tender and the juice runs.
3 Sweeten to taste.
4 Lift out of the juice with a draining spoon and place in a blender or food processor. Run the machine until smooth.
5 Pass through a sieve (strainer) to remove the seeds.
6 Thin with some of the cooking juice, as necessary.

- TO STEW AND PURÉE SOFTER VARIETIES:

1 Place in a saucepan and sprinkle with a little sugar.
2 Heat gently until the juice runs.
3 Tip into a sieve (strainer) and rub through to form a smooth purée. Taste and add a little icing (confectioners') sugar, if necessary. Thin with a little juice, liqueur or water, if liked.

- TO PURÉE RAW SOFT FRUIT (STRAWBERRIES, RASPBERRIES, ETC.):

1 Wash and place in a blender or food processor.
2 Run the machine until smooth, stopping and scraping down the sides, if necessary.
3 Pass through a sieve (strainer) to remove the seeds, if necessary.
4 Sweeten to taste with icing (confectioners') sugar.

- TO MAKE JAM (CONSERVE) FROM BERRIES:

Use equal quantities of fruit and sugar. For blackberries and strawberries, add the finely grated rind and juice of 1 lemon for every 1.5 kg/3 lb fruit.

1 Prepare the fruit, then place in a preserving pan.
2 Heat gently until the juice runs, then simmer, stirring gently until pulpy.
3 Stir in the sugar and boil until setting point is reached (see marmalade, page 201).
4 Pot and label.

Cook's tips for soft fruit

- Rhubarb cooks to a pulp very quickly. To keep its shape, cook in a casserole (Dutch oven) in the oven at 180°C/350°F/gas mark 4, sprinkled liberally with sugar but with no extra water.

- Canned soft fruits make excellent sauces when drained (reserving the juice), rubbed through a sieve (strainer), then thinned with a little of the reserved juice.

- To frost small sprigs of currants for decoration, brush gently with very lightly beaten egg white, then sprinkle liberally with caster (superfine) sugar. Leave to dry on non-stick baking parchment.

- To strip currants from a stalk, run a fork down its length, catching the fruit in the tines.

- When making jelly (clear conserve), don't be tempted to squeeze the fruit when leaving it to drip or the results will be cloudy.

- SOFT FRUIT JELLIES:

This is a basic, simple recipe; some are far more complicated. For less tart fruit, like blackberries, add the juice of 1 lemon for every 900 g/2 lb fruit. Use 600 ml/1 pt/2½ cups water for every 900 g/2 lb fruit.

1 Prepare the fruit (page 207) and place in a preserving pan with the water. Bring to the boil, reduce the heat and simmer until the fruit is pulpy.
2 Lay a new disposable kitchen cloth in a colander, suspended over a large bowl. Gently tip the pulp into the colander and leave to drip overnight.
3 Measure the juice and place in a preserving pan with 450 g/1 lb sugar for every 600 ml/1 pt/2½ cups juice.
4 Boil until setting point is reached (see marmalade, page 201).
5 Pot and label.

Stone fruit

These are all soft fruit that have a large stone (pit) in the middle, e.g. peaches; nectarines; apricots; all the varieties of plums, including greengages; all the varieties of cherries; damsons and sloes. All of these except sloes can be eaten either fresh or cooked in many delicious ways for desserts, in sauces and jams (conserves), and also be used to make delicious liqueurs.

Preparing stone fruit

- TO SKIN STONE FRUIT:

Plunge the fruit in boiling water for 30 seconds. Drain and peel off the skins.

- TO REMOVE THE STONE (PIT):

Cut in half and gently lift out the stone. If the fruit is ripe, the stone will come away easily. If not, gently ease round the stone with a sharp pointed knife. To stone cherries whole, a cherry stoner is required.

Cooking stone fruit

- TO POACH STONE FRUIT:

1 Peel, then halve or leave whole, as appropriate.
2 Make a sugar syrup. Put 300 ml/½ pt/1¼ cups water, wine, juice or a mixture in a saucepan or flameproof casserole (Dutch oven). Add 50 g/ 2 oz/¼ cup white or brown sugar.
3 Heat, stirring until the sugar dissolves. Add the fruit.
4 Bring to the boil, reduce the heat, cover and either simmer on top of the stove or in the oven at 160°C/325°F/gas mark 3 for 20–40 minutes until the fruit are just tender but still hold their shape. Larger fruits should be turned once in the juice during cooking.
5 Taste the juice and add more sugar, if necessary.
6 If liked, the fruit can then be removed from the juice and the liquid boiled until reduced and syrupy.
7 The fruit can be served hot or cold.

- TO STEW STONE FRUIT:

1 Halve and stone (pit) or leave whole if appropriate.
2 Place in a saucepan with enough water to cover the base.
3 Cover and cook gently until tender. Sweeten to taste.

Cook's tips for stone fruit

- Add a little thinly pared orange, lemon or lime rind when stewing stone fruit to bring out the flavour.
- Plum skins are often very tart. You will probably need to sweeten the juice more after cooking.

- TO MAKE JAM (CONSERVE) FROM STONE FRUIT:

Use equal quantities of sugar and fruit and 450–600 ml/¾ –1 pt/2–2½ cups water. For sweet fruit, add the juice of 1 lemon for every 1.5 kg/3 lb fruit.

1 Wash and halve the fruit and remove the stones (pits). Slice the fruit if appropriate. Crack the stones with a weight or nut crackers, but do not break up.
2 Place the fruit and their stones in a preserving pan with the water and simmer until the fruit is pulpy. Skim off the stones.
3 Add the sugar and boil rapidly until setting point is reached (see marmalade, page 201).
4 Pot and label.

Vine fruit

This group includes all the varieties of grape: green and red seedless varieties, fragrant muscat grapes and large, juicy black and green seeded varieties. The other family of vine fruit is the melon family: large, pink-fleshed, black seeded water melons; yellow honeydew melons and round chanterais; ogen; musk and cantaloupe varieties with green, pink or orange flesh. All are good served either as a starter or a dessert. They can be complemented with raw cured hams, ginger, other fruits and herbs like mint.

Preparing vine fruit

- TO SKIN GRAPES:

Plunge briefly in boiling water, drain and peel off the skins.

- TO REMOVE SEEDS FROM GRAPES:

Halve them and scoop out the seeds gently. Alternatively, if serving whole, insert the rounded end of a (clean!) hair-grip through the stalk end of the grape. Push down, then gently pull out. The seeds will come out with the grip.

- TO SERVE MELONS HALVED:

1 Cut in half and scoop out the seeds.
2 Place in small dishes and serve plain or with the centre filled with any of the following; ginger wine; port; fresh soft fruits; prawns; curls of raw, cured ham.

- TO SERVE MELON IN WEDGES OR SLICES:

1 Prepare as for halved melons, then cut into wedges or thinner slices.
2 Cut off the rind and lay the wedges or slices on plates and serve on their own or with any of the suggestions above.

- TO SERVE MELON BOATS:
1 Halve and seed the melon.
2 Cut lengthways into four or six 'boats'.
3 Cut down the length of the centre of the flesh, then cut the flesh away from the rind but leave in place.
4 Make cross cuts along the length of the fruit. Gently ease alternate pieces away from the centre to form a checkerboard effect.
5 If liked, thread an orange slice and a maraschino cherry on a cocktail stick and place in the centre to resemble a boat sail.

- TO PREPARE WATERMELON:

Simply cut into wedges to be eaten in the fingers. Alternatively, cut off the rind, cut into chunks, remove all the seeds and serve in fruit salad.

Tips for choosing fresh fruit

- Always pick very carefully. If pre-packed, look underneath the clear punnet or plastic bag. If there is a lot of juice, the fruit is damaged.

- Check that soft fruits have no discoloured patches or musty smell.

- To test if a melon is ready to eat, gently press one end: it should give slightly. Round varieties should have a sweet, fragrant smell.

- Stone fruit, including exotic varieties like mangoes, should give gently when squeezed in the palm of your hand and should smell very fragrant.

- Pineapples should be more yellow than green, feel firm but will give slightly when squeezed and have a sweet pineapple smell. If overripe, they will have a dark orange skin and feel soft.

- Bananas should be just yellow; if they are too green, they may not turn yellow at all before going black.

- Citrus fruits should feel heavy for their size.

- Check apples and pears for bruising. The skin should be taut, not wrinkly. Pears should give slightly when squeezed, but if soft, they will be inedible.

Freezing fruit

There are two ways of freezing fruit: dry freezing, with or without sugar, which is particularly good for berries and sliced fruit, and wet freezing, in syrup.

- TO DRY-FREEZE FRUIT:
1 Choose only top-quality fruit. Pick over and remove any hulls or stalks. Spread out on a tray that will fit in the freezer. Sprinkle with sugar, if liked.
2 Open-freeze until firm.
3 Pack into rigid containers or freezer bags, label and store in the freezer.

- TO FREEZE FRUIT IN SYRUP:
1 Prepare the fruit for stewing or poaching.
2 Stew or poach according to the type of fruit (pages 202–210).
3 Leave until cold, then turn into rigid containers, label and freeze.

Commercially frozen and canned fruit

Fruit bought ready-frozen and canned fruit are extremely useful. I always keep a selection of both to hand. My favourites are:

Frozen fruits
- Melon balls
- Cherries
- Mixed summer fruits and/or fruits of the forest
- Raspberries

Canned fruits
Choose fruits canned in natural juice rather than heavy syrup for a better flavour and texture.
- Apricots
- Blackcurrants
- Breakfast special (a fruit compôte)
- Mandarin oranges
- Pear halves
- Pineapple rings
- Raspberries
- Stoned (pitted) black cherries
- Whole peaches

Dried fruit

These are great energy food, having a high concentration of fruit sugar in them. They don't have the vitamin C content of fresh fruit but they do supply Vitamin A and various minerals. They are also an excellent source of fibre. They can complement all kinds of foods, including meat, poultry, salads, cheeses, desserts, biscuits (cookies) and cakes; they are excellent served on their own or mixed with cereals or yoghurt. They also make great snacks.

The group includes the cake fruits – large, stoned (pitted) and smaller seedless raisins, sultanas (golden raisins) and currants – and other fruits such as prunes, peaches, apricots, pears, apple rings, dates, figs, mangoes, bananas, blueberries, cranberries and dried fruit salad. Large dried fruits are now available in ready-to-eat varieties that don't need soaking before use.

Cooking dried fruit

* TO STEW DRIED FRUIT:
1 If the fruit needs soaking first, wash it and place it in a bowl with just enough water, fruit juice or a mixture of wine and water to cover. Leave to soak for several hours or overnight.
2 Tip into a saucepan. Bring to the boil, reduce the heat, part-cover and simmer for 15–20 minutes, until the fruit is tender but still holds its shape. Check frequently to make sure the fruit does not become pulpy.
3 Taste and sweeten with sugar or honey, if necessary. Serve hot or cold.

Cook's tips for dried fruit

* Soak cake fruit in a little fruit juice or any alcohol in the recipe for 1–2 hours before use to plump them up and improve their flavour.

* Prunes are great soaked in cold tea before stewing.

* It is often unnecessary to add extra sugar when stewing dried fruit as they are very sweet. It is best to cook, then taste and sweeten at the end.

* When stewing dried fruit, add the grated rind and a little of the juice from an orange or lemon for extra flavour.

* Sweet spices like cloves, cardamom pods or a piece of cinnamon stick give super flavour to a dried fruit salad when stewing.

Glacé (candied) and crystallised fruit

Cherries, oranges, lemons, figs, clementines, ginger, pineapple, angelica and mixed peel can all be all glazed in sugar syrup or crystalline sugar to preserve them. They are used for flavouring and decoration or as sweetmeats.

Nuts and seeds

High in protein, vitamins, iron, calcium and oils, nuts are highly nutritious. They are valuable for vegetarians as an alternative to meat, fish or poultry and invaluable to all cooks because they are so versatile!

The nuts most commonly used in cooking are walnuts, brazils, hazelnuts (filberts), almonds, coconut, chestnut, pistachios, macadamias, cashews, pecans and pine nuts. Peanuts are not really nuts but legumes – they grow in pods underground, not in trees like all other nuts.

Seeds, too, are highly nutritious. They can enhance many dishes, both sweet and savoury. The most popular seeds for cooking are sesame, poppy, black and yellow mustard, caraway, fennel, cumin, coriander, cardamom, fenugreek, pumpkin and sunflower.

Preparing nuts and seeds

- TO SKIN (BLANCH) ALMONDS OR WALNUTS:
1 Place in a bowl. Cover with boiling water.
2 Leave to stand for 1 minute. Drain and squeeze off the skins.

- TO SKIN HAZELNUTS (FILBERTS):
1 Spread the nuts out in a shallow baking tin (pan).
2 Place under a preheated grill (broiler) until the nuts begin to colour and the skins begin to loosen, turning occasionally.
3 Remove from the grill, place in a paper bag or clean tea towel (dish cloth) and rub off the skins.

- TO SKIN CHESTNUTS:
1 Split the hard skins with a sharp knife.
2 Place in a saucepan and cover with water. Bring to the boil and simmer for 5 minutes. Leave to cool in the water.
3 Drain and peel off both the hard outer skins and the brown skins inside.

- TO ROAST CHESTNUTS:
You really need an open fire, but this can be done under a grill (broiler).

1 Pierce the skin of each nut. Place on the fire shovel, or a baking tin (pan) for under the grill.

2 Place on the hot coals (or under the grill) and cook until the skins blacken and they 'pop', shaking the shovel or pan occasionally to turn the nuts.

3 Tip on to a piece of newspaper to cool, peel off the skins and dip the nuts in salt, if liked, before eating.

● TO TOAST NUTS AND SEEDS:

1 Place them in a non-stick frying pan (skillet) and toss over a moderate heat until golden brown.

2 Remove them from the pan as soon as they are cooked or they will burn.

Alternatively:

1 Spread them out on a plate.

2 Microwave on High (100 per cent power) until golden, tossing occasionally.

Cook's tips for nuts and seeds

● To prepare a coconut, drill two holes through the 'eyes' in the shell with a strong metal skewer or a bradawl and pour off the milk into a bowl. Then tap firmly with a hammer to split the shell. Prise the flesh off the shell and remove the brown skin. Eat raw or pare into shavings or grate for use in cooking.

● Nut butter is extremely useful for both cooking and spreading on bread. Simply purée any nuts, raw or toasted, in a blender or food processor until they form a smooth paste. Stop the machine and scrape down the sides from time to time. Season with salt, if liked, and store in an airtight container in the fridge.

● Tahini is a paste made from sesame seeds. It is not worth making, but keep a jar of ready-made tahini in your fridge: it will last for ages and adds depth to many meals, especially dips and sauces.

Nut and seed oils

Peanuts are the basis of the common groundnut oil and, of course, sunflower oil is widely used but many of the other nuts and seeds make delicious, well-flavoured oils for use on their own or mixed with another oil, such as sunflower or olive, to enhance many dishes. My favourites are sesame and walnut oils. Use these speciality oils sparingly because they are strong (and expensive!) – just a spoonful can make all the difference.

Recipes
Fresh Orange Jelly
Serves 4

Use the finely grated rind and juice of 2 lemons and use pineapple instead of orange juice to make a lemon jelly.

Finely grated rind and juice of 1 orange
15 ml/1 tbsp powdered gelatine
Pure orange juice

1 Put the orange rind and juice in a measuring jug and sprinkle the gelatine over. Leave to soften for 5 minutes.
2 Stand the jug in a pan of hot water and stir until the gelatine has dissolved or heat briefly in the microwave.
3 Make up to 600 ml/1 pt/2½ cups with pure orange juice.
4 Turn into a 600 ml/1 pt/2½ cup jelly (jello) mould and chill until set.
5 Dip briefly in hot water, then turn out on to a serving plate and serve cold.

Pears in Spiced Red Wine
Serves 4

15 ml/1 tbsp light brown sugar
5 ml/1 tsp lemon juice
5 cm/2 in piece of cinnamon stick
300 ml/½ pt/1¼ cups red wine
4 pears, peeled

1 Put the sugar, lemon juice, cinnamon and wine in a saucepan and heat until the sugar dissolves.
2 Cut a thin slice off the bottom of each pear so it will stand upright and gently cut out the cores.
3 Stand the pears in an ovenproof dish and pour over the wine. Cover with foil and bake in a preheated oven at 160°C/325°F/gas mark 3 for 30 minutes, turning once. Remove the cinnamon stick. Serve hot with the wine spooned over, or cool, then chill.

Tropical Compôte

Serves 6

100 g/4 oz/½ cup granulated sugar
150 ml/¼ pt/⅔ cup water
2 pomegranates
1 passion fruit
2 oranges
1 mango
2 kiwi fruit
1 small pineapple

1 Put the sugar and water in a saucepan and heat gently until the sugar has dissolved. Bring to the boil and boil for 3 minutes.
2 Meanwhile, halve the pomegranates and passion fruit and squeeze out the juice as you would for a lemon. Strain into the syrup.
3 Hold the oranges over the saucepan and cut off all the rind and pith, then slice and halve the slices.
4 Peel the mango and cut all the flesh off the stone in long strips. Halve if very big and add to the syrup.
5 Peel and slice the kiwi fruit and add to the syrup. Cut all the skin off the pineapple, slice the fruit, then cut into chunks, discarding any thick, central core.
6 Mix all the fruit and juices together and leave until cold. Transfer to a glass serving dish and chill for at least 2 hours to allow the flavours to develop.

Fresh Fruit Salad

Serves 4–6

Make the fruit salad at least 1 hour in advance to let the flavours develop. Allow about 45 ml/3 tbsp prepared fresh fruit per person. Leave any edible peel (on apples, peaches, nectarines or plums) for colour and texture.

300 g/11 oz/1 small can of mandarin oranges in natural juice
150 ml/¼ pt/⅔ cup pure apple or orange juice
5 ml/1 tsp lemon juice
A mixture of fresh fruits, chopped or sliced as necessary

1 Put the mandarins and their juice in a glass bowl. Stir in the fruit juices.
2 Add the prepared fresh fruits. If using juicy berries such as raspberries or
   blueberries, add these at the last moment so that the colour does not run
   too much. Chill until ready to serve.

. . . .

Pineapple Flambé   Serves 4

For a banana flambé, use four large bananas instead of the pineapple and
replace the kirsch and brandy with orange juice and rum.

1 ripe pineapple
50 g/2 oz/¼ cup butter or margarine
45 ml/3 tbsp kirsch
30 ml/2 tbsp caster (superfine) sugar
45 ml/3 tbsp brandy
Whipped cream, to serve

1 Cut all the rind off the pineapple and cut the fruit into eight thin slices.
2 Cut out the hard central core of each slice.
3 Melt the butter or margarine in a large frying pan (skillet).
4 Add the fruit and sprinkle with the kirsch and sugar. Cook for 2 minutes,
   then turn over.
5 Add the brandy, ignite and shake the pan until the flames subside.
6 Serve immediately, straight from the pan, with whipped cream.

. . . .

Mango Fool   Serves 4

1 ripe mango
45 ml/3 tbsp lemon juice
15 ml/1 tbsp caster (superfine) sugar
425 g/15 oz/1 large can of custard
150 ml/¼ pt/⅔ cup double (heavy) cream, whipped
Angelica 'leaves', to decorate

1 Peel the mango and cut all the flesh off the mango stone (pit).
2 Purée in a blender or processor with the lemon juice and sugar.
3 Fold in the custard and half the whipped cream.
4 Spoon into four wine goblets. Decorate each with a swirl of the remaining cream and an angelica 'leaf'. Eat within 2 hours.

Blueberry Almond Crumble

Serves 4

350 g/12 oz blueberries
175 g/6 oz/¾ cup caster (superfine) sugar
10 ml/2 tsp lemon juice
75 g/3 oz/¾ cup ground almonds
75 g/3 oz/¾ cup plain cake crumbs
2.5 ml/½ tsp ground cinnamon
50 g/2 oz/¼ cup unsalted (sweet) butter, melted
30 ml/2 tbsp flaked (slivered) almonds
Crème fraîche, to serve

1 Place the blueberries in a shallow, ovenproof dish with 75 g/3 oz/⅓ cup of the sugar and all the lemon juice.
2 Mix together the remaining sugar, the ground almonds, cake crumbs and cinnamon.
3 Stir in the melted butter, then sprinkle the mixture over the blueberries and press down lightly.
4 Bake in a preheated oven at 180°C/350°F/gas mark 4 for 20 minutes.
5 Sprinkle the flaked almonds over the top and bake for 15–20 minutes more until golden brown on top. Serve hot with crème fraîche.

Lemon Sorbet

Serves 6–8

600 ml/1 pt/2½ cups water
225 g/8 oz/1 cup granulated sugar
Thinly pared rind and juice of 2 large lemons
Bottled lemon juice
2 egg whites

1 Put the water and sugar in a saucepan. Heat gently, stirring, until the sugar has dissolved.
2 Bring to the boil and boil for 10 minutes until thick but not coloured. Add the lemon rind and leave until cold.
3 Make the freshly squeezed lemon juice up to 450 ml/¾ pt/2 cups with bottled lemon juice. Stir into the syrup.
4 Strain into a freezerproof container and freeze for about 1½ hours until frozen round the edges. Whisk with a fork to break up the ice crystals.
5 Whisk the egg whites until stiff and fold in with a metal spoon.
6 Return to the freezer and freeze until firm.

Orange Sorbet

Serves 8

Prepare as for lemon sorbet (above) but use the thinly pared rind and juice of 2 oranges instead of lemons and pure orange juice from a carton instead of freshly squeezed lemon juice. Sharpen with lemon juice, if liked.

Pink Strawberry Sparkle

Serves 4

225 g/8 oz strawberries, hulled and sliced
20 ml/4 tsp caster (superfine) sugar
Juice of ½ lime
½ bottle of sparkling rosé wine, chilled

1 Divide the strawberries between four champagne cups.
2 Sprinkle with the sugar and add a little lime juice to each.
3 Chill for at least 30 minutes.
4 When ready to serve, top up with the sparkling wine and serve straight away.

Melon Glacé
Serves 4

Drizzle with raspberry sauce (see Cook's tips for soft fruit, page 208) instead of ginger wine, if liked.

  2 small ogen, cantaloupe, galia or charentais melons
  4 scoops of vanilla ice cream
  30 ml/2 tbsp ginger wine

1 Cut the melons into halves, scoop out the seeds and place the melons in four serving dishes.
2 Add a scoop of ice cream to the cavity in each and spoon the ginger wine over. Serve straight away.

Gooseberry Fool
Serves 4

Try this with rhubarb, apples or greengages.

  450 g/1 lb gooseberries, topped and tailed
  45 ml/3 tbsp water
  100 g/4 oz/½ cup granulated sugar
  300 ml/½ pt/1¼ cups double (heavy) cream

1 Put the gooseberries in a saucepan with the water and sugar.
2 Heat gently, stirring until the sugar dissolves, then cover and simmer gently until the gooseberries are very soft.
3 Purée in a blender or food processor. Leave until cold.
4 Whip the cream into soft peaks. Fold in the puréed gooseberries.
5 Spoon into glasses and chill for 1–2 hours before serving.

Blackcurrant Mousse

Serves 4

Try this with other well-flavoured canned fruits with matching or contrasting jellies.

    1 packet blackcurrant-flavoured jelly (jello)
    300 g/11 oz/1 small can of blackcurrants in fruit juice
    170 g/6 oz/1 small can of evaporated milk, chilled
    170 g/6 oz/1 small can of cream

1 Dissolve the jelly in 150 ml/¼ pt/⅔ cup boiling water.
2 Stir in the juice from the can of blackcurrants and chill until on the point of setting.
3 Meanwhile, whisk the chilled evaporated milk until thick and fluffy.
4 When the jelly is the consistency of egg white, whisk in the fluffy milk.
5 Turn into four glasses and chill until set.
6 Spread the cream over and top with the blackcurrants.

Simple Pesto

Serves 4

Try this added to cooked pasta and tossed over a gentle heat before serving, or spread on slices of ciabatta bread and grill (broil) until melted, or use as a stuffing for chicken breasts or fish.

    20 fresh basil leaves
    1 large sprig of fresh parsley
    50 g/2 oz/½ cup pine nuts
    1 large garlic clove, halved
    90 ml/6 tbsp olive oil
    30 ml/2 tbsp grated Parmesan cheese
    A pinch of salt
    Freshly ground black pepper
    15 ml/1 tbsp hot water

1 Put the herbs, nuts and garlic in a blender or food processor. Run the machine briefly to chop.
2 Gradually add the oil in a thin trickle with the machine running to form a thick paste. Stop the machine and scrape down the sides a few times.

3 Add the cheese, salt and some pepper and run the machine again, adding the water to form a glistening paste.
4 Store in a screw-topped jar in the fridge for up to 2 weeks.

. . . .

Walnut and Sesame Dip   Serves 4

You can use almost any vegetables for the 'dippers': try small broccoli florets, sticks of carrot, celery and cucumber, strips of (bell) peppers, cherry tomatoes, mangetout (snow peas) and slices of apple, dipped in lemon juice.

1 large garlic clove
25 g/1 oz/¼ cup walnut pieces
1 slice of white bread
15 ml/1 tbsp sesame seeds, toasted
6 fresh basil leaves
15 ml/1 tbsp lemon juice
175 ml/6 fl oz/¾ cup mayonnaise
120 ml/4 fl oz/½ cup crème fraîche
Salt and freshly ground black pepper
A selection of vegetables, to dip

1 Put the garlic, walnuts, bread and sesame seeds in a blender with the basil and lemon juice. Run the machine until the mixture forms a paste, stopping the machine and scraping down the sides.
2 Add the mayonnaise and crème fraîche and run the machine until smooth.
3 Season to taste, then tip into a small bowl, cover and chill until ready to serve with the dippers.

. . . .

Basic Nut Roast   Serves 4

150 g/5 oz/1¼ cups chopped mixed nuts
75 g/3 oz/1½ cups fresh wholemeal breadcrumbs
1 small onion, finely chopped
15 ml/1 tbsp soy sauce
2.5 ml/½ tsp dried oregano

5 ml/1 tsp lemon juice
25 g/1 oz/2 tbsp butter or margarine
5 ml/1 tsp sunflower oil, plus a little for greasing
5 ml/1 tsp Marmite or Vegemite
150 ml/¼ pt/⅔ cup hot water
Mashed potatoes and a green vegetable and gravy (pages 263 and 266), to serve

1 Mix together everything except the Marmite or Vegemite and water.
2 Blend the Marmite or Vegemite and water together and stir in thoroughly.
3 Turn into a greased baking dish.
4 Bake in a preheated oven at 190°C/375°F/gas mark 5 for 30–40 minutes until golden brown and hot through.
5 Serve with mashed potatoes, a green vegetable and gravy.

....

Spinach and Peanut Loaf   Serves 4

225 g/8 oz frozen spinach, thawed
1 large onion, quartered
1 garlic clove
175 g/6 oz/1½ cups peanuts
4 slices of wholemeal bread, torn into pieces
1 egg
5 ml/1 tsp Marmite or Vegemite
5 ml/1 tsp dried thyme
Salt and freshly ground black pepper
A little sunflower oil, for greasing
450 ml/¾ pt/2 cups passata (sieved tomatoes)
Plain potatoes and sweetcorn (corn), to serve

1 Squeeze out the spinach to remove as much moisture as possible.
2 Place in a blender or food processor. Run the machine and drop in the onion, garlic, peanuts and bread. Alternatively, pass the ingredients through a coarse mincer (grinder), mincing the bread last.
3 Beat the egg with the Marmite or Vegemite and stir into the mixture with the thyme and a little salt and pepper.
4 Turn into a greased 450 g/1 lb loaf tin (pan) and cover with foil.

5 Bake in a preheated oven at 180°C/350°F/gas mark 4 for 1 hour or until firm to the touch.
6 Meanwhile, heat the passata with a good grinding of pepper.
7 Leave the loaf to cool for 3–4 minutes, then turn out on to a warm serving dish.
8 Serve sliced with the passata, potatoes and sweetcorn.

....

Chestnut and Mushroom Pie   Serves 4

700 g/1½ lb potatoes, cut into small pieces
30 ml/2 tbsp milk
65 g/2½ oz/scant ⅓ cup butter or margarine
1 onion, chopped
225 g/8 oz chestnut mushrooms, quartered
25 g/1 oz/¼ cup plain (all-purpose) flour
250 ml/8 fl oz/1 cup vegetable stock, made with 1 stock cube
30 ml/2 tbsp dried milk powder (non-fat dry milk)
430 g/15½ oz/1 large can of chestnuts, quartered
Salt and freshly ground black pepper
30 ml/2 tbsp chopped fresh parsley
5 ml/1 tsp dried thyme
50 g/2 oz/½ cup Cheddar cheese, grated
Baked or canned tomatoes, to serve

1 Cook the potatoes in boiling, lightly salted water until tender. Drain and mash with the milk and 15 g/½ oz/1 tbsp of the butter or margarine.
2 Meanwhile, melt the remaining butter or margarine in a saucepan. Add the onion and mushrooms and fry (sauté) for 3 minutes, stirring.
3 Add the flour and cook for 1 minute.
4 Remove from the heat and blend in the stock and milk powder. Return to the heat, bring to the boil and cook for 2 minutes, stirring.
5 Add the chestnuts and season to taste. Stir in the herbs.
6 Turn into an ovenproof serving dish. Top with the potato, fluff up with a fork and sprinkle with the cheese.
7 Bake in a preheated oven at 190°C/375°F/gas mark 5 for about 30 minutes until golden brown. Serve hot with baked or canned tomatoes.

....

soups and sandwiches

This chapter is all about quick bites for those times when you don't want a full-blown meal but need something nutritious and tasty. Soups are a great way of getting vegetables, protein and carbohydrates into you in one go. Sandwiches, providing they don't have too much butter or margarine in them, can also supply all the elements of a balanced main meal quickly and easily.

Cook's tips for snacks

- A snack meal should be as nutritious as a main one.
- The main part of your snack should be starchy carbohydrate – bread, pasta, etc. – to give you slowly-released energy and keep you going longer.
- Include plenty of fruit and vegetables in snacks. You can't have too much!
- Avoid snacks that are high in added sugar. They will give you a quick burst of energy, but then you'll feel hungry again.
- Snacks that are high in fat are also bad news. Your body will use only the fat it needs and then simply store the rest, probably around your hips and stomach!

Really useful soups

Soups can be divided into two main categories: thin and thick.

Thin soups

There are two types: broths, or semi-clear soups, made from brown or white stock with meat, vegetables, rice or barley added; and clear soups or consommés, which have been cleared by having whisked egg white added to collect all the particles that make them cloudy. They are then strained through muslin (cheesecloth), leaving them sparklingly clear.

Thick soups

Thick soups may be made in two ways. The ingredients may be cooked until soft, then puréed in a blender or food processor or passed through a sieve (strainer). Alternatively, they may be thickened and enriched after cooking by the addition of butter, cream or sometimes egg yolks.

All the soups in this chapter are simple and easy to make, so you won't find a recipe for consommé here; it's not the sort of thing I would suggest you busy yourself making for a quick snack (but the canned ones are great!). Some recipes use up the bones from the Sunday roast, and cooked, leftover vegetables. Others make the most of that last tired carrot or potato in the vegetable rack or the piece of 'mousetrap' cheese left over from a dinner party.

- NOTE:

Quantities are not vital. If you have an extra carrot you want to use, put it in. If you have a bit less cheese than the recipe asks for, or a small onion where a large one is required, it really doesn't matter. Also, if you don't have a meat bone, just add an extra stock cube and cook just until everything is tender.

Cans and packets have their place on the snack menu too, but they tend to be fairly unexciting. So I've come up with some great ways to tart them up, and make them look and taste great. Serve all of them with lots of crusty bread for a complete snack meal.

Super sandwiches

Sandwiches can be made with pittas, bagels, rolls, baguettes, naan bread, flour tortillas, croissants or brioches (to name but a few), as well as the more usual sliced breads. This section gives you a whole range of fillings in suggested breads, but you can put the filling in any bread receptacle you fancy. The quantities are up to you.

- CHEESE BLUSHER:

Crumble or grate some mild white cheese (e.g. Wensleydale), mix with sliced red onion, sliced baby beetroot (red beets) and mayonnaise, and use to fill split croissants.

- CHILLI BEAN WRAPS:

Mash drained red kidney beans with a pinch of chilli powder. Stir in chopped green (bell) pepper, chopped cucumber and chopped tomatoes. Spread flour tortillas with the bean mixture. Top with a little soured (dairy sour) cream or yoghurt, then shredded lettuce and a little grated Cheddar cheese. Add hot chilli sauce, if liked. Roll up and eat.

- CHINESE CHICKEN:

Chop some cooked chicken and mix with beansprouts, grated carrot and green (bell) pepper and a small piece of chopped stem ginger in syrup (optional), tossed in soy sauce; use to fill a baguette, spread with fromage frais.

- GREEK SALAD:

Shred white cabbage and lettuce, mix with finely chopped tomato and cucumber, sliced black olives and a little finely chopped onion. Toss with olive oil, a dash of wine vinegar and some black pepper and finally mix with some crumbled Feta cheese, and pack into seeded rolls or hunks of seeded bread.

- GRILLED (BROILED) BACON, TOMATO, MUSHROOM AND LETTUCE:

Grill some smoked back bacon, sliced tomato and sliced mushrooms; layer hot in a sandwich, lined with lettuce and mustard, and topped with a little mayonnaise, between slices of stoneground wholemeal bread.

- ITALIAN ROASTED VEGETABLE WITH PESTO:

Slice different coloured (bell) peppers and red onion, and fry (sauté) in olive oil until tender. Mix with a spoonful of pesto sauce, to taste. Pile into hunks of ciabatta bread, or rolls, and top with thinly sliced Mozzarella cheese.

- MINTED CURRIED LAMB:

Mix a little plain yoghurt with dried mint, salt and pepper. Stir in some finely diced cooked lamb and finely chopped cucumber. Mash a little curry paste with some butter and spread on naan breads. Lay lettuce leaves and sliced tomatoes on top. Spread the lamb mixture over and roll up.

- SMOKED MACKEREL AND CREAM CHEESE:

Cut a small smoked mackerel fillet into small pieces, discarding the skin, if preferred. Spread a halved bagel with cream cheese, top with a thin spreading of horseradish sauce and then the mackerel. Sprinkle with lemon juice and add a good grinding of pepper. Top with salad cress and serve.

- TUNA CRUNCHY CORN:

Mix some drained, canned tuna drained, canned sweetcorn (corn), a little chopped celery and a spoonful of pine nuts, moistened with tomato relish; pack into pittas.

Hot sandwiches

- CHEESE AND HAM CRESCENTS:

Fill split croissants with slices of ham and Cheddar or Gruyere (Swiss) cheese. Cook under a moderate grill (broiler) until the cheese melts, turning once.

- CROQUE MONSIEUR:

Sandwich a slice of ham and cheese together between two slices of bread. Butter the outsides. Grill (broil) or fry (sauté) until golden on both sides and the cheese is melting. Cut into halves and serve hot.

- CROQUE MADAME:

Sandwich a slice of cheese, a few slices of onion and a little chopped sage between two slices of bread. Butter the outsides. Grill (broil) or fry (sauté) until golden brown on both sides and the cheese is melting.

- GOLDEN MELTIES:

Spread two slices of bread with corn relish. Sandwich together with a slice of cheese and thin slices of yellow (bell) pepper. Butter the outsides. Grill (broil) or fry (sauté) until golden on both sides and the cheese is melting.

- HAM AND TOMATO CRESCENTS:

Split croissants and fill each with a slice of ham and half a sliced tomato. Sprinkle with dried basil. Cook under a moderate grill (broiler), turning once, until hot through and the croissants are crisp.

Recipes

Simple Scotch Broth   Serves 4

1 roast lamb bone from the Sunday joint
A handful of pearl barley
1 onion, finely diced
1 carrot, finely diced
1 potato, finely diced
A piece of swede (rutabaga) or a turnip, finely diced
1 bouquet garni sachet
1 chicken or lamb stock cube
Salt and freshly ground black pepper

1 Place the lamb bone in a saucepan.
2 Add the pearl barley, onion, carrot, potato and swede or turnip.

3 Pour in just enough water to cover, add the bouquet garni sachet, stock cube and some salt and pepper.
4 Bring to the boil, reduce the heat, part-cover and simmer very gently for 1½ hours.
5 Remove the lamb bone and bouquet garni sachet. Cut any meat off the bone and return to the pan. Taste and adjust the seasoning, if necessary, before serving.

· ·

Creamy Chicken and Vegetable Soup Serves 4

The quantity of vegetables doesn't matter – just use whatever you have.

1 roast chicken carcass
1 bay leaf
1 chicken stock cube
Salt and freshly ground black pepper
Cooked leftover vegetables, chopped
60 ml/4 tbsp dried milk powder (non-fat dry milk)
30 ml/2 tbsp plain (all-purpose) flour
75 ml/5 tbsp water

1 Break up the carcass and place in a saucepan.
2 Cover with water, add the bay leaf, stock cube and some salt and pepper.
3 Bring to the boil, cover and simmer for 1 hour. Strain the liquid and return to the saucepan.
4 Pick off any meat from the carcass and add to the liquid.
5 Add the vegetables and simmer for 5 minutes.
6 Blend the dried milk powder, flour and water together to form a smooth paste and stir into the pan.
7 Bring to the boil and simmer for 2 minutes, stirring, until thickened. Taste and adjust the seasoning.

· ·

Beef, Carrot and Onion Soup with Mustard Dumplings

Serves 4

3 onions, chopped
2 carrots, chopped
65 g/2½ oz/generous ¼ cup butter or margarine
30 ml/2 tbsp light brown sugar
1 roast beef bone
1 beef stock cube
Salt and freshly ground black pepper
100 g/4 oz/1 cup self-raising (self-rising) flour
15 ml/1 tbsp made English mustard

1 Place the onions and carrots in a large saucepan with 25 g/1 oz/2 tbsp of the butter or margarine. Fry (sauté), stirring, for 3 minutes until golden.
2 Stir in the sugar and fry for 2 minutes. Add the beef bone and enough water to cover. Crumble in a beef stock cube and add salt and pepper.
3 Bring to the boil, cover, reduce the heat and simmer gently for 1½ hours.
4 Lift out the beef bone. Cut off any meat, chop and return to the pan. Taste and adjust the seasoning.
5 Put the flour in a bowl. Add a little salt and pepper and rub in the remaining butter or margarine.
6 Blend the English mustard with 15 ml/1 tbsp water. Stir into the flour mixture with enough extra water to form a soft but not sticky dough.
7 Shape into small balls and drop round the top of the simmering soup. Cover and simmer for 15 minutes until the dumplings are fluffy. Serve hot.

··

Pork and Cabbage Soup with Caraway

Serves 4

1 roast pork bone
1 pork or chicken stock cube
Salt and freshly ground black pepper
2.5 ml/½ tsp dried mixed herbs
12 baby potatoes, scrubbed
½ small green cabbage, finely shredded
15 ml/1 tbsp caraway seeds
30 ml/2 tbsp plain yoghurt or soured (dairy sour) cream

1 Put a roast pork bone in a saucepan and cover with water.
2 Add the stock cube, a little salt and pepper and the herbs. Bring to the boil, reduce the heat and simmer gently for 1½ hours.
3 Remove the bone and cut off any meat. Chop and return to the pan.
4 Add the potatoes and simmer for 10 minutes.
5 Add the cabbage and caraway seeds. Bring back to the boil, reduce the heat, cover and simmer for 10–15 minutes until everything is soft. Taste and adjust the seasoning, if necessary.
6 Serve ladled into bowls with a spoonful of yoghurt or soured cream on top.

Blue Cheese and Celery Soup   Serves 4

You can use the outer, damaged celery sticks for this. The flavour is just as good, and it doesn't matter what they look like!

2–3 celery sticks, chopped
1 onion, chopped
1 potato, chopped
1.2 litres/2 pts/5 cups chicken or vegetable stock, made with 2 stock cubes
100 g/4 oz/1 cup blue cheese, crumbled
Salt and freshly ground black pepper
15 ml/1 tbsp cornflour (cornstarch)
30 ml/2 tbsp milk or single (light) cream
30 ml/2 tbsp chopped fresh parsley or a few celery leaves, to garnish

1 Place the celery, onion and potato in a saucepan and add the stock.
2 Bring to the boil, reduce the heat and simmer for 30 minutes.
3 Purée in a blender or food processor. Add the blue cheese and process again.
4 Strain back into the saucepan (to remove any celery strings), if liked.
5 Blend the cornflour with the milk or single cream. Stir into the pan, bring to the boil and cook for 1 minute, stirring.
6 Taste and adjust the seasoning. Serve garnished with chopped parsley or celery leaves.

Brie and Broccoli Potage

Serves 4

Use Camembert instead, if you prefer.

15 g/½ oz/1 tbsp butter or margarine
1 large onion, chopped
2 large potatoes, chopped
1.2 litres/2 pts/5 cups chicken or vegetable stock, made with 2 stock cubes
Salt and freshly ground black pepper
100 g/4 oz/1 cup Brie, chopped
100 g/4 oz raw or cooked broccoli, chopped
30 ml/2 tbsp milk or single (light) cream

1   Melt the butter or margarine in a saucepan. Add the onion and potato and fry (sauté) for 2 minutes until slightly softened but not browned.
2   Add the stock and season lightly.
3   Bring to the boil and simmer for 20 minutes.
4   Add the Brie and stir in with the broccoli. Simmer for 5 minutes, stirring.
5   Purée in a blender or food processor. Return to the pan. Taste and adjust the seasoning, if necessary. Stir in the milk or cream and reheat but do not boil. Ladle the soup into bowls and serve.

....

Crab and Potato Bisque

Serves 4

25 g/1 oz/2 tbsp butter or margarine
1 large potato, finely chopped
1 carrot, finely chopped
1 small onion, finely chopped
43 g/1¾ oz/1 small can of dressed crab
45 ml/3 tbsp plain (all-purpose) flour
900 ml/1½ pts/3¾ cups fish, chicken or vegetable stock, made with
    1 stock cube
5 ml/1 tsp celery salt
30 ml/2 tbsp dry sherry
150 ml/¼ pt/⅔ cup milk
150 ml/¼ pt/⅔ cup single (light) cream
170 g/6 oz/1 small can of white crabmeat
Chopped fresh parsley, to garnish

1 Melt the butter or margarine in a saucepan.
2 Add the potato, carrot and onion. Stir, then cover and cook very gently for 5 minutes until softened but not browned.
3 Stir in the dressed crab and flour and cook for 1 minute.
4 Remove from the heat and gradually blend in the stock.
5 Bring to the boil, stirring, reduce the heat and simmer for 10 minutes, stirring occasionally.
6 Stir in all the remaining ingredients and heat through. Sprinkle with parsley before serving.

• •

Green Velvet Soup   Serves 4

1 onion, finely chopped
1 potato, finely chopped
225 g/8 oz frozen broad (fava) beans
225 g/8 oz frozen spinach
900 ml/1½ pts/3¾ cups vegetable or chicken stock, made with 1 stock cube
Salt and freshly ground black pepper
A little grated nutmeg
60 ml/4 tbsp plain yoghurt

1 Put all the vegetables and stock in a saucepan. Bring to the boil, reduce the heat and simmer gently for 10 minutes until everything is tender.
2 Purée in a blender or food processor and return to the pan. Add salt, pepper and nutmeg to taste. Reheat.
3 Ladle into warm bowls and add a spoonful of yoghurt to each. Serve hot.

• •

Triple Tomato Soup   Serves 4

295 g/10½ oz/1 medium can of condensed tomato soup
400 g/14 oz/1 large can of chopped tomatoes
425 g/15 oz/1 large can of haricot (navy) beans, drained
2 sun-dried tomatoes, finely chopped
2.5 ml/½ tsp dried basil

1 Empty the can of condensed tomato soup into a saucepan.
2 Fill the same can with water and whisk into the soup.
3 Stir in the chopped tomatoes, beans, sun-dried tomatoes and basil.
4 Heat through until almost boiling. Ladle into bowls and serve.

• •

Cheese, Celery and Corn Chowder Serves 4

295 g/10½ oz/1 medium can of condensed celery soup
Milk
200 g/7 oz/1 small can of sweetcorn (corn)
100 g/4 oz/1 cup Cheddar cheese, grated
Freshly ground black pepper

1 Empty the celery soup into a saucepan.
2 Fill the same can with milk and add to the soup.
3 Stir in the contents of the can of sweetcorn and heat through, stirring.
4 Add the cheese and heat, stirring until melted.
5 Thin with a little more milk, if liked, and heat through again. Season to taste with pepper and ladle into warm bowls to serve.

• •

Crunchy Mushroom Soup Serves 4

295 g/10½ oz/1 medium can of condensed mushroom soup
Milk
170 g/6 oz/1 small can of sliced mushrooms, drained
2 slices of wholemeal bread
A little butter or margarine, for spreading
50 g/2 oz/½ cup Cheddar cheese, grated

1 Empty the soup into a saucepan.
2 Fill the same can with milk and stir in.
3 Add the mushrooms to the pan. Heat through, stirring.
4 Meanwhile, toast the bread on both sides. Spread one side with butter or margarine and cover with the cheese. Grill (broil) until melted. Cut into dice.
5 Ladle the soup into bowls, top with the diced cheese 'toasties' and serve.

• •

Cheesy Bean Bite

Serves 2–4

400 g/14 oz/1 large can of baked beans with pork sausages
1 Weetabix
4 pitta breads
2 tomatoes, sliced
50 g/2 oz/½ cup Cheddar cheese, grated

1 Heat the beans in a saucepan.
2 Crumble in the Weetabix and stir until thickened.
3 Warm the pittas either in a toaster, under the grill (broiler) or in the microwave. Make a slit along the edge of each one.
4 Line with tomato slices and cheese. Spoon in the bean mixture and serve straight away.

Hot Salmon Special

Serves 2–4

185 g/6½ oz/1 small can of pink or red salmon
30 ml/2 tbsp mayonnaise
10 ml/2 tsp capers, chopped
2.5 cm/1 in piece of cucumber, chopped
4 slices of wholemeal bread
Butter or margarine, for spreading
50 g/2 oz/½ cup Mozzarella cheese, grated
Freshly ground black pepper

1 Drain the fish, discard any skin and mash well. Remove the bones if you like but they are very good for you!
2 Mix in the mayonnaise, capers and cucumber.
3 Toast the bread on both sides. Leave on the grill (broiler) rack. Spread one side with butter or margarine, then top with the salmon mixture.
4 Sprinkle the cheese over and add a good grinding of pepper. Grill (broil) under a moderate heat until the cheese melts and bubbles, then serve.

Hot Mushroom Bakes
Serves 4

These make delicious little appetisers, cut into pinwheels before baking.

    8 slices of bread, crusts removed
    Butter or margarine, for spreading
    170 g/6 oz/1 small can of creamed mushrooms
    5 ml/1 tsp dried oregano
    Carrot, celery and cucumber, cut into matchsticks, to serve

1 Spread the bread on one side only with butter or margarine.
2 Place buttered sides down on a baking (cookie) sheet and spread with the creamed mushrooms. Roll up, making sure the sealed edges are underneath.
3 Bake in a preheated oven at 190°C/375°F/gas mark 5 for about 10 minutes or until golden. Serve hot with carrot, celery and cucumber sticks.

Hot Chilli Ham Bakes
Serves 4

These can also be cut into pinwheels to make appetisers.

    8 slices of bread, crusts removed
    Butter or margarine, for spreading
    8 slices of ham
    Chilli relish
    Cherry tomatoes, radishes and chunks of cucumber, to serve

1 Spread the bread on one side with butter or margarine.
2 Place buttered sides down on a baking (cookie) sheet and top each with a slice of ham. Spread with chilli relish to taste.
3 Roll up and make sure the sealed sides are underneath.
4 Bake in a preheated oven at 190°C/375°F/gas mark 5 for about 10 minutes or until crisp and golden. Serve hot with cherry tomatoes, radishes and chunks of cucumber.

breads, biscuits, cakes and puddings

Baking a loaf of bread, a cake or a batch of biscuits (cookies) is probably one of the most rewarding of experiences – and you can't go wrong if you follow my foolproof recipes! There is nothing nicer than that freshly baked aroma filling the kitchen and permeating the whole house. And when you see a cooling rack piled high with golden delights, well, you just have to tuck in!

All the goodies in this section will keep in an airtight container for several days. But if you think they won't be eaten that quickly, freeze some to be brought out, fresh, for another time. This chapter will also show you how to make your favourite puddings with bread, biscuit and cake bases.

Breads, biscuits, cakes and puddings are all high-energy foods. They tend to be high in simple carbohydrates or sugars, which, if eaten in excess, will cause weight gain and possibly tooth decay. Having said that, I believe a slice of home-made cake, a meltingly crisp home-made biscuit or a small finger of bread pudding, laden with fruit, is definitely worth indulging in from time to time. The key is 'Everything in moderation'.

Bread

Bread is a staple food in our diet and everyone should eat lots of it. Not only does it act as a filler, but also it is high in complex carbohydrates and so gives you lots of long-term energy and fibre (especially the wholemeal and whole grain varieties). It will also provide essential minerals (some are enriched with extra calcium too) and vitamins, especially the B-group ones.

There are now dozens of types of bread available: good old sliced white and wholemeal loaves; brown breads made with a mixture of white and wholemeal flours; tin loaves; sandwich loaves; farmhouse crusties and cobs, sometimes sprinkled with flour; bloomers (the oval ones with slashes on the top or with seeds); milk loaves; soft batch and granary loaves, made with malted wholegrain flour. And that's just the start of the list!

Speciality breads include French sticks and baguettes; Italian ciabatta, made with olive oil and sold either plain or flavoured with sun-dried tomatoes or olives; focaccia, a round Italian bread, flavoured with onions, garlic, herbs, mushrooms, sun-dried tomatoes or walnuts, and European pumpernickel, light and dark rye breads. There are also all the individual breads, such as Middle Eastern pitta breads and Indian naan, chappatis and puris; corn breads, flour tortillas, shiny crusted bagels and sour doughs of the Americas; humble bridge rolls; English muffins and crumpets; French croissants and brioches. These and many more are readily available. Enjoy all their various textures and flavours. You can't have too much of such a good thing!

Cook's tips for bread

- Buy in quantities that you can enjoy while fresh. If you are on your own, cut a loaf in half and freeze half for later use. That way you won't have to keep throwing away half a stale, mouldy loaf.

- A bread crock or bin helps keep bread fresh. If you don't have one, keep it in a plastic bag or plastic container with a sealable lid.

- Most bread freezes well, with the exception of French sticks: if they are frozen for any length of time, the crust tends to come away when thawed.

- Keep rolls, pitta breads, naan, etc., in your freezer; they can be easily separated when you need only one or two.

- Bread thaws quickly in the microwave. Thaw on Medium-low (30 per cent power) in short bursts.

- Bread, especially rolls, heats well from frozen.

- Sliced bread can be toasted from frozen.

- Keep part-baked rolls, baguettes and ciabatta in your storecupboard (but keep an eye on the sell-by dates). They can also be frozen.

- Turn stale bread into breadcrumbs, either in a food processor or blender, or by rubbing it on a grater, then store in manageable quantities in plastic bags in the freezer. Use for coating foods before frying (sautéing), as toppings for sweet and savoury dishes, or to make into stuffing (pages 274–5), bread sauce (page 260) or puddings.

Bread bits and bites

If you have leftover bread, it need not go to waste: there are lots of ways to use it up. All these ideas are equally good made with fresh, of course.

● BAKED BREAD CASES:

Cut the crusts off slices of bread and spread on both sides with butter or margarine. Press into the sections of a tartlet tin (patty pan). Bake in a preheated oven at 190°C/375°F/gas mark 5 for about 25 minutes until crisp and golden brown. Cover loosely with foil if over-browning. Store in an airtight container if they are not to be used immediately. If they are added to fillings for fruit or dessert fillings, serve immediately, or they will go soft.

● BUTTERED BREADCRUMBS:

Melt a little butter in a frying pan (skillet). Add enough crumbs to absorb the butter. Toss over a moderate heat until golden and crisp. Sprinkle over steamed vegetables or pasta as a garnish or serve with roast game.

● CROÛTONS:

Cut the crusts off slices of bread (if preferred) and cut the bread into neat cubes. Heat a little oil and butter or margarine in a frying pan (skillet). Fry (sauté) the bread cubes, tossing all the time until crisp and golden. Drain on kitchen paper (paper towels). Serve with soup.

● MELBA TOAST:

Cut the crusts off thin slices of bread from a sliced loaf. Roll them flat with a rolling pin. Place on a baking (cookie) sheet. Bake in a preheated oven at 190°C/375°F/gas mark 5 for about 15 minutes or until crisp and golden and curling at the edges. Alternatively, cut off the crusts, then toast the slices on both sides. Cut the slices in halves, widthways, to achieve two even thinner slices. Toast the cut sides until crisp and golden. Serve with pâté or dips.

● RUSKS:

Cut fairly thick slices of bread into fingers. Place on a baking (cookie) sheet and bake at 190°C/375°F/gas mark 5 until golden. Store in an airtight container.

● TOASTED CRUMBS:

Either dry-fry crumbs in a heavy-based frying pan (skillet) or grill (broil) in a shallow baking tin (pan) until golden, tossing all the time. Alternatively, bake whole slices of bread on a baking (cookie) sheet in a preheated oven at 190°C/ 375°F/gas mark 5 until crisp and golden. Place in a plastic bag and crush with a rolling pin. Store in an airtight container.

Quick breads and scones (biscuits)

These have baking powder or bicarbonate of soda (baking soda) added to make the dough rise as it cooks. Unlike yeast dough, the mixture reacts immediately with heat and moisture so there is no lengthy proving time. For best results, they should be baked as soon as they are prepared.

Cook's tips for scones

- Handle as little as possible to keep the mixture light and spongy.

- Bake as soon as prepared or the raising agent will begin to lose its effectiveness.

- Quick breads and scones are best eaten on the day they are made. If not, always warm before serving. They can be frozen.

Cakes

Making cakes

There are several different methods for making cakes, each giving a different texture to the finished cake.

- ALL-IN-ONE METHOD:

The fat must be soft (preferably soft tub margarine). It is beaten together with the sugar, sifted flour and eggs in one go, with the addition of extra baking power to aerate the mixture. The skill is not to over-mix: beat only until the ingredients are thoroughly combined. This will give a similar texture to a creamed method cake.

- CREAMING METHOD:

The softened fat and sugar are beaten together (creamed) until light and fluffy, then the eggs are beaten in. Finally, the dry ingredients are folded in very gently, so that the air is not knocked out. This produces a rich, spongy texture.

- MELTING METHOD:

The fat and sugar are melted over a gentle heat, then stirred into the dry ingredients with the beaten eggs. Baking powder is also added to aerate the mixture. This gives a sticky, open texture.

- RUBBING-IN METHOD:

The fat is rubbed into the dry ingredients, then the eggs are beaten in and the mixture is softened with a little extra liquid to form a soft, dropping consistency. This gives a coarser, slightly drier-textured cake.

- WHISKING METHOD:

The eggs and sugar are whisked until thick and pale, incorporating a lot of air. The well-sifted flour is then very gently folded in and, sometimes, melted fat added. This produces an exceptionally light, spongy texture.

To line a cake tin (pan)

Line the base only for sandwich tins (pan). Line the sides as well (step 2) for a fruit cake.

- GREASING AND LINING:

1 Cut a circle or square of greaseproof (waxed) paper the same size as the base.
2 Measure the distance round the tin with a piece of string and cut a strip of greaseproof paper slightly longer and about 5 cm/2 in deeper than the tin.
3 Lightly oil the tin and use the cut paper to line the sides, and base, if appropriate. Brush the surfaces of the paper with a little more oil.

- FAT-FREE LINING:

Prepare as above but use non-stick baking parchment and wet the tin instead of greasing it. There is no need to oil the paper after lining the tin.

Cook's tips for cakes

- Cake mixtures with baking powder added should be baked as soon as prepared for best results.

- Always make sure your tin (pan) is the correct size for the quantity of mixture: too large and the cake will be dry and hard; too small and the cake will be soggy and may rise over the top of the tin.

- Always level the surface of cakes before cooking. For rich fruit cakes, make a slight hollow in the centre after levelling.

- Sponge cakes need to cool slightly and should then be turned out on to a wire rack to cool. Rich fruit cakes (such as Christmas cake) should be left in the tin to cool for at least 2 hours before turning out.

Biscuits (cookies)

Making biscuits

Like cakes, there are several different methods for making biscuits.

- ALL-IN-ONE METHOD:

The fat used must be soft (preferably soft tub margarine). It is worked together with the sugar, flour and any other ingredients, using a fork, wooden spoon or food processor, until the mixture forms a firm dough. This produces a similar texture to the creaming method.

- CREAMING METHOD:

The fat and sugar are beaten together (creamed) until light and fluffy, then the dry ingredients are worked in to form a firm dough. The mixture may be enriched with egg yolk or softened with milk. It can be rolled and cut into shapes or pressed into a tin (pan), marked into shapes and baked, then cut. This produces a rich, meltingly crumbly biscuit.

Cook's tips for biscuits

- Always lightly grease your baking (cookie) sheet, or line with non-stick baking parchment when cooking biscuits.

- When baking biscuits made by the melting method, always use non-stick baking parchment.

- Keep an eye on all biscuits when cooking. The ones round the edge of the baking sheet may cook more quickly, so remove them as they brown and slide the others out to the edges.

- Don't overcrowd biscuits on a baking sheet or they may spread and run in together, spoiling their shape.

- Remember, many biscuits will crisp on cooling, so don't overcook.

- For the best flavour, use butter for shortbread biscuits.

- MELTING METHOD:

The fat and sugar or syrup are heated in a pan until melted, then the dry ingredients are stirred in. Runny mixtures may be dropped in spoonfuls on to a baking (cookie) sheet. Firmer mixtures can be shaped into balls and baked (they will spread as they cook), or pressed into a shallow baking tin (pan) and baked in one slab, then cut into shapes. The biscuits may be sticky, sometimes chewy, or thin and crisp, depending on the recipe.

- RUBBING-IN METHOD:

The fat is rubbed into the dry ingredients until crumbly, then moistened with egg yolk and/or milk to form a firm dough. This produces a crisp, crunchy biscuit.

Bread-based puddings

Many popular puddings are made with bread in one form or another. My favourites are given on pages 254–7. They are all extremely simple to make and beat the bought varieties hands down.

Recipes

Basic Yeast Bread Dough   Makes a 450 g/1 lb loaf

Basic bread dough is easy to make by hand – and very therapeutic! However, if you are short of time, use a food processor: mix the dough, then run the machine for 1 minute to 'knead' it. Then continue from step 5.

    450 g/1 lb strong white (bread) flour
    5 ml/1 tsp salt
    10 ml/2 tsp easy-blend dried yeast
    15 ml/1 tbsp sunflower or olive oil, plus a little for greasing
    250 ml/8 fl oz/1 cup hand-hot water

1　Sift the flour and salt into a bowl and stir in the yeast and oil.
2　Mix with the water to form a soft but not sticky dough, adding a little more if necessary.
3　Knead gently on a lightly floured surface for about 5 minutes until smooth and elastic.
4　Wrap in a lightly oiled plastic bag and leave in a warm place until doubled in bulk, about 45 minutes.
5　Knock back (punch down) and shape into a roll to fit a lightly oiled 450 g/1 lb loaf tin (pan). Place in the tin and leave in a warm place until the bread reaches the top of the tin.
8　Brush with beaten egg or milk to glaze. Bake in a preheated oven at 220°C/425°F/gas mark 7 for about 25 minutes until it is risen and golden; the base should sound hollow when the loaf is tipped out of the tin and the base tapped with your knuckles.
9　Cool on a wire rack.

Garlic and Herb Bread   Serves 4–6

Replace the garlic with 15 ml/1 tbsp of chopped, fresh thyme to make a herb baguette.

1 small baguette
50 g/2 oz/¼ cup butter or margarine
1–2 garlic cloves, crushed
15 ml/1 tbsp chopped fresh parsley
15 ml/1 tbsp chopped fresh tarragon

1 Cut the bread into 12 slices, not quite through the base crust.
2 Mash the fat with the garlic and herbs.
3 Spread between each slice and spread any remainder over the top.
4 Wrap in foil and bake in a preheated oven at 200°C/400°F/gas mark 6 for about 15 minutes until the crust feels crisp and the centre soft when squeezed.

....

Banana Bread   Makes 1 loaf

2 ripe bananas
5 ml/1 tsp bicarbonate of soda (baking soda)
50 g/2 oz/¼ butter or margarine, plus extra to serve
100 g/4 oz/½ cup caster (superfine) sugar
275 g/10 oz/2½ cups self-raising (self-rising) flour
2.5 ml/½ tsp ground cinnamon or mixed (apple-pie) spice
1 egg

1 Put the bananas in a food processor and run the machine until smooth.
2 Add all the remaining ingredients and run the machine to blend.
3 Turn into a lined 900 g/2 lb loaf tin (pan).
4 Bake in a preheated oven at 180°C/350°F/gas mark 4 for about 50 minutes until risen, golden and a skewer inserted in the centre comes out clean.
5 Cool slightly. Remove from the tin, take off the paper and leave to cool on a wire rack. Serve sliced and spread with butter or margarine.

....

Oven-fresh Scones

Makes 8

225 g/8 oz/2 cups self-raising (self-rising) flour
10 ml/2 tsp baking powder
25 g/1 oz/2 tbsp butter or margarine
15 ml/1 tbsp caster (superfine) sugar
A little milk, to mix

1 Sift the flour and baking powder into a bowl.
2 Rub in the fat. Stir in the sugar and mix with enough milk to form a soft but not sticky dough.
3 Knead very briefly on a lightly floured surface. Pat out to about 2 cm/¾ in thickness and cut into 8 scones (biscuits), using a 5 cm/2 in biscuit (cookie) cutter.
4 Transfer to a lightly greased baking (cookie) sheet and bake immediately in a preheated oven at 230°C/450°F/gas mark 8 for about 10 minutes until risen and golden. The bases should sound hollow when tapped. Transfer to a wire rack to cool slightly. Serve warm, if possible.

Minted Teacup Loaf

Makes 1 loaf

This recipe needs no scales – just use the same teacup for all the ingredients.

1 teacup raisins
1 teacup sultanas (golden raisins)
½ teacup currants
½ teacup light brown sugar
½ teacup pure apple juice
½ teacup cold black tea
5 ml/1 tsp dried mint
¼ teacup butter or margarine
2 teacups self-raising (self-rising) flour
Butter, to serve

1 Put all the ingredients except the flour in a saucepan and heat gently until the fat melts, then bring to the boil and boil for 2 minutes.
2 Leave until lukewarm, then stir in the flour.
3 Turn into a greased and base-lined 900 g/2 lb loaf tin (pan). Bake in a preheated oven at 180°C/350°F/gas mark 4 for 1¼ hours or until risen, golden and a skewer inserted in the centre comes out clean.
4 Leave to cool in the tin for a few minutes, then turn out on to a wire rack, remove the paper and leave to cool. Serve sliced and buttered.

Boiled Fruit Salad Cake

Makes 1 cake

100 g/4 oz/½ cup butter or margarine
175 g/6 oz/¾ cup dark brown sugar
120 ml/4 fl oz/½ cup pure orange juice
75 ml/5 tbsp water
250 g/9 oz/1 small packet of dried fruit salad, chopped and any stones (pits) removed
5 ml/1 tsp bicarbonate of soda (baking soda)
10 ml/2 tsp mixed (apple-pie) spice
225 g/8 oz/2 cups self-raising (self-rising) flour
5 ml/1 tsp baking powder
1 large egg, beaten
30 ml/2 tbsp milk

1 Grease and line an 18 cm/7 in square cake tin (pan).
2 Put everything except the flour, baking powder, egg and milk in a saucepan.
3 Bring to the boil and boil for 1 minute. Remove from the heat and leave to cool for 5 minutes.
4 Stir in the flour, baking powder, egg and milk. Turn into the prepared tin and bake in a preheated oven at 180°C/350°F/gas mark 4 for about 1 hour 10 minutes or until a skewer inserted in the centre comes out clean.
5 Cool for 10 minutes, then turn out, remove the paper and leave to cool. Serve cut into fingers.

Chocolate Walnut Brownies   Makes 12

50 g/2 oz/½ cup plain (all-purpose) flour
15 ml/1 tbsp bran
1.5 ml/¼ tsp baking powder
50 g/2 oz/½ cup walnuts, chopped
65 g/2½ oz/good ¼ cup butter or margarine
50 g/2 oz/½ cup plain (semi-sweet) chocolate, broken into pieces
175 g/6 oz/¾ cup dark brown sugar
2 eggs, beaten
2.5 ml/½ tsp vanilla essence (extract)

1 Dampen a 28 × 18 cm/11 × 7 in shallow baking tin (pan) and line with non-stick baking parchment.
2 Mix together the flour, bran, baking powder and nuts. Melt the fat with the chocolate and sugar.
3 Cool slightly, then beat in the eggs and vanilla essence. Pour into the flour mixture and mix well. Turn into the prepared tin and bake in a preheated oven at 180°C/350°F/gas mark 4 for 35 minutes until risen and the centre springs back when lightly pressed.
4 Leave to cool in the tin, then cut into squares.

Baking Powder Bread   Makes 2 small loaves

25 g/1 oz/2 tbsp butter or margarine
450 g/1 lb plain (all-purpose) flour
20 ml/4 tsp baking powder
300 ml/½ pt/1¼ cups skimmed milk

1 Rub the butter or margarine into the flour and baking powder.
2 Mix with enough of the milk to form a soft but not sticky dough.
3 Divide the dough in half. Shape each into a loaf and place in two greased 450 g/1 lb loaf tins (pans).
4 Bake in a preheated oven at 230°C/450°F/gas mark 8 for 20–25 minutes until risen and golden and the bases sound hollow when tapped.
5 Turn out on to a wire rack and leave to cool.

Fat-free Jam Sponge
Makes 1 cake

This mixture can also be cooked in a lined Swiss roll tin (jelly roll pan). Once baked, turn out, trim the edges with a knife, quickly spread with the jam (conserve) and roll up.

2 eggs
50 g/2 oz/¼ cup caster (superfine) sugar
A few drops of vanilla essence (extract)
50 g/2 oz/½ cup self-raising (self-rising) flour
45 ml/3 tbsp raspberry jam
5 ml/1 tsp icing (confectioners') sugar

1 Put the eggs, sugar and vanilla in a bowl. Whisk with an electric beater until thick and pale and the whisk leaves a trail when lifted out of the mixture.
2 Sift the flour over the surface and fold in gently with a metal spoon. Do not over-mix.
3 Turn into two non-stick 18 cm/7 in sandwich tins (pans), base-lined with non-stick baking parchment. Bake in a preheated oven at 200°C/400°F/gas mark 6 for about 8–10 minutes until risen, golden and the centres spring back when lightly pressed.
4 Cool slightly, then turn out on to a wire rack to cool. Sandwich the cakes together with the jam, transfer to a serving plate and sift the icing sugar over the surface.

All-in-one-Victoria Sandwich
Makes an 18 cm/7 in cake

175 g/6 oz/¾ cup caster (superfine) sugar
175 g/6 oz/¾ cup soft tub margarine
175 g/6 oz/1½ cups self-raising (self-rising) flour
5 ml/1 tsp baking powder
3 eggs
Jam (conserve)
A little icing (confectioners') sugar or extra caster sugar, to decorate

1 Put all the ingredients except the jam in a bowl and beat with a wooden spoon until smooth and fluffy. Alternatively, blend in a food processor until just mixed.
2 Turn into two greased 18 cm/7 in sandwich tins (pans), base-lined with greased greaseproof (waxed) paper. Level the surfaces.
3 Bake in a preheated oven at 190°C/375°F/gas mark 5 for about 20 minutes until risen and golden. The centres should spring back when pressed.
4 Cool slightly, then turn out on to a wire rack, remove the paper and leave to cool. Sandwich together with jam.
5 Dust with icing or caster sugar, if liked.

Chocolate Sandwich

Makes an 18 cm/7 in cake

Prepare as All-in-one Victoria sandwich (pages 249–50) but substitute 15 g/½ oz/2 tbsp of the flour with cocoa powder and add an extra 2.5 ml/½ tsp baking powder. Sandwich together with whipped cream instead of jam (conserve).

Fast Sultana Cake

Makes 1 cake

Use mixed dried fruit (fruit cake mix), currants or raisins, if you prefer.

225 g/8 oz/2 cups self-raising (self-rising) flour
175 g/6 oz/¾ cup caster (superfine) sugar
175 g/6 oz/¾ cup soft tub margarine
3 eggs
5 ml/1 tsp mixed (apple-pie) spice
50 g/2 oz/⅓ cup sultanas (golden raisins)
15 ml/1 tbsp milk

1 Grease and line an 18 cm/7 in loose-bottomed cake tin (pan) with greased greaseproof (waxed) paper.
2 Put the flour, sugar, margarine, eggs and spice in a food processor. Run the machine until just blended. Alternatively, put in a bowl and beat with a wooden spoon until smooth.

3 Fold in the fruit and add the milk, to give a soft, dropping consistency.
4 Turn into the tin and level the surface.
5 Bake in a preheated oven at 160°C/325°F/gas mark 3 for about 1½ hours until golden, risen and a skewer inserted in the centre comes out clean.
6 Leave to cool in the tin for 10 minutes, then turn out, remove the paper and leave to cool completely.

Date and Walnut Cake   Makes 1 cake

For a nuttier texture, substitute half the flour with self-raising (self-rising) wholemeal flour.

225 g/8 oz/2 cups self-raising flour
5 ml/1 tsp mixed (apple-pie) spice
100 g/4 oz/½ cup butter or margarine
100 g/4 oz/½ cup caster (superfine) sugar
75 g/3 oz/½ cup chopped cooking dates
30 ml/2 tbsp chopped walnut halves
1 egg, beaten
75 ml/5 tbsp milk

1 Sift the flour and spice into a bowl. Add the fat and rub in with your fingertips until the mixture resembles breadcrumbs.
2 Stir in the sugar, dates and walnuts.
3 Stir in the egg and enough milk to form a soft dropping consistency.
4 Turn into a greased and lined 450 g/1 lb loaf tin (pan).
5 Bake in a preheated oven at 180°C/350°F/gas mark 4 for about 1¼ hours until risen and golden and a skewer inserted in the centre comes out clean.
6 Cool slightly, then turn out on to a wire rack, remove the paper and leave to cool.

Viennese Fingers
Makes 12

150 g/5 oz/⅔ cup butter
75 g/3 oz/½ cup icing (confectioners') sugar, sifted
150 g/5 oz/1¼ cups plain (all-purpose) flour, sifted
100 g/4 oz plain (semi-sweet) chocolate
A few drops of vanilla essence (extract)

1 Grease two baking (cookie) sheets.
2 Beat 100 g/4 oz/½ cup of the butter with 25 g/1 oz/3 tbsp of the icing sugar, then work in the flour. Place in a piping bag with a large star tube (tip) and pipe 12 strips, about 5 cm/2 in long, on to each baking sheet.
3 Bake in a preheated oven at 190°C/375°F/gas mark 5 for 10–15 minutes until a pale golden brown. Transfer to a wire rack to cool.
4 Melt the chocolate in a bowl over a pan of hot water or in the microwave. Beat the remaining butter and icing sugar together with the vanilla.
5 Sandwich the fingers in pairs with the butter icing (frosting), then dip one end in melted chocolate. When set, dip the other ends in the chocolate.

Shortbread Triangles
Makes 8

100 g/4 oz/1 cup plain (all-purpose) flour
A pinch of salt
25 g/1 oz/¼ cup rice flour or cornflour (cornstarch)
65 g/2½ oz/scant ⅓ cup caster (superfine) sugar
100 g/4 oz/½ cup butter

1 Sift the flour, salt and rice flour or cornflour into a bowl.
2 Add 50 g/2 oz/¼ cup of the sugar and the butter, cut into small pieces, and rub in with your fingertips until the mixture resembles fine breadcrumbs.
3 Press into an 18 cm/7 in sandwich tin (pan). Prick all over with a fork and mark into eight equal triangles. Chill for 1 hour.
4 Bake in a preheated oven at 150°C/300°F/gas mark 2 for about 1 hour until a very pale golden brown.
5 Sprinkle with the reserved caster sugar. Leave to cool in the tin, then transfer to a wire rack and break, or cut, into triangles before serving.

Macaroons
Makes 12

2 egg whites
150 g/5 oz/⅔ cup caster (superfine) sugar
A few drops of almond essence (extract)
150 g/5 oz/1¼ cups ground almonds or hazelnuts (filberts)
Rice paper
12 whole blanched almonds or hazelnuts, to decorate

1 Lightly whisk the egg whites.
2 Add the sugar, almond essence and ground nuts. Mix to a paste. Roll into balls and place well apart on a baking (cookie) sheet lined with rice paper.
3 Top each with a whole nut. Bake in a preheated oven at 190°C/375°F/gas mark 5 for about 20 minutes until pale biscuit coloured.
4 Leave to cool for 10 minutes, then cut or tear the rice paper round each macaroon and transfer to a wire rack to cool completely.

Speciality Flapjacks
Makes 18

75 g/3 oz/⅓ cup butter or margarine
25 g/1 oz/2 tbsp light brown sugar
30 ml/2 tbsp golden (light corn) syrup
175 g/6 oz/1½ cups crunchy oat and fruit cereal
50 g/2 oz/½ cup plain (all-purpose) flour

1 Melt the butter or margarine, sugar and syrup in a saucepan.
2 Stir in all the remaining ingredients until well mixed.
3 Turn into a non-stick 18 cm/7 in square baking tin (pan) and press down well.
4 Bake in a preheated oven at 190°C/375°F/gas mark 5 for about 12 minutes or until golden.
5 Cool slightly, then mark into 18 fingers. Leave until completely cold before removing from the tin.

Forkies

Makes about 20

65 g/2½ oz/scant ⅓ cup soft tub margarine
50 g/2 oz/¼ cup caster (superfine) sugar
5 ml/1 tsp vanilla essence (extract)
100 g/4 oz/1 cup self-raising (self-rising) flour
Halved glacé (candied) cherries, to decorate

1 Put all the ingredients except the cherries in a bowl and mix with a fork until the mixture forms a dough.
2 Shape into walnut-sized balls and place on a greased baking (cookie) sheet.
3 Flatten with a fork dipped in cold water.
4 Bake in a preheated oven at 190°C/375°F/gas mark 5 for about 15 minutes until pale golden brown.
5 Top each with a halved cherry and leave until firm, then transfer to a wire rack to cool completely.

Sticky Toffee Plum Pan

Serves 4

50 g/2 oz/¼ cup butter or margarine
225 g/8 oz/1 cup light brown sugar
15 ml/1 tbsp lemon juice
A few drops of almond essence (extract)
4 thick slices of bread, crusts removed and cubed
450 g/1 lb ripe plums, stoned (pitted) and quartered
Crème fraîche, to serve

1 Melt the butter or margarine in a large frying pan (skillet).
2 Add the sugar and lemon juice and a few drops of almond essence and stir until the sugar has melted.
3 Fold the bread gently through the toffee mixture until evenly coated.
4 Add the plums, stir gently, then cover and cook over a gentle heat for about 5 minutes until the plums are soft.
5 Serve hot, or cooled then chilled, with crème fraîche.

Super Rich Bread Pudding

Serves 6–8

100 g/4 oz bread, cubed
150 ml/¼ pt/⅔ cup milk
3 eggs
50 g/2 oz/¼ cup dark brown sugar
5 ml/1 tsp ground cinnamon
5 ml/1 tsp grated nutmeg
5 ml/1 tsp ground mace
175 g/6 oz/1 cup mixed dried fruit (fruit cake mix)
20 g/¾ oz/1½ tbsp butter or margarine, melted
Caster (superfine) sugar, for dusting
Cream or custard, to serve

1　Put the bread in a bowl.
2　Add the milk and leave to soak for 30 minutes. Beat well with a fork.
3　Lightly beat the eggs and mix in with the sugar, spices and fruit. Brush a 1.2 litre/2½ pt/6 cup ovenproof dish with some of the butter.
4　Turn the mixture into the dish and level the surface. Drizzle with the remaining butter.
5　Bake in a preheated oven at 180°C/350°F/gas mark 4 for about 1 hour or until golden brown and set.
6　Cool slightly, dust with caster sugar and serve cut into pieces with cream or custard.

• •

Rhubarb Charlotte

Serves 4–5

450 g/1 lb rhubarb, cut into short lengths
100 g/4 oz/½ cup demerara or light brown sugar
5 slices of bread
75 g/3 oz/⅓ cup butter or margarine, melted

1　Mix the rhubarb with three-quarters of the sugar.
2　Cut four of the slices of bread into triangles and dip in the melted butter or margarine. Use to line a 1 litre/1¾ pt/4¼ cup ovenproof dish.

3 Fill with the rhubarb and sugar. Dice the remaining bread and toss in the remaining butter or margarine. Scatter over the top and sprinkle with the remaining sugar.
4 Cook in a preheated oven at 180°C/350°F/gas mark 4 for about 40 minutes until golden brown and cooked through.

. . . .

Christmas Pudding   Makes 1 pudding

100 g/4 oz/1 cup plain (all-purpose) flour
100 g/4 oz/1 cup breadcrumbs
A pinch of salt
5 ml/1 tsp mixed (apple-pie) spice
100 g/4 oz/1 cup shredded (chopped) beef or vegetable suet
150 g/5 oz/⅔ cup dark brown sugar
500 g/18 oz/3 cups dried mixed fruit (fruit cake mix)
1 large egg, beaten
120 ml/4 fl oz/½ cup brown ale or stout
Butter or oil, for greasing

1 Mix everything in a large bowl. Cover with a cloth and leave to stand for 24 hours.
2 Stir again and turn into a greased 900 ml/1½ pt/3¾ cup pudding basin, base-lined with a circle of greased greaseproof (waxed) paper.
3 Cover and steam for 6–7 hours, topping up with boiling water as necessary. Leave to cool.
4 Re-cover and store in a cool dark place.
5 When required, steam for a further 2½ hours before serving.

. . . .

A Dash of Sherry Trifle   Serves 4

4 trifle sponges
300 g/11 oz/1 medium can of strawberries
30 ml/2 tbsp sherry
425 g/15 oz/1 large can of custard
170 g/6 oz/1 small can of cream
Toasted flaked (slivered) almonds

1　Crumble the sponges into the base of a glass serving dish.
2　Empty the can of strawberries over and gently mash into the sponges.
3　Sprinkle the sherry over. Spoon on the custard. Gently spread the cream over.
4　Sprinkle with toasted almonds and chill until ready to serve.

Summer Pudding

Serves 6

900 g/2 lb soft fruit such as raspberries, blackberries, blackcurrants, strawberries
Finely grated rind of ½ orange (optional)
45 ml/3 tbsp water
100–175 g/4–6 oz/½–¾ cup granulated sugar
8 slices of white bread, crusts removed

1　Slice or quarter the fruit if large and put in a saucepan with the orange rind, if using, the water and 100 g/4 oz/½ cup of the sugar.
2　Heat gently until the juices run and the fruit is soft but still holding its shape. Taste and add more sugar, if necessary.
3　Line a large pudding basin with some of the bread, cutting to fit.
4　Spoon in the fruit and juice and cover with the remaining bread, trimming to fit and filling in any gaps.
5　Stand the basin on a plate and cover with a saucer or small plate. Top with weights or a couple of cans to squeeze the juice through the bread. Chill overnight.
6　Turn out on to a shallow serving dish.

sauces, dressings and stuffings

Plain meat, poultry, vegetables and salads can be rather bland and desserts, too, sometimes need a little added flavour. However, with the right sauce, dressing or stuffing, they can be transformed. Here is every little recipe you'll need to make those inspirational accompaniments.

Cook's tips for sauces

- If you need to keep a sauce warm in a saucepan, cover it with a circle of wet greaseproof (waxed) paper. This will prevent a skin forming.

- For milk-based sauces, use a non-stick pan – much easier to clean!

- Do not boil egg- or cream-based sauces or they will curdle.

- Prepare oil-based dressings in a screw-topped jar. They can then be shaken to blend beautifully and can be stored in the same container.

- Make more dressing than you need and store it in the fridge.

- Bread sauce can be cooked in the oven. Place the ingredients in a small covered ovenproof dish on a low shelf for 15–20 minutes. Remove the onion and clove and beat well before serving.

All the stuffings can be used to stuff boned joints of meat, poultry, fish or game or cooked in a separate dish. If using to stuff a turkey, double the quantities. A good tip, too, is to keep a packet of stuffing mix in the cupboard. Make up as directed on the packet, then enhance it by adding a freshly chopped onion or a handful of fresh chopped herbs or chopped nuts.

Recipes
Apple Sauce

Serves 4

450 g/1 lb cooking (tart) apples, sliced
15 ml/1 tbsp water
30 ml/2 tbsp granulated sugar, plus extra to taste
A knob of butter or margarine

1　Put the apples in a saucepan with the water and sugar.
2　Cover and cook gently, stirring occasionally, until pulpy.
3　Beat in the butter or margarine and sweeten with more sugar, if liked.

Basic White Sauce

Serves 4

45 ml/3 tbsp plain (all-purpose) flour
300 ml/½ pt/1¼ cups milk
A small knob of butter or margarine
1 bouquet garni sachet
A pinch of salt
Freshly ground black or white pepper

1　Put the flour in a saucepan and gradually whisk in the milk until smooth.
2　Add the butter or margarine and the bouquet garni sachet.
3　Bring to the boil and cook for 2 minutes, stirring all the time, until thickened and smooth.
4　Squeeze the bouquet garni sachet against the side of the pan to extract the maximum flavour, then discard.
5　Season the sauce to taste with salt and pepper. Use as required.

Caper Sauce

Serves 4

Prepare as for basic white sauce (page 259) but add 30 ml/2 tbsp chopped capers before seasoning the sauce. Serve with lamb or fish.

Bread Sauce
Serves 4

50 g/2 oz/1 cup fresh white breadcrumbs
1 small onion
1 clove
A good pinch of grated nutmeg
Salt and freshly ground black pepper
300 ml/½ pt/1¼ cups milk

1 Put the breadcrumbs in a non-stick saucepan.
2 Press the clove into the onion and put in the pan with the nutmeg, a little salt and pepper and the milk.
3 Bring to the boil, stirring. Reduce the heat and simmer for 5 minutes, stirring all the time.
4 Cover with a circle of wetted greaseproof (waxed) paper and leave to cool. Just before serving, remove the paper, bring back to the boil, stirring, discard the onion and clove and spoon into a small serving bowl.

• •

Cheese Sauce
Serves 4

Prepare as for basic white sauce (page 259) but add 50 g/2 oz/½ cup Cheddar cheese, grated, after step 4. Serve with fish, pasta or vegetables.

• •

Chilli Sauce
Serves 4

For a hotter sauce, add more chilli powder or a few drops of Tabasco sauce.

2 spring onion (scallions), finely chopped
10 ml/2 tsp grated fresh root ginger
1 garlic clove, crushed
60 ml/4 tbsp medium-dry sherry
20 ml/1½ tbsp caster (superfine) sugar
30 ml/2 tbsp tomato purée (paste)
2.5 ml/½ tsp chilli powder
A good pinch of Chinese five spice powder
60 ml/4 tbsp chicken stock

10 ml/2 tsp cornflour (cornstarch)
15 ml/1 tbsp water

1 Mix all the ingredients except the cornflour and water in a saucepan.
2 Blend the cornflour with the water and stir in.
3 Bring to the boil and cook for 1 minute, stirring. Use hot or cold as required.

....

Curry Sauce
Serves 4–6

295 g/10½ oz/1 medium can of condensed celery or mushroom soup
90 ml/6 tbsp water
30 ml/2 tbsp tomato purée (paste)
5 ml/1 tsp garlic purée
5 ml/1 tsp dried onion granules
15 ml/1 tbsp curry paste
5 ml/1 tsp garam masala
5 ml/1 tsp ground turmeric
30 ml/2 tbsp mango chutney
50 g/2 oz creamed coconut
Salt and freshly ground black pepper

1 Put all the ingredients in a saucepan. Heat gently, stirring, until the coconut is melted and the mixture is bubbling. Thin with a little more water, if necessary.
2 Season to taste and serve with grilled (broiled) chicken or hard-boiled (hard-cooked) eggs. Alternatively, add chicken, turkey or vegetables to the sauce, heat through until piping hot and serve with rice.

....

Cucumber and Dill Sauce
Serves 4

Prepare as for basic white sauce (page 259) but add ¼ cucumber, finely chopped, and 5 ml/1 tsp dried dill (dill weed). Serve with fish or chicken.

....

Fast Barbecue Sauce

Serves 4

30 ml/2 tbsp wine or malt vinegar
30 ml/2 tbsp tomato ketchup (catsup)
30 ml/2 tbsp golden (light corn) syrup
15 ml/1 tbsp Worcestershire sauce
Salt and freshly ground black pepper
2.5 ml/½ tsp garlic granules (optional)

Whisk all the ingredients together. Use to brush food while grilling (broiling) or frying (sautéing) or serve with plain cooked meats, poultry or fish.

Green Cress Sauce

Serves 4

Prepare as for basic white sauce (page 259) but add 1 bunch of finely chopped watercress to the sauce and a pinch of cayenne. Serve with fish or chicken.

Hollandaise Sauce

Serves 4

2 eggs
30 ml/2 tbsp lemon juice
100 g/4 oz/½ cup butter, melted
A pinch of cayenne

1 Whisk the eggs in a saucepan with the lemon juice.
2 Gradually whisk in the melted butter.
3 Whisk over a gentle heat until thickened. Do not boil or it will curdle. Whisk in the cayenne and use as required.

Meat Gravy

Makes 450 ml/¾ pt/2 cups

The juices from roasting a joint, still in the roasting tin (pan)
45 ml/3 tbsp plain (all-purpose) flour
450 ml/¾ pt/2 cups vegetable water or stock, made with a stock cube
Gravy block or browning
Salt and freshly ground black pepper

1 Put the tin of juices on top of the stove. Remove all but 15 ml/1 tbsp of the fat.
2 Stir in the flour and cook, stirring, for 1 minute.
3 Remove from the heat and gradually blend in the liquid.
4 Return to the heat and bring to the boil and cook for 2 minutes, stirring.
5 Add gravy block or browning and seasoning to taste.

Mint Sauce

Serves 4

If fresh mint is not available, use 15 ml/1 tbsp dried mint instead.

30 ml/2 tbsp chopped fresh mint
15 ml/1 tbsp caster (superfine) sugar
30 ml/2 tbsp boiling water
Malt vinegar, to taste

1 Put the mint in a small bowl.
2 Add the sugar and stir in the boiling water until the sugar dissolves.
3 Leave to stand for at least 30 minutes, preferably longer, to allow the flavour to develop.
4 Just before serving, stir in vinegar to taste.

Mustard Sauce

Serves 4

Prepare as for basic white sauce (page 259) but stir in 10 ml/2 tsp made English mustard, 15 ml/1 tbsp light brown sugar and malt vinegar to taste. Serve with boiled beef, boiled ham or oily fish, such as mackerel.

Mushroom Sauce
Serves 4

4–5 button mushrooms, finely chopped
30 ml/2 tbsp water
1 quantity of basic white sauce (page 259)
A squeeze of lemon juice (optional)

1 Stew the mushrooms in the water in a covered pan for 3 minutes.
2 Remove the lid and boil rapidly, if necessary, to evaporate any liquid.
3 Stir into the cooked white sauce and add a squeeze of lemon juice, if liked.
4 Serve with chicken, fish, vegetables, pork or pasta.

Onion Sauce
Serves 4

2 onions, finely chopped
30 ml/2 tbsp water
1 quantity of basic white sauce (page 259)
Salt and freshly ground white or black pepper

1 Stew the onions in a saucepan with the water gently for 10 minutes until really soft.
2 Stir into the cooked white sauce, taste and adjust the seasoning.
3 Serve with lamb, pork or chicken or vegetables.

Parsley Sauce
Serves 4

Prepare as for basic white sauce (page 259) but add 30 ml/2 tbsp chopped fresh parsley to the sauce once cooked. Serve with fish, chicken or vegetables.

Sweet and Sour Sauce   Serves 4

For a chunky sauce, use a small can of pineapple chunks in natural juice instead of the pineapple juice and add a 2.5 cm/1 in piece of finely chopped cucumber and a coarsely grated carrot.

  30 ml/2 tbsp soy sauce
  45 ml/3 tbsp tomato ketchup (catsup)
  90 ml/6 tbsp clear honey
  60 ml/4 tbsp malt vinegar
  60 ml/4 tbsp pineapple juice
  60 ml/4 tbsp orange juice
  30 ml/2 tbsp cornflour (cornstarch)
  30 ml/2 tbsp water

1 Blend the soy sauce, ketchup, honey, vinegar and the fruit juices.
2 Blend the cornflour with the water and stir in.
3 Bring to the boil and cook for 1 minute until thick and clear. Serve hot.

Tomato Sauce   Serves 4

  15 ml/1 tbsp sunflower or olive oil
  1 onion, finely chopped
  1 garlic clove, crushed (optional)
  400 g/14 oz/1 large can of chopped tomatoes
  15 ml/1 tbsp tomato purée (paste)
  2.5 ml/½ tsp caster (superfine) sugar
  A pinch of dried basil or oregano
  Salt and freshly ground black pepper

1 Heat the oil in a saucepan and fry (sauté) the onion and garlic, if using, for 2 minutes, stirring.
2 Add the tomatoes, tomato purée and sugar.
3 Bring to the boil and boil rapidly for about 5 minutes until pulpy.
4 Season to taste and serve hot with any meat, fish, poultry or pasta.

Tomato Sauce with Fresh Basil   Serves 4

Prepare as for tomato sauce (page 265) but omit the dried basil or oregano and stir in 6–8 chopped, fresh basil leaves before seasoning after cooking.

....

Vegetable Gravy   Makes 300 ml/½ pt/1¼ cups

If you have no vegetable water, use stock made with a vegetable stock cube.

    50 g/2 oz/¼ cup butter or margarine
    2 onions, chopped
    30 ml/2 tbsp plain (all-purpose) flour
    300 ml/½ pt/1¼ cups vegetable water
    5 ml/1 tsp Worcestershire sauce
    5 ml/1 tsp Marmite or Vegemite
    Salt and freshly ground black pepper

1   Melt the fat in a saucepan. Add the onions and cook, stirring, for 5 minutes until soft and golden brown.
2   Blend in the flour and cook for 1 minute.
3   Remove from the heat and gradually blend in the stock, Worcestershire sauce and Marmite or Vegemite.
4   Return to the heat, bring to the boil and cook for 2 minutes, stirring. Season to taste. Strain, if liked.

....

Blue Cheese Mayonnaise   Serves 4

    100 g/4 oz/1 cup Danish Blue cheese, crumbled
    60 ml/4 tbsp mayonnaise
    45 ml/3 tbsp crème fraîche
    5 ml/1 tsp lemon juice
    Salt and freshly ground black pepper

1   Mash the cheese with 15 ml/1 tbsp of the mayonnaise until fairly smooth.
2   Beat in the remaining mayonnaise, the crème fraîche, lemon juice, salt and pepper to taste. Use as required.

....

Cheese Dressing

Serves 4

60 ml/4 tbsp cream cheese
10 ml/2 tsp snipped fresh chives
10 ml/2 tsp chopped fresh parsley
30 ml/2 tbsp milk
5 ml/1 tsp dried onion granules
Salt and freshly ground black pepper

Whisk all the ingredients together with salt and pepper to taste. Thin with a little more milk, if necessary. Use as required.

....

Creamy Garlic Dressing

Serves 4–6

15 ml/1 tbsp olive oil
75 ml/5 tbsp crème fraîche
15 ml/1 tbsp lemon juice
1 garlic clove, crushed
15 ml/1 tbsp chopped fresh parsley
A pinch of salt
Freshly ground black pepper
5 ml/1 tsp clear honey
A little cold milk

Whisk all the ingredients together, adding enough milk to thin to a pouring consistency. Chill until ready to serve.

....

Curried Mayonnaise

Serves 4

60 ml/4 tbsp mayonnaise
15 ml/1 tbsp curry paste
15 ml/1 tbsp sultanas (golden raisins)
15 ml/1 tbsp chopped fresh coriander (cilantro)
Milk

Mix the mayonnaise mixture with the curry paste and stir in the sultanas and coriander. Thin with a little milk, if necessary.

....

French Dressing   Serves 4

45 ml/3 tbsp olive oil
15 ml/1 tbsp red or white wine vinegar
2.5 ml/½ tsp Dijon mustard
A pinch of salt
A pinch of caster (superfine) sugar
Freshly ground black pepper

1 Shake all the ingredients together in a screw-topped jar until well blended.
2 Taste and adjust the seasoning. Use as required.

Honey Nut Dressing   Serves 4

30 ml/2 tbsp clear honey
30 ml/2 tbsp sunflower oil
15 ml/1 tbsp lemon juice
30 ml/2 tbsp finely chopped mixed nuts
15 ml/1 tbsp chopped fresh parsley
Salt and freshly ground black pepper

Put all the ingredients in a screw-topped jar and shake vigorously until well blended. Use as required.

Mayonnaise   Serves 4

I've included this recipe, but I'm not convinced it's not worth making your own as you can buy such good-quality mayonnaise in jars. Store in the fridge once opened.

1 egg
1 egg yolk
30 ml/2 tbsp lemon juice
15 ml/1 tbsp white wine vinegar
2.5 ml/½ tsp mustard powder
Salt and freshly ground black pepper
375 ml/13 fl oz/1½ cups sunflower or olive oil

1 Blend or whisk the egg, egg yolk, lemon juice, wine vinegar, mustard, salt and pepper.
2 Add a little of the oil and blend or whisk again.
3 Gradually add the remaining oil, a little at a time, blending or whisking continuously until the mayonnaise thickens.

••

Minted Yoghurt and Cucumber   Serves 4

Use this as a dip with pitta breads, or to top jacket-baked potatoes or to serve with curries.

5 cm/2 in piece of cucumber, grated
5 ml/1 tsp dried mint
1 small garlic clove, crushed (optional)
150 ml/¼ pt/⅔ cup plain yoghurt
Salt and freshly ground black pepper

1 Squeeze the grated cucumber to remove excess moisture. Place in a bowl.
2 Add all the remaining ingredients and mix thoroughly.
3 Chill until ready to serve.

••

Oriental Soy Dressing   Serves 4

30 ml/2 tbsp light soy sauce
45 ml/3 tbsp sunflower oil
15 ml/1 tbsp sesame oil
15 ml/1 tbsp medium-dry sherry
10 ml/2 tsp light brown sugar
5 ml/1 tsp grated fresh root ginger
Freshly ground black pepper

Whisk all the ingredients together and use as required.

••

Rosy Dressing   Serves 4

60 ml/4 tbsp mayonnaise
15 ml/1 tbsp tomato ketchup (catsup)
2.5 ml/½ tsp Worcestershire sauce
Freshly ground black pepper
A few drops of Tabasco sauce

Mix all the ingredients together and use as required.

....

Sweet Creamy Dressing   Serves 4

15 ml/1 tbsp light brown sugar
60 ml/4 tbsp crème fraîche
2.5 ml/½ tsp made English mustard
A pinch of salt
Freshly ground black pepper
Malt vinegar, to taste

1 Whisk the sugar, crème fraîche, mustard, salt and lots of pepper together
   in a small bowl or jug.
2 Whisk in vinegar to taste.

....

Vinaigrette Dressing   Serves 4

30 ml/2 tbsp white wine vinegar
30 ml/2 tbsp olive oil
1 shallot, very finely chopped
2.5 ml/½ tsp Dijon mustard
10 ml/2 tsp chopped fresh parsley
5 ml/1 tsp caster (superfine) sugar
Salt and freshly ground black pepper

1 Put all the ingredients in a screw-topped jar and shake until well blended.
2 Store in the fridge until ready to use.

....

Yoghurt Mayonnaise

Serves 4

30 ml/2 tbsp mayonnaise
30 ml/2 tbsp plain yoghurt
2.5 ml/½ tsp lemon juice
A pinch of salt
A pinch of caster (superfine) sugar
A good grinding of freshly ground black pepper

Blend all the ingredients together and chill until ready to serve.

· ·

Basic Vanilla Sauce

Serves 4

15 g/½ oz/2 tbsp cornflour (cornstarch)
300 ml/½ pt/1¼ cups milk
1.5 ml/¼ tsp vanilla essence (extract)
15 ml/1 tbsp caster (superfine) sugar

1 Blend the cornflour with a little of the milk in a saucepan.
2 Stir in the remaining milk, the vanilla and sugar.
3 Bring to the boil and cook for 1 minute, stirring, until thickened and smooth. Serve with any hot puddings.

· ·

Cheat's Custard

Serves 4

I usually use canned or carton custard, but if you haven't any (and don't have any custard powder), this makes a good alternative.

Prepare as for basic vanilla sauce (above) but add a few drops of yellow food colouring when blending the milk and cornflour.

· ·

Hot Chocolate Caramel Sauce   Serves 2–4

1 chocolate caramel bar
90 ml/6 tbsp milk
15 g/½ oz/1 tbsp butter or margarine
15 ml/1 tbsp drinking (sweetened) chocolate powder

1 Cut the bar into pieces and place in a saucepan.
2 Add all the remaining ingredients and heat gently, stirring all the time, until smooth and thickened.
3 Serve hot over ice cream, fruit or profiteroles.

Hot Lemon Sauce   Serves 4–6

15 g/½ oz/2 tbsp cornflour (cornstarch)
25 g/1 oz/2 tbsp caster (superfine) sugar
300 ml/½ pt/1¼ cups water
Juice of 2 lemons

1 Blend the cornflour and sugar with a little of the water in a saucepan.
2 Add the remaining water and the lemon juice.
3 Bring to the boil and cook for 2 minutes, stirring, until thickened and clear. Serve hot with steamed puddings, pancakes or apple pie.

Hot Orange Sauce   Serves 4

Prepare as for hot lemon sauce (above) but use oranges instead of lemons. Add a dash of lemon juice, if liked, to sharpen the taste. Serve as for hot lemon sauce.

Instant Chocolate Sauce

Serves 1

Make sure you use chocolate powder with milk powder added – the sort that makes an instant hot chocolate drink.

45 ml/3 tbsp instant drinking (sweetened) chocolate powder
Boiling water

1 Put the instant chocolate powder in a small jug.
2 Whisk in boiling water, 5 ml/1 tsp at a time, to form a smooth paste.
3 Keep adding water until you have a thick, pouring consistency.
4 Serve over ice cream or fruit – it's particularly good with bananas or pears.

· ·

Jam Sauce

Serves 4–6

Use any flavour of jam (conserve).

60 ml/4 tbsp jam
30 ml/2 tbsp caster (superfine) sugar
Finely grated rind and juice of ½ lemon
75 ml/5 tbsp water

1 Finely chop any pieces of fruit in the jam.
2 Blend all the ingredients in a saucepan and heat gently, stirring, until the sugar has dissolved.
3 Simmer for 5 minutes. Serve hot with sweet omelettes, steamed or milk puddings.

· ·

Peppermint Custard

Serves 4

Prepare as for basic vanilla sauce (page 271) but add a few drops of peppermint essence (extract) and green food colouring and omit the vanilla. Great with steamed chocolate pudding.

· ·

Syrup Sauce

Serves 4

90 ml/6 tbsp golden (light corn) syrup
30 ml/2 tbsp lemon juice

Heat the syrup and lemon juice in a saucepan until hot but not boiling. Serve hot with steamed puddings or pancakes.

• •

Velvet Chocolate Sauce

Serves 4

For a dark chocolate sauce, substitute cocoa (unsweetened chocolate) powder for the drinking (sweetened) chocolate powder and add caster (superfine) sugar to taste.

30 ml/2 tbsp cornflour (cornstarch)
30 ml/2 tbsp drinking chocolate powder
300 ml/½ pt/1¼ cups milk

1 Blend the cornflour and chocolate with a little of the milk in a saucepan.
2 Blend in the remaining milk.
3 Bring to the boil and cook for 2 minutes, stirring all the time, until thickened and smooth. Thin with extra milk, if necessary

• •

Herby Ham Stuffing

Serves 4

50 g/2 oz/1 cup fresh wholemeal breadcrumbs
1 small onion, finely chopped
50 g/2 oz/½ cup finely chopped cooked ham
2.5 ml/½ tsp dried mixed herbs
15 ml/1 tbsp chopped fresh parsley
Salt and freshly ground black pepper
1 small egg, beaten

Mix all together and use as required.

• •

Nutty Rice Stuffing

Serves 4

100 g/4 oz/1 cup cooked long-grain rice
30 ml/2 tbsp raisins
25 g/1 oz/¼ cup walnuts, chopped
15 ml/1 tbsp snipped fresh chives
15 g/½ oz/1 tbsp butter or margarine, softened
Salt and freshly ground black pepper

Mash all the ingredients together and use as required.

Parsley and Thyme Stuffing

Serves 4

To double the quantities, use one whole egg to bind instead of 2 egg yolks.

50 g/2 oz/1 cup fresh white breadcrumbs
30 ml/2 tbsp chopped fresh parsley
15 ml/1 tbsp chopped fresh thyme
Salt and freshly ground black pepper
1 egg yolk
15 ml/1 tbsp boiling water

Mix all the ingredients together and use as required.

Sage and Onion Stuffing

Serves 4

50 g/2 oz/1 cup fresh white breadcrumbs
1 small onion, finely chopped
8 fresh sage leaves, finely chopped
Salt and freshly ground black pepper
15 ml/1 tbsp melted butter or margarine
1 egg yolk
15 ml/1 tbsp milk

1 Mix the breadcrumbs with the onion, sage and some salt and pepper.
2 Stir in the melted butter, egg yolk and milk. Use as required.

----

index